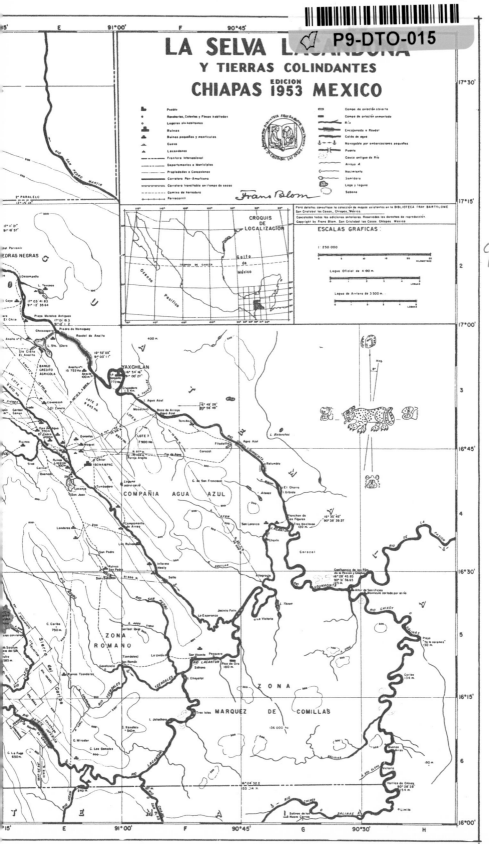

LA SELVA LACANDONA
Y TIERRAS COLINDANTES
CHIAPAS EDICION 1953 MEXICO

Frans Blom

SACRED MONKEY RIVER

SACRED MONKEY RIVER

A Canoe Trip with the Gods

CHRISTOPHER SHAW

W. W. NORTON & COMPANY

NEW YORK LONDON

For information about permission to reproduce selections from this
book, write to Permissions, W. W. Norton & Company, Inc.,
500 Fifth Avenue, New York, NY 10110

The text of this book is composed in Perpetua
with the display set in Chevalier Open
Composition by Thomas Ernst
Manufacturing by Quebecor World Book Services
Book design by Chris Welch
Cartography by Hannah Hinchman

Drawings on pages 132–133 by Linda Schele, from *The Blood of Kings*,
used by permission of the Kimbell Art Museum.

Library of Congress Cataloging-in-Publication Data
Shaw, Christopher.
Sacred monkey river : a canoe trip with the gods / by Christopher Shaw.
p.   cm.
ISBN 0-393-04837-3
1. Mayas—Usumacinta River Valley (Guatemala and Mexico)—
Antiquities. 2. Mayas—Usumacinta River Valley (Guatemala and
Mexico)—Religion. 3. Lacandon Indians—Social life and customs.
4. Shaw, Christopher—Journeys—Usumacinta River Valley (Guatemala
and Mexico) 5. Usumacinta River Valley (Guatemala and Mexico)—
Description and travel. 6. Usumacinta River Valley (Guatemala and
Mexico—Antiquities. I. Title.
F1435.S53 2000
972'.6—dc21   00-037221

W. W. Norton & Company, Inc., 500 Fifth Avenue, New York, N.Y. 10110
wwww.wwnorton.com

W. W. Norton & Company Ltd., 10 Coptic Street, London WC1A 1PU

1 2 3 4 5 6 7 8 9 0

for Noah and Sue

It is not certain that space is empty and shapeless though it must seem so, just as it must seem we are nowhere except as we occupy space and shape it. Whether we look at the surface of the earth which is endless though not infinite, or at the spaces beyond, whose limits we cannot see or perhaps think of, the need for a sense of place is so strong that we try to limit the vastness, however arbitrarily, and fill the emptiness if only by naming places such as a mountain, a water, or certain stars.

—WILLIAM BRONK

We (the undivided divinity operating within us) have dreamt the world. We have dreamt it as firm, mysterious, visible, ubiquitous in space and durable in time; but in its architecture we have allowed tenuous and eternal crevices of unreason which tell us it is false.

—JORGE LUIS BORGES

By and large, the Maya were a riverine people who transported goods and people in dugout canoes. On four bones from [a] tomb at Tikal, life and death are symbolized as a canoe trip with the gods.

—LINDA SCHELE AND MARY ELLEN MILLER,
The Blood of Kings

CONTENTS

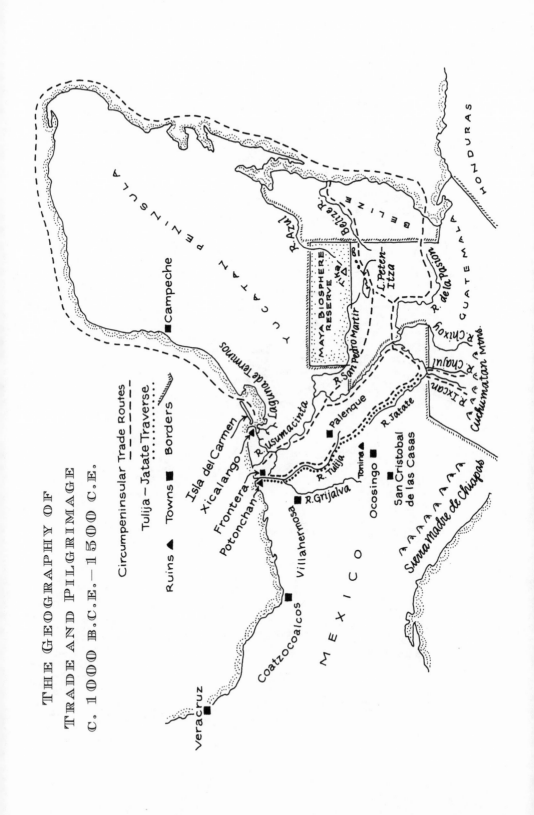

THE GEOGRAPHY OF
TRADE AND PILGRIMAGE
c. 1000 B.C.E. – 1500 C.E.

Circumpeninsular Trade Routes - - - -
Tulija – Jatate Traverse ....
Ruins ▲ Towns ■ Borders - - -

Campeche

YUCATAN PENINSULA

R. Azul

MAYA BIOSPHERE RESERVE

BELIZE

R. Hondo

L. Peten-
Itza

R. de la Pasion

GUATEMALA

HONDURAS

R. Chixoy

R. Choyul

Cuchumatan Mtns.

R. Ixcan

R. San Pedro Martir

Laguna de Terminos

Isla del Carmen

Xicalango

Frontera

Potonchan

R. Usumacinta

Palenque

R. Jatate

R. Tulija

Tonina ▲

Ocosingo

San Cristobal
de las Casas

R. Grijalva

Villahermosa

MEXICO

Sierra Madre de Chiapas

Coatzocoalcos

Veracruz

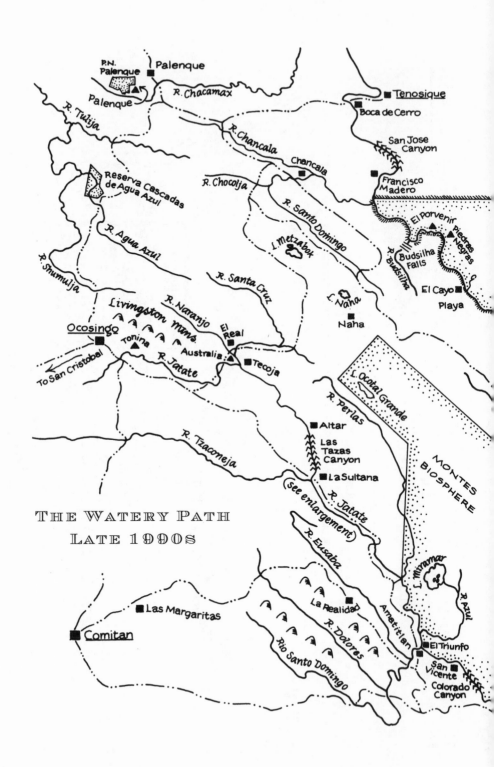

THE WATERY PATH
LATE 1990s

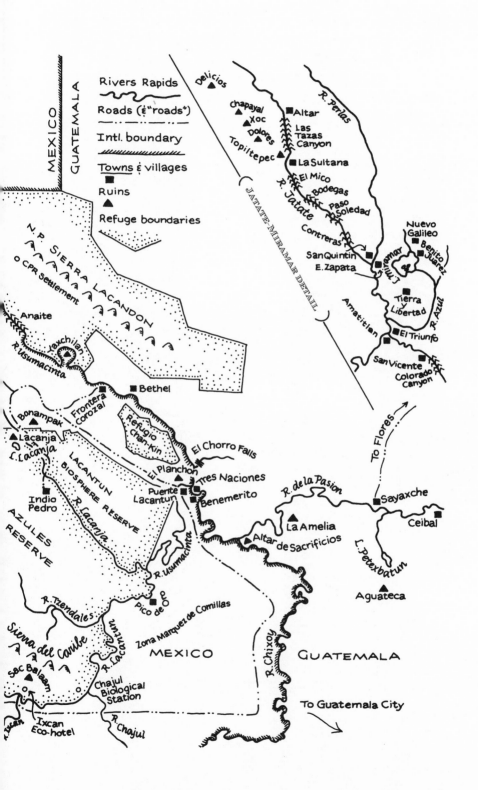

Rivers Rapids
Roads (& "roads")
Intl. boundary
Towns & villages ■
Ruins ▲
Refuge boundaries

MEXICO
GUATEMALA

Delicios ▲

Chapayal ▲
Xoc ▲
Dolores ▲
Topiltepec ▲

■ Altar
Las Tazas Canyon
■ La Sultana
El Mico
Bodegas
Paso Soledad
Contreras
San Quintin
E. Zapata

R. Perlas
R. Jatate

JATATE-MIRAMAR DETAIL

Nuevo Galileo ■
Benito Juarez ■
Miramar

Amatitlan
Tierra y Libertad
R. Azul
El Triunfo ■
San Vicente Colorado Canyon

N.P. SIERRA LACANDON
○ CPR Settlement

Anaite ▲
Yaxchilan ▲
R. Usumacinta

■ Bethel

To Flores

Bonampak ▲
Frontera Corozal
Lacanja ▲
L. Lacanja
Refugio Chan-Kin
El Chorro Falls
■ Planchon
Tres Naciones ▲
Puente Lacantun
Benemerito
R. de la Pasion
Sayaxche ■
Ceibal ■

LACANTUN BIOSPHERE RESERVE
R. Lacanja
Indio Pedro
AZULES RESERVE

La Amelia ▲
Altar de Sacrificios ▲
L. Petexbatun
Aguateca ▲

R. Usumacinta
R. Tzendales
Pico de Oro
Sierra del Caribe
Sac Balaam
R. Lacanja
Zona Marquez de Comillas
MEXICO
GUATEMALA
R. Chixoy

Chajul Biological Station
Ixcan Eco-hotel
R. Chajul

To Guatemala City

SACRED MONKEY RIVER

One

FOUNDATION

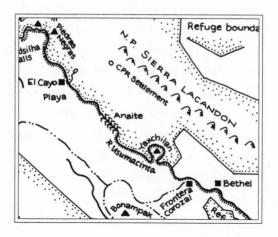

D RIVING EAST FROM VERACRUZ, YOU COME DOWN OUT OF THE
green volcanic Tuxtla Mountains immediately onto the Isthmus
of Tehuantepec, a torrid flatland of savannas and wetlands traced with
estuaries, shallow lakes, and slow-moving rivers. At a village of
Zoque Indians, teenagers dressed as monkeys extort change from
motorists forced to halt by enormous speed bumps called topes.
From here on, despite the veneer of North American–style sprawl
that afflicts most of the western hemisphere, everything alters. The

shapes of finite topographies layered deep in time and history, and honored in spatial and temporal configurations by people all over the region, mirror universal forms.

The road bypasses the sprawling and fetid oil port of Coatzacoalcos on the gulf. To unaccustomed eyes the landscape appears undifferentiated, shapeless, a flat, featureless expanse of sawgrass and amoeboid watercourses meandering under a vaulting sky. Less than 150 miles separates the Pacific from the Gulf of Mexico. Along the sluggish creeks and estuaries, and on the wide rivers draining the highlands, men pass up and down in dugout canoes called cayucos. (In Eisenstein's documentary, *Que Viva Mexico!*, comely Zapotecas plied cayucos through the estuaries of Tehuantepec.)

Leaving the isthmus, you pass La Venta, a ceremonial center of the early culture known to the Aztecs as Olmec—the Land-of-Rubber People—who inhabited the littoral and adjacent highlands in the first millennium B.C.E. The Olmec comprehended the watercourses in minute detail, depended on them for travel, agriculture, and fish, and accommodated their frequent shifts due to storms, erosion, and other telluric whims. The waters carried them to the sea, and up the steepening rivers inland to the mountains for flint, jade, feathers, and other precious materials and trade goods.

At La Venta, now overshadowed by a gargantuan oil refinery, the Olmec built the first known temple-mountain—one of the hundreds of earth and stone pyramids dotting Mesoamerica—symbolizing the volcanoes of the Tuxtlas, the cleft mountains they saw as the sources of creation. The pyramids typically surrounded enclosed plazas, each offering doorways, "portals," through symbolic caves on the summits or primordial oceans under the plazas, to the Place of Awe, the Otherworld. Their arrangement centered the universe and concentrated divine forces. They also replicated the shape of the cosmos and the story of creation.

During the so-called formative period of Mesoamerican civilization (approximately 1500 B.C.E. to the beginning of our era), the Olmec dispersed, following the watersheds, and settled in widely separated pockets throughout the region. They carried with them their distinctive, and, in the archaeological record, novel religion, characterized in burials both at home and in settlements outside the core area by figurines depicting strange almond-eyed supernaturals with cleft foreheads, fetal effigies, cosmic toads, and miniature canoes.

Each of these articles symbolized some aspect of the soul's transformation in shamanic trance, or under the influence of ritual bloodletting and drugs, from mundane reality to the alternate plane, where its possessor could consult with his ancestors and come to know their wishes. This transformation was the religion's fundamental sacrament. The model canoes probably served as vehicles, or "snuffboards," for ingesting psychotropic substances used to carry the soul on its ineffable journey.

The Olmec laid down principles that influenced religious and royal practice in Mesoamerica for two thousand years. The classical Maya, the architects of the grand ruins now crawling with tourists and New Age pilgrims from Honduras to Cancún, subscribed to the Olmec worldview as conscientiously and deliberately as we look to Greece and the Old Testament. Central to this shared view was the principle of the Watery Path connecting the sacred world in the sky with the earthly face of the cosmos. The means of travel from one to the other, metaphysically speaking, was the canoe; its avatar a celestial canoe in the sky, the Milky Way.

Theirs was a religion of transformation, of death into life, rooted in geography. The shape of the Olmec and later the Maya cosmos reflected the interconnecting waterways of the isthmus, the nearby delta of the Usumacinta and Grijalva rivers, and their tributary highlands. It was the land of origination, the known world, and it mirrored a larger reality.

Out of the amorphous universe it formed a "here with meaning," the necessary conceptual underpinning of all human identity, and of consciousness itself.

———

RESIDENTS CALL THE Usumacinta delta and the surrounding lowlands Chontalpa, "Place of the Chontals," after the (ethnically dubious) "Maya" Chontal Indians. When Juan de Grijalva anchored off the river's mouth in 1517, a far-reaching trade empire based in the delta controlled most of the gulf coast and the coastal waters of Yucatán, all the way to the Caribbean coast of Honduras. It probably reached the Antilles and the gulf and southeast coasts of North America. The seagoing dugout "as long as a galley" that greeted Columbus off the Honduran Bay Islands in 1502 most likely held Chontal traders from the Grijalva/Usumacinta delta.

The Chontalpa is a low, hot expanse of wetland, rain forest, petroleum seeps, mangrove swamps, cacao plantations, and rich savannas called centlas. Its annual floods and rainfall—over a hundred inches, among the highest on the planet—makes it seem marginal as human habitat. It discourages foot travel, as Cortés's 1525 Honduran expedition found to its peril.

But its hundreds of rivers, streams, canals, seasonal lakes, and side channels create networks connecting to coastal and inland waters, many navigable solely by cayuco. As late as the sixteenth century, glyph-painted signboards fastened to trees pointed the way through the watery maze, like those marking routes and portages in the Boundary Waters of Minnesota or the St. Regis Canoe Area of the Adirondacks.

The distributaries connected to overland trade routes that followed interior valleys south from central Mexico. Rivers flowing from the southwest connected to Mixe-Zoque and Chiapanec Indian lands, from the south with the Palencano Chol. From the southeast, they connected to the Manche, Lacandon, Itza, and Tzeltal Maya, as well as the Cuchumatan Mountains, with their priceless salt, flint, and obsidian deposits, their precious green stones and feathers. As early as the second century B.C.E., and possibly sooner, delta traders carried ceramics, shells, and cacao to the Usumacinta headwaters, along with razor-sharp spines from stingray tails, prized for the sacramental penis perforation that lay at the heart of the classic period's rituals of bloodletting and hallucination.

They also carried other, more exotic goods from the central highlands and beyond. On their return, they brought the interior's raw materials downstream to be collected and concentrated in the Chontalpa's free ports. Power accrued to these procurers of things from afar. Their travels, according to anthropologist Mary Helms, identified them with mythic travelers, and turned them in people's minds into "present-day transformers and culture-hero creators." Their journeys recapitulated ancient journeys, making each commercial excursion a kind of pilgrimage. The trunk line of inland commerce was the Usumacinta River.

In *The Maya Chontal Indians of Acalan-Tixchel,* written in the 1930s, Franz Scholes and Ralph Roys portrayed a number of different ethnic and linguistic communities occupying the Chontalpa at the time of European contact, reaching as far as Tenosique, a few day's paddle up the Usumacinta. The different tribes lived in separate towns or villages, or in segregated neighborhoods in neutral free ports like Xicalango.

A tapestry of tribes and cultures attracted by trade settled in multiethnic trading ports along the coast and the immediate inland estuaries: Zoques and Mixes, Mayas, and, from the central Mexican highlands, speakers of Nahuatl—for a long time the lingua franca of delta traders. Xicalango, on the Isla del Carmen, the barrier island at the mouth of the Laguna de Términos, was a neutral Nahua entrepôt with ethnically distinct neighborhoods.

All of the era's cultures partook of the delta's opportunities. "Water transportation was everywhere available," wrote Scholes and Roys. "Aztecs [and, before them, Toltecs and 'Olmecs'] brought handsome fabrics, ornaments and spindle cups of gold, articles of copper and obsidian, dyed rabbit hair, and slaves." They carried home cacao, tanned jaguar and cougar pelts, tortoiseshell, amber, and jade, products that flowed to the delta via the circumpeninsular routes and the

Usumacinta loop. (Thus Moctezuma learned every detail of the Córdoba and Grijalva voyages.) Slave labor, Scholes and Roys suggested, obtained through trade or war with neighboring tribes, was especially profitable in a country where the principle crop, cacao, ripened and was harvested year-round, and where long-distance commerce required many paddlers or carriers.

Of the classical era, Scholes and Roys suggested that superior canoemanship determined the rise of the dominant lowland city-states, with their pyramids and inscriptions. By the time the first dates were being carved in limestone along the Usumacinta River, around 200, the canoe routes of the Usumacinta watershed and across Peten to the sea were well established and storied among the generations of paddlers. In their minds the watershed existed as a totality, something definitive and absolute, rather than fragmentary, local, contingent. Analogies with the Homeric Aegean are not far-fetched.

To the Olmec, both canoe travel and spirit travel led to communication with one's ancestors and the transformation of the flesh into spirit and back again. The trader's journey outward from the known world corresponded to the shaman's journey to the Otherworld, the land of the dead. Both voyagers mediated between realms, returning from a Beyond—from death—with valuable goods and information. Travel over long distances, primarily by water, was the central feature of this ritual symbiosis of mundane commerce and sacred pilgrimage, "each bringing blessings on the other," according to Mayanist Nancy Fairiss.

AT VARIOUS TIMES during the Maya classical period, Nahuatl-speaking traders from the central Mexican highlands established footholds in the Chontalpa. By the fourteenth century the Mexica—the Aztecs—controlled part of the trade.

The name Usumacinta probably originated in the Nahua town of that name about a hundred miles upriver from the gulf, not far from

Tenosique, where the swift waters of the upland watershed join the torpid estuary. It is easy to imagine canoe traders bound upriver from the mouth at Potonchan calling the river, one of the delta's many broad winding channels, the "Usumacinta," the one that would take you upstream to Usumacinta town.

The Austrian explorer Teobert Maler, the most exhaustive chronicler of the river's natural and cultural history around the turn of the century, took an early stab at the name's derivation. "The Aztec name . . . means 'place of monkeys,'" he wrote. "*Osumatli,* monkey; *tsintla,* near, under, behind, etc. . . . [Locals are] not willing to pronounce *ts* or *tl,* because it demands too great a lingual effort on the part of this ease-loving people. Therefore...they simply say *sinta*, and this reminds them—ridiculous as it is—of the word cinta, ribbon. . . ." He claims the villagers of Usumacinta changed the name to Cabecera, meaning the principal set-tlement of a district, "not wanting to be named for monkeys."

Maler, as usual, at least had it close. Linguist Ricardo Salvador reads the name this way: *ozoma(tli)*, monkey, plus *-tzin*, a reverential or diminutive suffix, plus *-tlan(tli)*, place, equals Ozomatzintlan, place of sacred monkeys. No mention of a river. You would have to say *ozomatzinatl* to get sacred monkey water, *ozomatzinapantli* for sacred monkey watercourse, or *ozomatzinatoyatl,* sacred monkey river. If the original word were *ozomatzintla(h)*, Salvador concludes, then the literal reading would refer to an abundance of sacred monkeys.

Mesoamericanist Richard Haley thinks "sacred" too strong a trans-lation for *-tzin*. The honorific distinguishes one monkey from another as being in some way more important or at least distinguishable, though hardly sacred. *-Tzin* may also come from *-tzinco,* meaning new, as in *New* Mexico. Nicholas Hopkins, an anthropologist, opts for the meaning "small," to distinguish spider monkeys from the larger howler monkeys. Contradicting Maler, he says it was characteristic of gulf coast Nahua dialects, though not central Mexican ones, to replace the *tl* sound with *t,* and so this probably predated any influ-ence of the later-arriving Aztecs.

-Tzin may also be derived from *-tzintli,* buttocks, referring to a base or foundation, and arriving at "Monkeys, Place of Origin."

In any case, Maler was not far off.

Other names predated the Nahuatl. Maya of the lowland classical period, approximately 200 to 800 c.e., when Palenque and Tikal thrived, probably called the river Xocolha, "Water of the Xoc," after a mythical water monster. (Today's Lacandon call it Xoklá. A tributary near Piedras Negras is called Chocolha.) Later it may have shared the name Ayin, "Crocodile," with its principle upstream tributary now called the Pasión, after Christ's Passion.

In postclassic and colonial times the river bore numerous names and epithets depending on which end you viewed it from. Highlanders referred to the main river as the Sacapulas, or the Tuhalha. The lower river, below present-day Tenosique, went by Ixcolay and Cactocom, and the estuarial reaches, the Ixaccha.

Something edenic or arcadian clings to all these readings. Crocodiles, prominent in creation stories, represent the earth. Monkeys themselves, without redundant honorifics, possess mythic overtones lying deep in the Mesoamerican consciousness. In the *Popol Vuh,* the origin myth and scripture of the Quiche Maya, we are told that three creation cycles preceded the present one, each including a progressively more successful effort by the gods to fashion creatures who could keep the calendar, remember their creators, and offer them appropriate deference and sacrifice. Monkeys, in a curiously Darwinian slant, are remnants of the second creation cycle.

According to the *Popol Vuh,* the first people, made of mud, melted when exposed to rain. The gods tried wood, but the creatures were rigid, unfeeling, and lacked awareness. When that cycle succumbed to flood, the "wooden people" survived as monkeys, and as living remnants, emblems, of the previous creation.

Today monkeys represent everything irrational, unsocialized, irreverent, earthy. In the Festival of Games that marks the five lost days in the 260-day Maya calendar, held every February in San Juan

Chamula, near San Cristóbal de las Casas, men in monkey costumes cavort and taunt the spectators and participants with obscene and disruptive gestures and behavior. During the festival, the Chamulans, Tzotzil-speaking Mayas of an independent and largely traditional mien, "destroy the old world and create a new one," according to Mayanist Linda Schele. The monkeys (and foreigners) symbolize that lost, prior world. Schele calls them "pre-cultural beings who tear down the order of the world in order to prepare for its re-creation."

The name tells us that to these nature-oriented people, monkeys, the most visible and audible of the region's fauna, emblematized the vast, sprawling basin of the Usumacinta. That a place of monkeys, with all their associations, should refer to the Usumacinta generally—both river and watershed—is hardly surprising. Local Nahuatt-speaking Indians and Maya alike would regard it as a place of origins, with its great ruined cities, former glory and calamities, impenetrable forests, canyons, and rapids—numinous attributes that set the watershed apart as geographically distinct from its surrounding territories. It faces inward, like one of the region's monumental ceremonial complexes: a highland perimeter and an interior bowl forming "a break in the homogeneity of space"—Mircea Eliade's definition of sacred geography. For those reasons we must grant the watershed its significance as a sacred space, and render the meaning of the Usumacinta as "Sacred Monkey River."

IN MESOAMERICA THE matter of origins relates to canoes and canoeing, as well as to monkeys and crocodiles. Dugouts probably originated in Africa, where people from Gabon to Mozambique still ply the crocodile and hippo rivers, the coastal waters, and Rift Valley lakes in hardwood canoes. Eastward, in southern Asia, dugouts are used wherever navigable waters are warm and plentiful, fishing and trade fuel local and regional economies, and tropical hardwoods grow abundantly.

We may assume canoes crossed the Bering Strait with early northeast Asian tribespeople, ancestors of the first Americans, who perhaps followed the glacial or land-bridge coastline in large oceangoing dugouts or skin boats, or at least built them when they could to hunt seals, whales, and waterfowl, and to fish, while they skirted the coast on foot. Recent discoveries of early coastline migration have challenged the long-held paradigm in which manufacturers of distinctively fluted projectile points crossed the Beringian land bridge no earlier than the end of the last Ice Age, ten to twelve thousand years ago, and over generations followed an ice-free inland corridor south. The projectile points and the people who made them are known by the name Clovis, after one of their best-known sites in New Mexico.

Yet origin narratives throughout the western hemisphere contain stories of ancestors arriving by canoe from the west, the north, or the sky. In North America alone, canoe iconography surfaces widely in ancient art and stories. A pictograph carved beside a lake near Peterborough, Ontario, depicts half a dozen ancestor-like beings standing in a celestial dugout. The Iroquois Peacemaker comes from the northwest to upstate New York in a stone canoe, or a white canoe in some renderings, to establish the Great Peace and unite the Five Nations. The Muskogees and other southeastern tribes believe in twin Beings of Light (analogous to the Maya Hero Twins) who descended by canoe from a hole in the sky to teach the culture to the ancestors.

It was an unpeopled and unmediated ecosystem that they encountered, and that influenced the continuing evolution of human consciousness in the western hemisphere.

No direct archaeological evidence places canoes in Mesoamerica before the first millennium B.C.E.: wooden artifacts rarely survive the tropical climate. (In North America the oldest-known dugout, found buried in mud in Florida, dates to 5000 B.C.E.) Yet in South America numerous Amazonian tribes say their ancestors paddled the rivers—the "Paths of the Ancestors"—east to their homelands. Anthropologist Anna Roosevelt has found wood preserved in mud beside a river in eastern Brazil considerably older than ten thousand years and bearing all the earmarks of dugout fabrication.

Roosevelt's is one of many recently excavated sites (the Queen Charlotte Islands, Chile, and elsewhere) that challenge the Clovis paradigm of recent migration by land alone. She believes the migration from Eurasia to the Americas took place, at least in part, by canoe via coastal waters, following the southern shore of Beringia. This movement may have taken place before, during, and/or after the last glaciation. A coastal route would have been richer in game than an interior one, and the climate generally milder.

Traversing the land bridge itself would have been "impossible without water crossings," say anthropologists William Engelbrecht and Carl Seyfert. Beringia and the ice-free corridor inland would have been laced with thousands of square miles of meltwater sloughs, meanders, blind channels, and whitewater draining to the proto–Yukon River. "It is hard to imagine a mammal living there who was not an accomplished swimmer or a human who was not a skilled boatman," adds Peter Young of Vermont's Center for Northern Studies.

Equally waterlogged conditions would have confronted human migrants moving south by the interior route. Points retrieved from formerly submerged sites suggest Paleoindians probably hunted swimming caribou and mammoths from boats. Boats would have speeded the Clovis migration itself.

Watercraft must have existed in Asia in time to support the peopling of Australia at least forty thousand years ago. Human occupation of the Solomon Islands dates from thirty-three thousand to twenty-eight thousand years, requiring long ocean crossings at low Ice Age sea levels. By two thousand years ago seagoing canoe navigators had peopled most of the far-flung Pacific islands. Today, traditionally minded Pacific islanders ritualize and metaphorize canoecraft and navigation much as did the early Mesoamericans, who esteemed canoe navigators and considered long-distance canoe travel analogous with the shamanic journey of the spirit.

It would have taken far less sophisticated craft and skills than the island navigators possessed to follow the coastal waters of the land bridge and the low, now inundated coasts of British Columbia and the Northwest. And tribes of the Aleutian Islands, the Queen Charlottes, and the Pacific Northwest have developed and currently sustain some of the world's richest canoe cultures.

Whether or not subliminal memories of canoe-borne migration from Asia undergird certain western hemisphere creation narratives, we know that the Olmec and Maya associated canoes and long-distance canoe travel with ancestral arrivals and the making and shaping of the world.

The classical Maya Maize God, also called First Father rode a cosmic cayuco across the path of the sun to set in place the three cosmic hearthstones near the constellation Orion. There, he separated earth and sky at the dawn of the fourth creation cycle—ours, which approaches its end in the second decade of the twenty-first century. Two gods accompanied him whose images crop up frequently in classical depictions of birth, death, and royal accessions, kneeling at opposite ends of the galactic canoe.

Today, Lacandon Mayas brew their sacred intoxicant, the beverage called balche—their vehicle of communication with the gods—in a ritual dugout that stands outside the "god-house," a pole-and-thatch structure set off from the residential houses, where Lacandon men gather to drink and burn copal incense in braziers representing the gods. Their cosmology equates cayucos and crocodiles. Both are low and long, and liminal between the upper and lower worlds. Crocodiles derive from the cayucos of the wooden men, the lokin, who lived during the previous creation cycle.

At death Lacandons travel to Xibalba by paddling across a dangerous river, accompanied by a dog.

The canoe motif is continuous. The Olmec instigated the voyages of trade and pilgrimage into the highlands and along the gulf coast. Later gulf traders linked the city states of the Maya classical period, fostered their rise, and perhaps their decline as well.

By the classical period, canoe travel had long been perceived as a first principle of creation, preexisting the world itself. Voyaging the rivers, ancient paddlers recapitulated the journeys of gods and ancestors, retracing and thereby consecrating the Maya terrain. In the process of "entering the road"—the Watery Path—and transforming themselves from yeomen into pilgrims, they delineated and held together the world, and the land-based identity of the people.

The mental maps of the classical Maya, their cosmographs, were composed of mountains and lakes laced together by rivers. In practical terms, these rivers represented highways of war, commerce, and cultural exchange—the Usumacinta above all.

THE USUMACINTA PROPER begins in a nebulous region surrounding the convergence of its three main tributaries, the ríos Pasión, Chixoy, and Lacantun, somewhat less than two hundred miles upstream from the delta. Its headwater geography resembles an enormous amphitheater—the Chiapan highlands, the Cuchumatan Mountains, and the Alta Verapaz highlands of Guatemala forming a semicircle two hundred miles in diameter and rising to twelve thousand feet. (Guatemala accounts for 60 percent of the watershed.) The waters draining this expanse gather and concentrate in a single spout, which forms at barely five hundred feet above sea level and funnels their waters northwest to the gulf.

Teobert Maler claimed he had found the Usumacinta's source by 1895. He declared the Río Pasión an arm of the Usumacinta, followed it upstream to the ruin of Cankuen, near Seibal in Guatemala, and pronounced it "explored," at least from "an archaeological point of view." It was an era of heroic quests for the sources of heroic rivers—though major rivers seldom spring from single sources—and Maler wanted one for himself.

Maler knew his way around the Usumacinta better than any European, despite his rank as one of archaeology's blowhards. He never actually navigated the perilous Cañón San José, between Piedras Negras and Tenosique, but he traveled every other part of the river and some major tributaries by cayuco or steam launch. He also explored intensively around Budsilhá Falls and the mouth of the Río Chocolhá, an area often missed by other European and American explorers, who usually rushed to get to Tenosique and out of the territory as soon as possible after visiting the ruin of Yaxchilan.

Among the "three M's" of early Mesoamerican archaeology, Sylvanus Morley visited the Usumacinta more than once, in the 1920s and 1930s, and Alfred Maudslay beat Maler to Yaxchilan, then known as Menche Tinamit, in 1889. At the turn of the century Maler renamed the ruin on his own, incorrectly conflating the name of an arroyo across the river (Yalchilan) with a mistranslation of the Maya words for green or blue-green (yax) and priest (chilam). The name stuck, meaningless or not. He meant to leave an indelible mark, and since the Usumacinta composed the core of the classic world, no better place existed to leave it. It's only surprising that he didn't try to rename the river itself.

In quest of the Usumacinta's "source," Maler pushed upstream from a landing on the Pasión called Paso Real. The ascent, a distance Maler estimated at about 153 kilometers, took eight days. This was the era of the big mahogany camps, called monterías. Maler and his guide navigated their cayuco through flotillas of mahogany logs drifting downstream two hundred miles to the mills at Tenosique. When he reached what he considered the head of navigation, at a point where some smaller rivers converged, Maler pronounced his exploration complete.

In a report he later wrote for Harvard's Peabody Museum, Maler termed the exploration "a stupendous piece of work, accomplished at great expense of money, vast labor, and many annoyances." I doubt he exaggerated. He went on, describing himself as "wandering about from one year's end to another in these inaccessible wildernesses in search of remnants of bygone civilizations, denying myself the joys of life, subjected to strenuous labor, many dangers, and the daily annoyances resulting from the perpetual discontent of my men." He viewed his workers—Mayas from Tenosique, mostly—through a strong Social Darwinist lens. He considered them degenerate, yet possessing at least one redeeming quality. "However lazy and shiftless [they] may be in other respects," he wrote, "they display great aptitude on the water. It seems indeed as if [paddling] were the only occupation which they do not object to, for they perform all other labor with the greatest reluctance." Apparently he considered this ability genetically determined.

His map, published in the Peabody report, details the Pasión's twists and turns with admirable accuracy, but refuses to distinguish its course from the Usumacinta's. Today the Pasión is still called the Pasión and the Usumacinta is still generally acknowledged to begin where the Pasión and the Chixoy rivers, both flowing out of Guatemalan highlands, come together. The ruin called Altar de Sacrificios, discovered and named by Maler, stands at their confluence.

But you could call it either way. From the confluence—depending on the season and the water level, and which direction you were traveling in—the Pasión could be an arm of the Usumacinta. Maler usually arrived there moving upstream. On one trip he paddled up from the mouth of the Lacantun and found the current backing up into the Pasión because of heavy rains on the upper Chixoy.

So Maler's idiosyncratic hydrology may be partly forgiven. We may even accept his claim of having explored the entire Usumacinta from "an archaeological point of view," though he neglected the tributaries of the Lacantun, Lacanjá, and Jatate almost completely. (Bonampak— unknown to Westerners until 1946—and Toniná, among smaller ruins, lie at the headwaters of these tributaries, yet the sheer density of their ruins is far less than the Pasión's.) He discovered, surveyed, photographed, and named more ruins in the watershed than anyone before him, and most since. Some of these have seldom or never been visited again. By mapping the upper Usumacinta, its tributaries and ruins, he demonstrated the river's central importance in classical Maya geography. And though we would hardly call him a canoeist, or a boatman for that matter—clearly he depended on native paddlers for that service— he took to water for his explorations rather than following the river-banks on muleback. That way he absorbed a sense of geographic scale, distance, and difficulty unavailable to landbound explorers.

In 1889 Desirée Charnay and Alfred Maudslay explored the Usumacinta (in part) from opposite directions, met in the middle, and published highly descriptive accounts of their travels. At about the same time, clerics and scholars from Guatemala and Mexico passed through and wrote about the area. But none of them spent as much time on the river itself or investigated it as thoroughly as Maler did, nor with his breadth of knowledge and passion. Until Morley, and later the Danish anthropologist Frans Blom, came on the scene in the 1920s, Maler's travels in the watershed were unequaled.

Maler was an adept birder, and undaunted by the watershed's many poisonous and otherwise incorrigible fauna. He exhaustively cata-logued species according to their local names, and matched them tax-onomically with their Latin designations wherever possible. His knowledge included geology, and he seems to have been aware of the watershed as a distinct geographical entity, recognizing its intercon-necting human and wild systems. He knew where he stood at any given point in relation to every other place in the drainage. And where Charnay observed and described the river's wild beauty, its wealth of vegetation and wildlife, in lyrical prose, Maler did so with a natural-ist's eye and discipline. His on-site descriptions paint pictures of great natural beauty without resorting to overheated rhetorical flourishes.

Yet he was a bully and a prig in his personal and business relations. The Peabody dropped his services in 1905. He died in Mérida, Yucatán, in 1917.

Since Maler's time, the Usumacinta has been photographed from space, the images magnified and pored over by governments and nongovernmental agencies—and prospective looters—looking for ruins, ancient roads, canals and raised beds, mineral wealth, illegal logging and settlement. Satellite images documenting the watershed's shrinking forests have depressed *National Geographic* readers and North American high school students. Its flow has been measured to the decimal point by interests intent on damming it for hydroelectric power. At least from on high, it has been reduced to a sum of known quantities. But in its essence, its nature as a place apart, it remains a dimly perceived and shapeless expanse. In the 1920s the German expatriate writer B. Traven, while riding muleback to the Usumacinta and back, wrote in his notebook that the Usumacinta was thought to be mysterious for being so little explored. The observation remains only slightly less true today.

MY FIRST RECOLLECTION of the Usumacinta is of color: pale jade shot with turquoise and slightly clouded with silt; three hundred yards wide at low water. We had arrived by van from Palenque for a five-day raft trip beginning at Frontera Corozal, Chiapas, a Chol Maya border village with a ramshackle customs office and a small military garrison. We were headed seventy-five miles downstream through wild canyons and forests, with stops at the ruins of Yaxchilan, in Mexico, and Piedras Negras, on the Guatemalan side.

This was in February 1989. I had stolen a couple of weeks from my job editing a regional magazine in the Adirondacks to run the river with Victor Perera, the Guatemalan journalist who wrote *The Last Lords of Palenque*, a lament on the Lacandon Maya, their cultural decline and the shrinking of their forest homeland, the selva lacandona of southern Mexico and Guatemala.

His book had renewed my fascination with the area, begun when I read the novels and short stories of B. Traven (nom de plume of the Bavarian anarchist Ret Marut), reclusive author of *The Treasure of the Sierra Madre* and the so-called Jungle Novels, in high school. *Last Lords* brought back the Travenesque aura of ancient culture and wilderness persisting side by side in a modern nation, and of economic exploitation, peasant resistance, and rebellion. It added to my interest that I had been a rafting and canoeing guide in the Adirondack Park of northern New York and had once considered running the Usumacinta as a possible winter business venture. My guiding days had passed, though I still felt the Usumacinta's commercial attraction.

The magazine I edited—an advertising-driven, low-budget bimonthly—tried valiantly to cover the Adirondack Park's thorny environmental issues. At the time, the most pressing of these concerned property rights activists who angrily protested visionary and successful, if imperfect, land-use structures of long duration, which preserved the region's character. Their arguments relied on debatable readings of the Constitution, and boiled down to the blanket statement: "Don't tell me what to do with my land." My own feelings ran generally, though not entirely, counter to those of people I had known for decades. For those and other reasons it was a good time to get away.

Coincidentally, the Usumacinta faced a hydroelectric threat that would have rivaled Egypt's Abu Simbel dam project on the Nile in the scale of its archaeological and biological destruction. Across the river, rebels controlled the wild Guatemalan shore as far as the Mexican border at La Línea. The two countries had quarreled over logging rights and borders along the river for more than a century. The insurgency had undermined the corridor's already shaky security. The parallels between the Adirondacks and the Usumacinta, if any existed, were tenuous at best. I nevertheless sensed or imagined undercurrents connecting them.

On a wide gravel bar, forty-foot rib-and-plank boats called lanchas awaited tourists for day trips to Yaxchilan. We launched two kayaks, a paddle raft, and two "snout" rafts—a couple of inflatable Army-surplus bridge pontoons overlaid with a platform and oar frame—and drifted down the swift, flat expanse. High forest grew to the shore on both banks and echoed with the calls of howler monkeys. The big rafts lumbered ponderously but steadily downcurrent, fast enough to make Yaxchilan within three hours. I paddled one of the kayaks, and Tom Harper, an outdoor educator who had organized the trip with Victor Perera, paddled the other one.

Around the first bend, a cayuco came in sight, moving slowly up the current in front of the high green wall on the Mexican side. The boatmen, or vogas, stood at each end, alternately paddling and poling with long mahogany paddles called cañaletes. An alternate term, remo, refers more accurately to oars. A woman sat amidships, beside a tarp-covered mound. Their pace upstream against the stiff flow could not have been more than a mile an hour, if that, and they carried little more than three inches of freeboard. It looked as if they were floating *in* the water rather than on it.

They were a father, daughter, and son-in-law, the father paddling in the stern—the position known as gobernador. A dónde vas? he said. Tenosique, we answered. Ah, Tenosique. 'Ta bueno. He commented on our strange boats and we explained they were modeled upon those used by native people of the Arctic, the Inuit, who built them for running rapidos. Ah, sí, he said. To describe the Inuit we used the word winik, Maya for "people," which is what they call themselves and Native Americans generally. The Inuit we termed winik del alto norte, Indians of the high north, who lived amid mucho nieve, mucho frio, lots of snow and cold. Ah, sí, the man said.

At the time, I knew nothing of the metaphysic of canoes.

It was an old boat of darkened mahogany, about eighteen feet long, patched with sheet metal and rivets, with a low, graceful sheer line rising toward the bow, and a stern that barely cleared the water. They stood in place, holding water while we talked despite the force of the current. The whole arrangement seemed precarious. We asked what they carried under the tarp and the old man told the woman to fold back one corner, revealing a pile of waxy green-fading-to-orange serrano chiles freshly harvested from a jungle milpa somewhere between there and Yaxchilan. He spoke again and the woman scooped up a double handful of the chiles. We popped open our spray skirts to put the chiles inside, then we thanked them and turned our polymer-resin boats downcurrent, veering toward midriver to catch up with the rafts.

That evening I sat on the upturned bottom of a long cayuco that lay atop the high bank at Yaxchilan, sipping rum, mesmerized by the river's broad reach and the bronze light on the trees. Glassing the far shore, I saw a rebel appear, stumbling along the Guatemalan shore. He wore threadbare fatigues and carried on his shoulder an old assault rifle with the blueing worn off. I watched while he completed his reconnaissance and turned away from the river, into the trees.

In the morning we broke camp and put in the river just as the sun cleared the treetops. Immediately the man appeared again, standing with a couple outside their thatched hut nestled in the forest. He waved us to shore. Against the wishes of Scott Davis, the outfitter whose company, Ceiba Adventures, had provided the boats and guides for our trip, Victor insisted we should learn from the man as much as we could, and that we should at least honor his entreaty.

Victor's raft ferried toward shore. A second rebel came out of the hut, and both clambered aboard. We divided them between two rafts, hiding their firearms and supplying life jackets and spare baseball hats to disguise them in case of Guatemalan air patrols. The soldier in our raft was young and reticent, possibly non-Spanish-speaking, but Victor conversed with the older man in the other boat. The man said his group controlled the whole Guatemalan side of the river, and that they were now patrolling from Nuevo Jerusalem, just upstream, down to Piedras Niegras. He refused to be photographed.

We were in a shallow flat approaching the class 3 Anaite rapid, the water gliding languidly over exposed rocks, the gravel bottom clearly visible in the morning light. (The International Scale of River Difficulty runs from 1 to 6, with 1 being little rougher than flat and 6 meaning runnable only on penalty of drowning or worse. Classes 2 and 3 are the normal range for most open-canoe whitewater.) There was a silence as the young soldier in my boat pointed overhead and two scarlet macaws flew across the river from Guatemala to Mexico. Mo'ob, he said, speaking the Maya name for macaws.

The men rode with us through the Anaite rapid, with its train of three-foot waves, its large mid-current rock slightly river left, and narrow, twisting course. The rapid's reputation had been exaggerated, yet it excited our guests enough. Not far downstream we dropped them off near a milpa, or forest garden plot, where they would reprovision themselves.

As we continued downstream, the river felt familiar and strange at the same time, as if I had been there long before, or dreamed it. With every mile the canyons and forest grew deeper, the shores untracked, the corridor steep and winding, the current extremely fast. I found the rapids routine, but the *flat* water unnerving, broken by turbulent vortices and eddy lines caused by the river's steep limestone bed and deep, narrow channel. At one point I flipped the kayak and, unable to perform an Eskimo roll, swam down a long chute, bouncing off limestone blocks abrasive as sandpaper before being rescued.

We camped on a huge sandbar, or playa, on the Guatemalan side. Late that afternoon we hiked inland half a mile, following a creek to a small, slate-clear lake where Lacandons had lived in historical memory. A crocodile skull lay by the outlet. Again the low light struck an exposed ledge across the pond and cast a bronze glow over the treetops. It looked so much like home at that hour that it would not have surprised me if a loon had called. We got back to the sandbar at dusk, where a large aquatic animal—a crocodile, or possibly an anadromous tarpon—cavorted and splashed in a pool offshore in light too tenebrous to identify it by, and nighthawks (goatsuckers) darted under the stars.

In the morning a family of spider monkeys followed our rafts through the canopy for miles, climbing to the end of each branch's slenderest twig before launching and just catching the next. We found their effigies carved in the overgrown temples at Piedras Negras, where we camped that night.

We arrived at the landing late in the morning, as two rebels materialized from the understory. They quizzed us about the rafts, prompting concerns of a possible field requisition. Victor relayed our harmless intentions and sympathy with their cause. They were Cakchiquel Maya, again an older veteran and a younger soldier. They lived in the ruin, launching forays from there. They had sustained casualties a few days earlier.

The veteran's cheeks held patchy whiskers beneath sad eyes. He was in his forties but looked older. He wore a fatigue cap and the standard black rubber boots of the country, crisply military despite the rigors of the field. A plastic safety cap was in place on the muzzle of his well-maintained M-16, and he wore a .45 automatic Colt on his hip. (His subordinate carried a battle-scarred AK-47 with a broken stock.) He told us he had not seen his family in nine years, when he had been driven off his land and joined the rebels. He professed indifference to Marx. All either of them wanted, he said, was the right to work a parcel of land and live in peace.

The guides unpacked (keeping a watchful eye on the soldiers), arranged a kitchen, and laid out a lunch buffet while some of us pitched our tents on the beach. The men asked for cigarettes, which we didn't have, then for food. We invited them to join us for lunch. As we took our turns around the lunch table, two more rebels came out of the trees and began awkwardly assembling sandwiches from lunchmeats and soft white Mexican "Bimbo" bread. All four stayed for coffee before wishing us a pleasant visit and vaporizing into the forest under a load of leftover white bread and American cheese.

MALER VISITED AND described Piedras Negras in 1895, not long after its initial discovery by a mayor of Tenosique. Two decades later, archaeologist Sylvanus Morley, attempting to record all the hieroglyphic inscriptions in the lowlands, spent two long stretches taking photographs there. In the 1930s the University of Pennsylvania, under Linton Satterthwaite, undertook a controversial dig, mapping the layout of the ruin's main acropolis and pyramids. No further field-work had been done there in sixty years. The work to that point proved indispensible to Maya studies, nevertheless.

Tatiana Prouskouriakoff, a diligent and painstaking Harvard epigra-pher, spent twenty years poring over Maler's and Morley's detailed Piedras Negras drawings and photos, and the monumental pieces removed by the University of Pennsylvania. In the 1960s Prous-kouriakoff realized that the inscriptions recorded historical deeds by once-living rulers, rather than arid prophecies and astronomical com-putations, as existing theories contended. The discovery made possi-ble the decipherment and comprehension of Maya glyph writing, and opened a door to that remote and inscrutable people's collective con-sciousness. Her "historical thesis" began a chain reaction of learning that remains unexhausted.

The ruin brooded under a mature, unbroken canopy. The plazas and temples Proskouriakoff drew with such precision were totally obscured in the profusion of huge mahoganies and ceibas sprouting from the pyramid crowns, tendrils of parasitic strangler figs (mato palo) depending from their limbs. Fallen stelas—inscribed standing stones—velvety with moss, lay in the ferns. You might be admiring a heliconia blossom flashing in the dappled half-light when the figure of a sculpted monkey's head would emerge from the shadows before your eyes like a photograph developing. Other figures, which in a museum would have seemed at least marginally comprehensible, were indecipherable in that unbridled context, betraying assumptions concerning perception, scale, and substance conditioned by other landscapes, aesthetics, cosmovisions.

In the ruin we found an ingenious snare set by jaguar hunters, and a tractor used for hauling stelas and abandoned by University of Pennsylvania archaeologists in the 1930s. Rubble littered the bases of pyramids where someone had dug their way inside looking for arti-facts. (Later, a well-known archaeologist told me that the University of Pennsylvania's excavators had dug and left the rubble in their haste to get away with as many pieces as they could, as destructive in their way as the greediest looters.) In shallow caves we found freshly extinguished fires, refuse, and cartridge cases where our Cakchiquel hosts had camped, as Maler had a century earlier. A small banana patch grew in a clearing nearby. On returning to the beach, we surprised a basking iguana.

I photographed my tent pitched on the sand near a huge limestone slab carved with a circular design and known as the Sacrificial Rock, cantilevering over the landing as if it had fallen there, though it may always have rested at that angle. The sand was white, the water swirling ominously through its deep, narrow channel, the steep hillsides dark with thick growth. It was, as Morley found in the twenties, a fabulous campsite. I swam in the eddy behind a pile of slabs that had fallen in the river, wondering what large creature had been thrashing in the water the night before. I opened my eyes underwater to bars of sunlight flickering through an aqueous solution of pale milky jade.

In the evening the rebels returned with two tepescuintle—toothsome jungle woodchucks—roasted on a spit. They joined us for dinner and told us they had driven off engineers and surveyors engaged in staking out a nearby damsite. Victor Perera told them of an imminent plan to log old-growth mahogany in a section of the Sierra Lacandon nearby, a bit of intelligence that raised their eyebrows. They vowed to stop it. They said they belonged to the Rebel Armed Forces (FAR), one of four resistance groups then operating in Guatemala, all of which, while remaining autonomous, stayed in touch and coordinated their efforts. They claimed to have allies with similar aims in Belize and Chiapas, a bit of intelligence that in 1989 raised *our* eyebrows. I couldn't help seeing them as the first line of defense against the anything-goes resource extraction ravaging much of the watershed.

They returned in the morning as we broke camp, helping to carry some of the heavier items down the bank to the boats. Then they joined us as we held hands in a circle and Victor said a prayer for peace, the shy younger rebel and the seasoned veteran, their faces beaming. When Victor finished, the older man added words of his own. We must have presented a striking tableau from a distance, one that, as a northeasterner among Californians, made me cringe slightly, but that finally had a tonic effect on all present, if not on the course of peace. Flush with a sense of fellowship and the PR value of our meeting, the veteran went around shaking our hands and saying, When you get back to your university, please send the world greetings from the Cakchiquel nation.

With everything packed, we launched the rafts. The veteran held the bow of the kayak for me, his M-16 slung on his shoulder, while I settled myself in the cockpit. Adios, he said as I paddled into the current. Adios, I answered. Buena suerte. When I looked back from midriver, he and the young recruit were standing in the shadow of the Sacrificial Rock, waving. The current picked up and sucked me toward the first rapid below the ruin. When I looked back again, they were gone.

I relay their greeting now.

A FEW MILES downstream, on a deep bend between Budsilhá and San José Canyon, inside Mexico, we passed a cayuco factory at the landing for the village of Francisco Madero. Two unfinished boats stood in the stocks beneath a tamarind tree. Raw mahogany chips, russet-colored, littered the ground around them. The cayuco master and his team concentrated on a single boat, bent over their adzes. The other cayuco rested in a condition of half completion, its boatlike features emerging from the primal log.

Soon after Francisco Madero we ran the class 3 rapids under San José Canyon's spectacular thousand-foot walls and camped at Boca de Cerro ("Mouth of the Hill"), below the final drop. We passed out of the selva, and the swift water, into the delta.

The next day, drifting past dozens of small farms and river settlements on the wide flats, we saw more boats, and boys fishing. They paddled out to us standing in two exquisitely wrought cayucos, the hulls asymmetrical though harmonious (a fundamental principle of Maya art and design, according to my friend Moises Morales), the bows sheering gracefully upward, the sterns down, the adze and machete strokes still fresh on their hulls. Both cayucos were eleven or twelve feet long, with rounded chines, and the boys seemed comfortable with only three or four inches of freeboard, as if riding artful wood chips. They laughed and plied the water with narrow fluted paddles shaved delicately as violin bows. We were passing through the transition from the highland to the delta waters, the tidal and the swift, near Usumacinta town, where cultures had mixed in mutual self-interest for two thousand years. We gave them food and they asked us for pens. Early that afternoon we beached on a wide bar at a cane field near Tenosique, and drove on well-maintained country roads, past crop fields and pastures, back to Palenque.

Thirty-six hours later we drove all day over rough tracks to the Lacandon village of Naha, at the headwaters of three Usumacinta tributaries. There I met Chan K'in Viejo, the centenarian religious headman, or to'o'hil, of the unconverted, traditional Lacandons. As a service Chan K'in interpreted some of our dreams according to traditions meticulously recorded and cross-referenced by anthropologist Robert Bruce in his book *Lacandon Dream Symbolism*. To a rather insipid sex dream the old man offered a stock response, that the dreamer would "see game." Another member of our party complained about his job and speculated that he might become a mendicant seeker. It is good to work, the old man said.

The next day a rented Volkswagen van arrived in the village, improbably carrying Leon Shenandoah, Chan K'in's counterpart among the Haudenosaunee, the Longhouse People, of upstate New York and Canada—the Iroquois. Shenandoah told us an aged Onondaga woman had dreamed he should go to the jungle and find the old man who kept the old ways, and he had made his way to Naha by asking around Yucatán and Chiapas, accompanied by two Tuscarora helpers and a middle-aged white woman from Syracuse who paid the bills. It surprised Shenandoah not at all that he had found what he was looking for. Victor translated while the two men shared creation stories and prophesied the world's end, which they agreed would occur sometime in the next thirty or forty years.

A KIND OF end has come already to the Usumacinta, or come again, amid echoes of the classical Maya "fall." In almost every Mayanist's eschatological scenario, humans had populated the watershed so thickly by the eighth century that the forest had become a patchwork. The resulting climate changes and erosion depleted poor rain forest soils. Food demand outstripped the productivity of both the Mayas' sophisticated slash-and-burn agriculture and their elaborately maintained system of aquatic raised beds. Eighth-century burials show a widening nutritional gap between the elite royal classes—the *ahaus*—whose skeletons remained robust, and the common folk, whose remains grew smaller and showed signs of malnutrition. Wars ensued. The people lost faith in their rulers and abandoned the cities. Their populations returned to a sustainable level. It meant that large sections of the Lacandon forest and the contiguous forests of Petén and southern Yucatán were already mature second-growth, second-chance wildernesses long before Cortés hacked his way from Tenosique to Honduras in 1525. Classical culture had to decline in order for the ecosystem to recover.

Today, in Chiapas and Guatemala, the living heirs of the classical Maya endure outrages at landowners' hands similar to the ones that Traven depicted in his series of six Jungle Novels, written in the 1930s. In Chiapas, eighty years after the Mexican revolution, nineteen non-Indian familes own the greater portion—7 million hectares—of the state's best farmland. Before the peace of December 1996 in Guatemala, troops beholden to landowners massacred

Mayas. The Indians suffer at each other's hands as well. In both countries, politics, religion, and money divide the most traditional Maya communities, many of the fractures stemming from feuds and animosities dating back hundreds of years.

Runaway populations aggravate chronic conflicts. At various times since World War II, when driven to ease land pressures, the Mexican government has encouraged colonization in the lowlands. Thousands of Mayas left their homes in the high, cool tierra templada and started new lives on the frontier, in the jungle, the tierra caliente. Combined with legal and illegal logging and international aid incentives that rewarded land clearing, their market-driven (rather than subsistence) slash-and-burn agriculture methods recapitulated the classical period's cycle of destruction.

The historical echoes—and all Mesoamerica is a historical echo chamber—are too loud to miss. Yet a wild selva devoid of native forest dwellers would be open, in the Usumacinta, to wholesale exploitation.

Today highways slice across the rivers and encircle the forests, obscuring the ancient relationships of scale and distance, the perceptions dependent on the speed of canoe travel upstream or down, the trails and portages hewing to topography. Transits and bulldozers reconfigure the landscape, laying roads brutally straight and fast, carrying in tourists and settlers, carrying out timber and oil, disordering people's mental maps, disrupting social and cultural expectations.

Now you speed at dusk across the pale flat delta, the landscape's details fading in the light: the rich savannas, the narrow watercourses winding ambiguously to the Grijalva or the Usumacinta, the ceibas arching their crowns over the rangeland. Trucks flash their lights and pass each other with abandon. In the distance the front range of the Chiapas highlands casts a low profile against the sky.

Two

PALENQUE

I RETURNED TO THE USUMACINTA IN 1992, DRIVING AROUND THE
watershed's highland perimeter from Palenque to Antigua,
Guatemala, and back to Chiapas, where I revisited the Lacandon
headman Chan K'in Viejo and his son Kayum Ma'ax at Naha.

After Naha, hours from Ocosingo on brutal dirt roads, my com-
panions and I stopped at a bridge spanning the Río Santa Cruz near El
Real, the site of a historic Tzeltal Maya community, and the headquarters of the old Bulnes land grant, fictionalized by Traven. The Santa

Cruz, no bigger than a trout stream, ran blue-green and fragrant over an eight-foot drop before disappearing into a shadowy slot canyon. These were the far headwaters of the Usumacinta, two hundred river miles upstream from Yaxchilan. Steep, jagged mountains surrounded the valley, treeless but for the wind-whipped pines you could see nodding on their crests.

From the bridge I scouted the class 5 drop for a navigable line, running it and the next one in my mind, into the slot canyon, and beyond, to the Río Jatate of fearsome history and reputation, and beyond that to the Río Lacantun and the Usumacinta, four hundred miles to the mangrove sloughs guarding the mouth at the Gulf of Mexico.

The route, down four succeeding rivers, described three sides of a quadrangle heading progressively southeast, northeast, and northwest. It enclosed the Montes Azules Biosphere Reserve, the 1,270-square-mile remnant of the Lacandon rain forest, and skirted the Maya Biosphere Reserve in Guatemala, haunt of the Guatemalan rebels of Piedras Negras.

I wanted to infiltrate, to be absorbed into, and to absorb as much as possible the essence of that strange new place, however confusing and unwelcoming it might be. As I stood on the bridge, it seemed the most natural thing in the world to launch a boat and follow the rivers where they carried me, even necessary given their entry to the region's character—the quickest route to the heart of the country.

I formed a mental picture of the watershed as a capacious blue-green dish, distinct and set apart from the surrounding geography by mountains, rivers, and a persistent air of mystery (not simplistically "exotic," however, though outlandish within its own context). The dish had an elusive though definable character combining fine-grained landscapes of river and forest ecosystems, canyon and range, and a vast complex of history and myth "ubiquitous in space and durable in time" (Borges). I visualized it as the repository of a concentrated Americanness, a fount where grand and tragic experiments of reverberating interest and importance had taken place. Dense, enigmatic, it folded back on itself.

That unity, held together by the network of rivers, had sustained and nurtured classical culture. Today, such geographical and cultural isolation could help expedite the establishment of protective conventions for nature and monuments, and nowhere are the stakes higher for such conventions than in the Usumacinta. That isolation also increased the potential for dangerous fractures: political, ethnic, economic, ecological.

I harbored no pretensions of a "first descent," nor of discovery. Ancient traders, lumbermen, and modern recreationists had run the Usumacinta for centuries, down each of its half dozen major tributaries. Though it remained marginal and unknown, the region not only had been discovered, but had been photographed from space, digitized on GIS programs. In the grand scheme I was just another poseur aiming to "run the river X from its source to its mouth," a cliché of exploration literature.

All I could try to do was to slow and concentrate my perception, take in the basin—la cuenca—in its totality from top to bottom, at canoe speed, the speed of the ancients, and gain a sense of the step-by-step relations of distance and direction that undergird a basic knowledge of place. Along the way perhaps some adhesive element would draw together the pieces of the fabric, like a zipper, at least for the purposes of my own understanding, and show it to me whole.

I anticipated bearing witness to change and possibility, and hoped that somewhere in the Usumacinta's vast basin, its network of capillaries and backwaters, in a place where roads, deforestation, and speed had not distorted the relationships, I might find people who viewed the region as a cosmogram held together by canoes and river navigation and informed by the voyages of the ancestors. Only in this way did my purpose at all resemble the more scientific and fanciful ones of the *real* explorers, those priests, soldiers, and scholars who sought lost cities and uncontacted tribes, copied the inscriptions and stole the art, who catalogued its biological wealth and loss, or cased the joint for plunder.

Four years after standing on the bridge over the Santa Cruz, I rolled into Palenque from the Adirondacks carrying two canoes on the roof rack of a many-miled but durable Nissan Sentra. I took a room in a cheap hotel in the "cañada" section on the edge of the village. Then I ate a bad mole poblano, devoid of picante or character, in a new tourist restaurant on Calle Merle Green and followed the village's back streets out to the main drag.

The holiday binge drinking was in full cry, fireworks for sale on every corner. Billboards advertised chain saws and pesticides. On the retaining wall fronting the raised zócalo someone had painted a jungle scene and captioned it with the words "Protect our trees and rivers. They protect our natural lands." Another wall, painted in the heraldic tricolor (green, orange, and white) of Mexico's ruling party, the PRI, declared, "1996, the year of peace and reconciliation in Chiapas."

The mural alluded to tentative peace accords signed in recent weeks between Maya representatives of the EZLN—the Zapatistas— and the Mexican government at San Andrés Larráinzar, in the highlands, and currently being debated for approval in every remote outlying ejido and aldea that formed the movement's social base.

It illustrated how much had changed in the mountains and canyons of Chiapas since I had plotted my pilgrimage to understanding on the bridge at El Real. The dam threats on the Usumacinta had subsided, but in 1994 the war over land and power that had ravaged Guatemala for a generation had jumped the river like a forest fire and caught in the dry tinder of Chiapan inequities, confirming the reports of our informants at Piedras Negras in 1989. The Guatemalan conflagration had finally consumed its fuel and sputtered out, leaving more than 200,000 dead in a population of 11 million. That peace agreement, the fruit of five years of negotiations between Guatemalan authorities and representatives of four rebel organizations, had been finalized just weeks before my arrival. The Zapatista uprising was a dustup by comparison—two weeks of fighting in January 1994, less than 500 known dead, though thousands of others had died or been displaced in related activity.

Conditions in both countries had spun off criminal activity along the Usumacinta itself. Contraband traffic had increased, some of it run by sacked Guatemalan army officers. In Mexico, campesinos had turned piratical after suffering peso devaluations caused by former President Carlos Salinas's drastic NAFTA-induced economic policies. Villagers near San José Canyon on the Usumacinta poached mahoganies around Piedras Negras, smuggling out logs on motorized lanchas, and posed as Zapatistas to hijack raft trips and private boaters for cash and equipment.

Scott Davis, of Ceiba Adventures, had suffered one of the worst of these attacks. Fortunately, rumors reported a falling off in criminal activity along the Usumacinta. Upstream, in las cañadas, the forests and canyons of the Río Jatate, the first leg of my descent, the rebellion endured. There, Davis had received permission from military and Zapatista representatives to resume his five-day trips. The chain of trust forged by regular contact with the Indians had been broken, however, and it was unclear whether either of us could actually regain access to the river.

Tonight, Palenque showed few effects of the recent upheavals, at least on its surface. Alegría prevailed. Only the occasional olive drab truckload of uniformed soldiers riding down the street betokened unrest. State police circled the zócalo and the ring of downtown streets, young toughs in blue T-shirts and baseball caps riding in the beds of brand-new, blue Dodge pickups, brightly polished. They looked like an eager band of head-crackers. In the event of a confrontation, you never would have been able to distinguish gunfire from the constant explosions of cheap fireworks, sold by children on every street corner.

The town fathers probably financed the patrols out of their own pockets. It behooved them to moderate the polarities—Indian versus Ladino, ranching versus tourism—which they catered to equally. Tourism was catching up economically, but ranching still prevailed in the municipality, the consequence of aid incentives in the seventies which had paid by the hectare for cleared pasture. The programs dried up years ago, yet everybody kept a few beeves, even Indians, and bulls and semen were advertised on hand-lettered signs along the back roads.

The clearing had altered the surroundings dramatically in a generation, from high canopy forest with isolated ranch clearings to its reverse: open pasture with isolated forest patches. The village sprawled across a height of land separating Salto de Agua, on the Tulijá, and the head of a smaller river called the Chacamax, an Usumacinta tributary. The ruin, said to have been called Lacamja, "Place of Water," in ancient times, stood dramatically on a terrace of the highlands' front range, a few miles outside the village, surrounded by a national park. Everywhere Asian zebu cattle, long-horned and white, drifted like ghosts over the landscape.

On the outskirts the road ran through a ragged commercial strip boasting a Volkswagen dealership, numerous tire repair and lube joints, building supply outlets, convenience stores, restaurants, and cheap motels. Closer to town stood the airport, high school, and a two-year ag-and-tech college. Inexpensive taxis and combis—Volkswagen buses with row seating for passengers—ran continuously from a colonia called Pacal-Na, at the far end of the strip, to the zócalo, so despite the strung-out design of the suburbs, you could more or less get by without owning a car.

Downtown's main artery started at a hideous sculpture of a Maya head, called the cabeza, and ran for a mile to the other end of town. You could walk the distance in half an hour. For the first quarter mile it was a broad boulevard crowded with traffic, with a busy Pemex gas station, a health clinic and a cemetery. Crowds milled back and forth between adjacent bus stations where street vendors sold fresh mangoes, grilled meat, or audiotapes of salsa and rancheras, samples of the latter broadcast at full volume from nuclear-powered blasters. Beyond the Pemex station the boulevard narrowed and two side avenues converged.

A commercial smorgasbord flanked the next quarter mile; loud, smelly, abrasive. Most consumer goods available in Mexico could be found there, except for a decent newspaper, but including marijuana. Blasters, fireworks, and unmufflered Volkswagen Beetles competed for the highest decibel level. You could send a fax from twenty different shopfronts.

The travel agencies, knickknack shops, craft outlets, and tourist hotels all bore the names of major ruins, figures from the classical Maya pantheon, or one of the state's totemic but endangered animal species (Las Tucanes, Hotel Pacal, Viajes Bonampak). On the streets the ancestors' direct descendants—local Chol Maya and barefooted Tzotzil women and girls from the highland town of Chamula—sold belts, highland traje (traditionally woven wool and cotton garments), and Subcomandante Marcos dolls by the dozens. In the outlying ejidos and aldeas of the municipality the same women and girls, and their husbands and fathers, vied with cattlemen and developers over the diminishing availability of good and marginal agricultural land.

The municipal hall, located on the zócalo (and restored following riots over a baseball game the year before) displayed a new limestone seal over its portico, featuring the distinctive profile of Pacal, the eighth-century ruler whose reign encompassed the period of Palenque's greatest flowering, and whose tomb, with its heraldic and spectacular carved sarcophagus lid, lay in the bowels of the ruin's massive Temple of the Inscriptions.

The village's layout left much unspecified. Unlike the ruin, it expressed no cosmovision, no worldview except linearity—which was, after all, the chief expression of western commercial and civic art of the last fifty years. And nothing pointed to a landscape until recently defined by rivers and their navigation by canoe.

The first Americans in Palenque, a diplomat and a soldier named Walker and Caddy, had in fact traveled there by canoe from Belize, traversing the southern Yucatán peninsula along an ancient trade corridor in the 1830s. In 1839 another diplomat, the explorer John Lloyd Stephens, came via the highland trails from San Cristóbal de las Casas. Emerging from the mountains, Stephens passed through Palenque's pastoral suburbs and saw the village standing on a slight table of land, "consisting of one grass-grown street, unbroken even by a mule-path, with a few straggling white houses on each side, on a slight elevation at the farther end a thatched church, with a rude cross and belfry before it. A boy could roll on the grass from the church door out of the village." He called it "the most dead-and-alive place I ever saw." Stephens and his partner, the artist Frederick Catherwood, had just made a difficult passage from Ocosingo, during which they infamously traveled part of the distance by silla, a chair strapped to an Indian's back. Stephens observed that the Indians still lived in thatched huts in the surrounding country, and whites or mestizo Mexicans inhabited the village, a pattern that persists.

The village came into being around the end of the sixteenth century—oral tradition says 1598—when colonial authorities in Guatemala gathered scattered family groups living in the lowland forests, adjacent highlands, and the Río Tulijá valley to "administer" them better, exploit their labor, and protect them from apostasy. (Chiapas remained a Guatemalan department until early in the nineteenth century.) The task fell to Friar Pedro Lorenzo, whom Palencanos and residents of many nearby towns both native and mestizo remember and revere as a sympathetic figure.

The village's Indians rebelled from time to time, like others around Chiapas. In 1712 troops from Guatemala put down a band of backsliders who made "unseemly obeisances to a female deity." The last uproar before 1994 had occurred in the mid-nineteenth century.

IN THE MORNING I woke to an earthquake's gentle rocking at 7 A.M., then drove out past the cabeza toward the ruin. Yellow dabs of blossoming guanacaste trees brightened the surrounding hills. The ridgeline to the east, while green, had a ragged, skinned look. The ridge rose a thousand feet above the plain, its gentle karstic folds and corrugations fragmented by the erratic, immoderate use of chainsaws for clearing and milpa scars on the steep slopes. Below, expensive new hotels and restaurants built to serve a theoretical carriage trade of tourists had sprung up in the pastures. They bore the totemic names of threatened species or of classical Palenque's royal court, and they all appeared empty. Even the peso's nosedive the year before had failed to halt their construction.

That was the chief change from my last visit: more construction.

When Stephens came here in 1839, the mule ride to the ruin took two and a half hours. "Very soon we entered the forest, which continued unbroken to the ruins, and probably many miles beyond," Stephens wrote. "The road was a mere Indian footpath, the branches of the trees . . . hanging so low that we were obliged to stoop constantly. . . . From the thickness of the foliage the sun could not dry up the wetness from the deluge of the night before. The ground was very muddy, broken by streams swollen by early rains, with gullies in which the mules foundered and stuck fast, in some places very difficult to cross."

Now the forest was gone. It had vanished so fast, was still vanishing, that people my own age had a hard time internalizing the new reality. And Chol people in the vicinity, when you saw them along the road or disappearing into the undergrowth with machetes in hand, wore a look I came to associate with the landscape's radical transformation. It was the same look of stunned disbelief that you saw in photographs of the survivors of bombings, urban renewal, and other ravages—their fields salted, their wells poisoned, the world reconfigured in the blink of an eye.

At a small creek (still running clear), which Stephens called the Michol, I turned left. A sign read EL PANCHAN, VEG. CUISINE. CONTEMPLATION AND MEDITATION. Here a pocket of original forest stood thick and tall. The driveway led to a ford, shaded by a chicozapote with enormous root buttresses and bromelias as big as century plants sprouting from its limbs. My car still loaded, I declined the crossing, even though the water had receded since the recent rain. Instead I parked and crossed a footbridge in dappled shade.

Hundreds of scarlet ginger blossoms lined the drive for a hundred yards. Cars and vans from every part of North America were parked in front of the main house, a three-story confabulation of concrete piers called a champa, with wide mahogany floors and metal roofing open to the air and shaded by tall trees and vines. An elevated concrete walkway extended from the second-floor kitchen and common area to a small open-sided pole structure, called a palapa, with a thatched roof and screened walls built in the air—the study and retreat of Moises Morales: Mayanist, guide, hotelier, and raconteur. On the champa's third floor, a penthouse and azotea had been added for his companion, a German artist and spiritual adept named Rakshita.

Callipygian Euro-beauties in diaphanous shifts drifted around bare-foot. They all seemed tattooed and pierced in their navels, nostrils, and quien sabe where else. They returned my greetings with studied sangfroid or silent, serene expressions.

I stood on the ground-floor patio and called up to the kitchen. Rakshita looked over the railing wearing a quizzical expression. Her hair had gone from blond to gray. I reminded her of our meeting five years before, when I had interviewed Don Moises, and mentioned the names of some friends we had in common. I told her about my plan to run the Usumacinta, and asked if it would be possible to use Panchan as my base.

She remembered me, and told me in her silky German accent that she would have a cabaña opening the next day. Moises would be gone until then, she added. I asked after him. She said, He is the same as always: he starts things and doesn't finish, he forgets other things. But he has a big heart and will talk to you again. Some people don't have the patience to listen to everything he has to say. But he loves to give himself, and when he does he gives all of himself.

That was how I remembered him—along with qualities she didn't mention.

That evening, New Year's Eve, the scene on the zócalo hummed with anticipation and a hint of menace, the republic's hopes teetering on the edge of something, perhaps some improvement, perhaps not.

I called home from a pay phone. My fiancée, Sue Kavanagh, told me Victor Perera had left a message on the answering machine that old Chan K'in had died.

When I reached him in Berkeley, Victor sounded distraught. He had heard the news from Robert Bruce, his collaborator on *The Last Lords of Palenque*, who called from Mexico City. Chan K'in died three years to the day after the death at ninety-three of Gertrude (Trudi) Duby Blom, his close friend and mentor, a photographer, conservationist, explorer of the selva Lacandona, and the widow of the Danish explorer and anthropologist Frans Blom. Chan K'in's age was estimated at 103 or 104.

Victor lamented that fewer and fewer remained of the old guard who remembered the selva and had tried to protect it before the massive losses of the seventies, when the Lacandons themselves had traded hundreds of old-growth mahoganies for land; people like Bruce, the Bloms, the zoologist Miguel Alvarez del Toro, and the Belgian historian Jan de Vos.

I tried to listen on the Telmex pay phone while firecrackers exploded around my feet, thrown in the spirit of año nuevo by some of the village's future unemployed young men. Victor told me to ask around about Chan K'in's death and prospects for Naha.

The tribe had long endured the diseases and depredations of freelance lumberers, mestizo hunters, and chicle gatherers (chicleros), but in 1940 the Mexican government declared most of southeastern Chiapas government property and open to settlement. By the early fifties the Lacandons were feeling the encroachments of their more numerous and more fertile highland cousins. The newcomers' free-ranging livestock infested the Lacandons' benignly managed milpas, and their larger-scaled slash-and-burn agriculture laid waste large forested areas.

The Lacandons' territory encompassed isolated, patriarchal, extended-family homesteads called caribals, and their hunting and trading ground, which stretched from Tenosique to San Cristóbal, and from Palenque to Sayaxché, in Guatemala. Under pressure they coalesced into villages to protect their milpas from invaders, and to be eligible for government benefits.

Traditionally, their agricultural practice perfectly suited their habitat. They grew a hundred or more species of fruits and vegetables, rotating their plots. After clearing new milpa, they planted the usual three sisters—maize, beans, squash—and chiles, and rotated them with tobacco. After three years, when the soil wore out, they moved on, but they still used the old plot to grow fruit and attract small game like deer and tepescuintle. After a generation they could return and reuse the old plot. In normal times, the system maintained them in relative good health. They also practiced abortion and infanticide and maintained their population at an optimum level of between two hundred and four hundred people since colonial times.

Nominally Christian Maya of the highlands—Tzeltales, Tzotziles, and Tojolabales—on the other hand, valued high birth rates. Aided by government health-care initiatives dating from the sixties, they had one of the highest in the world, approximately 3.5 percent a year, and a diminishing base of arable land. Forced to pay high rents by Latino and Maya landlords, they farmed at least partly for cash, but the economy of scale, especially since NAFTA, undervalued their labor. To survive, they boosted production by the only means available: among them pesticides and herbicides. Ronald Nigh, an agrarian anthropologist in San Cristóbal, told me the use of herbicides drastically reduced the amount of time campesinos had to spend weeding, traditionally a job performed twice during each of three annual maize crops. By the time they completed a large plot, it was time to go back and do it again. With one application of Roundup, however, they accomplished the same thing in a matter of hours, leaving time to work on road crews or for wages on lowland plantations. The two farming approaches conflicted, and the slower, more compatible Lacandon method suffered.

In the middle fifties the Bloms—he an old-fashioned anthropologist, she a onetime intimate of Frida Kahlo—undertook to preserve a section of the selva as a Lacandon homeland and forest preserve, making nuisances of themselves with the federal government. Desperate not to be overrun, the Lacandons supported the campaign. In 1964 a lumber mill opened in the village of Chancala, near Palenque, bringing industrial forestry to the selva and ratcheting up the pressure. The trees retreated before roads and more settlers.

In 1971 the government, bowing to the Bloms and the tide of change, set aside 614,321 hectares, including non-Lacandon native communities and an enormous wealth of tropical hardwoods, as an indigenous reserve, to be managed communally by the Lacandons "for time immemorial." Immediately the national forestry agency began negotiating with tribal leaders for rights to harvest some of their last old-growth mahoganies, plying them with gifts and favors. The community divided, with the Bloms and others advising against the sale. In the end, Chan K'in's son, the current president of Naha, signed away the old trees in return for what amounted to barrels of cash for the tribe. It was a turning point not only for the three hundred or so Lacandons but for their paternalistic treatment by well-meaning advocates.

Bulldozers carved a road through the forest to Naha, erasing local memory accumulated over centuries of foot and canoe travel. Mahoganies fell and were trucked to anonymous markets. The tribe acquired one pickup truck, then others. More colonists followed the new road.

In *Last Lords* Perera had described the psychic shock the lumbering brought to the more traditional members of the community, but the deal devastated the gringo old guard he now mourned. The Lacandons pleaded pragmatism in their defense: if they had turned down the offer, they reasoned, the government would have taken the trees for nothing—probably true. Ironically, the Lacandon grant became the basis of the Montes Azules Biosphere Reserve in 1978, when an additional 331,200 hectares were added to the original grant. The designation forever confused how the protected area should be managed—as a wilderness reserve, a Lacandon homeland, or for resource extraction.

Today Montes Azules and the surrounding lowlands make up a patchwork of vaguely delineated jurisdictions managed communally by the Lacandons, as well as by Chol and Tzeltal residents who agitated for and won inclusion in the original grant. A large but shrinking core area protects the selva's old-growth vestiges and wildlife. Representatives from Conservation International, Ecosur, an organization headquartered in San Cristóbal, and smaller groups, counsel the communities on sustainable agriculture, community development, and ecotourism. Below the surface many other interests—extractive, military, religious—vie for influence and power in the lowlands. Compatible, prosperous indigenous communities are clearly preferable to these.

Now, however, you saw Lacandons wearing the traditional tunics and long hair with Rolex watches on their wrists as they sold bows and arrows and other crafts on the streets of San Cristóbal and Palenque. Others had Mexicanized, cutting their hair and adopting jeans and sneakers as their dress. All viewed skeptically the Zapatistas—the descendants of colonists—and their hunger for land.

On the zócalo I took a bench and joined the crowd. The church and plaza flanked it on the west; the municipal building on the north; the colonnaded cabildo, once the seat of colonial administration, now a museum and arts center, on the south. In front of the cabildo a dozen marimba students ranging in age from twelve to fifteen offered a recital, their instruments lined up side by side. They made a harmonious counterpoint to the fireworks. Grackles answered antiphonally in the box-trimmed arbors. Families watched each other from the benches with their toddlers on their laps, couples strolled in silent communion. The midnight Mass congregation poured onto the plaza from the open church portal.

However calming, the scene had a chaotic edge, the kind that in a suspense film you know presages some disorder. Where had the securidad's pickup trucks gone? I felt like I wasn't the only one who sensed an impending dislocation, some spectacle celebrating or condemning the third anniversary of the Zapatista uprising: perhaps a sudden, stealthy appearance by masked guerrillas, a lecture, a riot. We watched and listened for sounds of danger amid the marimbas and fireworks.

I got up and joined the overflow crowd on the plaza in front of the church, the same Stephens had mentioned, its roof thatch replaced by tiles. New Year's marked the Feast of the Circumcision, a holy day of obligation for those faithful not yet converted to fundamentalist Protestantism and singing pop gospel tunes down the street in the evangelical hall next door to the restaurant Las Tinajas. I pressed my way to the wide-open door. Other gringos were sprinkled through the crowd and there were some Indians as well, including the Chamulan craft dealers and their daughters. They stood barely four feet tall in their blue embroidered huipiles, long black skirts, and bare feet, the daughters carrying infants in slings across their bodies. Inside the worshipers listened to a decidedly non-Mexican cleric of Bishop Samuel Ruiz Garcia's progressive diocese. Bearded and taller than six feet, he resembled a Russian monk more than a Mexican priest. From what I could hear, he voiced seasonal platitudes peppered with references to justice and equality.

Outside I joined a dozen or so family members crowded onto a bench. The family's abuelo and abuelita, wrinkled, grizzled, and resigned, sat stoically and nearly invisible, surrounded by their numerous offspring—a dozen distributaries branching from their main channel. A woman I took to be their daughter, a no-nonsense type who would have sold real estate in the States (and may have here), bore two toddlers on her lap. She wore a low-cut, fashionable print dress, high heels, makeup, and wished me feliz año nuevo. The next generation ran in the high teens and young twenties, mostly female and stuffed just shy of suffocation into the Palencana uniform of designer jeans and see-through blouses with black lingerie and four-inch red heels.

Inside, the priest ended his homily. Out here I hobnobbed at ease with the western hemisphere's new majority, the vanguard of an indisputably new world. The grandparents viewed this irruption in time from a grand and benign remove. They faded to ancestorhood before my eyes. Far away in Berkeley, Victor Perera mourned losses vague and specific that belonged to all of us. He wrote once—and reminded me often—of the time he watched some Lacandons felling a mahogany they would carve for a new cayuco, one of those trees reserved for the community's use under the agreement. The massive trunk lay in a new clearing near stumps of its fallen neighbors, the earth scarred by skidder tracks, while he rhapsodized out loud to his hosts about the tragedy of the selva and the parallel and precipitate decline of their own ancient culture.

Kayum, one of Chan K'in's sons, a painter of naïve but arresting jungle scenes with one-man shows from Barcelona to Seattle to his credit, looked up from his ax work and gently scolded Victor that he must let go of the world. It is creaking and groaning like an old man, he said. Everything prefigured the imminence of xu'tan, he said, the Lacandon apocalypse. The proper attitude of a hach winik was to welcome it and the new era of creation it anticipated. He spoke with the deep calm and conviction of a believer. Victor never forgot it, though he never accepted it either, Kayum's willingness to watch and welcome while a thousand generations of accumulated beauty and uncatalogued nonhuman life got traded for the shortest term of gains, or in many cases no gain at all.

One of the toddlers next to me spread her five fingers in a wide fan and extended her arm in my direction. Loss on a scale like that which the selva had undergone overwhelmed me and I couldn't accept it myself. But my energy to mourn it had been spent on other battles. The best thing I could think of was to get ready for the next cycle of creation and whatever degree of recovery it afforded.

I PLANNED A swift, self-contained, self-propelled, low-impact descent in the go-light tradition of the north woods, an economical mode of wilderness travel and best for apprehending the cuenca whole hog.

Of old, expeditions engaged teams of mules, porters, and vogas, cumbersome affairs that searched mostly for ruins and inscriptions but lost sight of geography. (There were exceptions.) They carried heavy camera and film-processing equipment, heavy kitchens. They stayed for weeks, living off the land, hunting, fishing, and cutting trees. Armed, they assumed a measure of safety against freelancing banditos that I could not. Today, arms and hunting were illegal in the selva (army and police patrols who searched me never cared about drugs, only guns), yet it was a risky moment to be wandering at large. My speed and small size would be my best defense, if any were needed.

Similar considerations precluded my using a traditional cayuco. Most cayucos were heavy and slow. To locate and purchase a suitable one would take weeks. An average eighteen-foot cayuco weighed hundreds of pounds, necessitating costly manpower. Furthermore, I faced considerable whitewater on the lower Jatate and Usumacinta. While I believed the ancient Maya had the capacity to run class 3 rapids (with teams of paddlers), I had no idea whether I could find contemporary dugouts that were designed appropriately—though to do so was one of my goals.

Building one would be harder yet. The proper sizes and species of trees—especially mahogany—were hard to come by, and to cut them required permission from local or communal governments, unlikely to be granted. I wanted no part in felling trees big enough to make cayucos. A few old-time cayuco masters remained who had once overseen the crafting of boats for commercial use, however, as in

Francisco Madero, where I had seen the Chol cayuco builders working in 1989, and they were the ones who most diligently preserved traditional practices.

The carving process varied little whether undertaken by teams overseen by masters, village groups, or individuals. Trees were selected for straightness, width, durability, and ease of working. The preferred species included mahogany, cedar, and a species known as mankhote in Chol, which lasted in the water for thirty years.

The tree's location hardly mattered: some were cut ten or twelve miles from water. After receiving permission to fell the tree, the crew erected a platform to sever the trunk above the swelling root buttresses common in rain forest species. The first cuts, made with ritual care, were placed to guard against splitting and to guide the tree's fall. Then the master examined the fallen trunk for defects and decided how best to cut around them. Cutaway sections were saved, and carved into bowls and troughs (called canoas).

With the log laid out, the master cut transverse grooves at the point where the sheer line would rise toward the peaks, then ran a cord for cutting the trunk down to the level of the gunwales. Axes, machetes, and curved and straight adzes accomplished the work. Next he marked the chine, the angle at which the sides were cut, and strung another line down the center of the trunk, on either side of which he drew the critical bow and stern shapes—the sheer and rocker, the characteristic banana curve of whitewater craft, adjusted for whether the boat would be used primarily in swift water or flat. (In an older technique, one side of a large leaf would be folded over the bow and traced onto the wood, echoing the craft's organic, dendritic roots.) He roughed out the ends with a machete.

The master marked the sides and interior and they were cut, thicker along the bottom, thinner along the gunwales, the thickness monitored through holes bored in the hull. Finally the boat was inverted using a winch to shape the bottom for rocker and side-to-side stability, another critical step that determined performance.

The process took up to two weeks. When the holes were plugged and the boat finished, the crew ate a ceremonial meal and transported the canoe to water by pushing it across poles used as rollers, the method by which ancient traders portaged cayucos overland.

Lacandons followed similar procedures, mythic overtones imbuing every step. The slabs cut from the hull they made into stools for the god house.

But my romance was with the idea of canoes and their capabilities, and not with specific types, which were remarkably consistent around the world. My boats followed design principles evolved in the western hemisphere, and diverged from native designs only in their materials and their creators' ethnicity. No serious canoeist, native or gringo, would fail to appreciate their advantages of weight, performance, and durability.

I moved to Panchan on New Year's morning, taking numerous trips with my equipment back and forth across the footbridge, and down the driveway and a branching path. Eventually I sat on the porch of my cabaña surrounded by canoes and gear. It pleased me to see it all spread out, a visual assurance that I could subsist in the jungle for more than a month and move unfettered through the landscape.

I had two large portage packs and a waterproof, hard-plastic box with a backpack harness carrying more than a month's supply of organic freeze-dried food. For kitchen equipment there were two MSR stoves, blue enamel dishware for four, four nesting aluminum pots, and numerous plastic jars and bottles containing fuel, oils, and spices. I had brought paddles for every eventuality: two whitewater blades of heavy-duty fiberglass, two wooden bent shafts for the flats, and spares. I had life jackets, a helmet, carabiners, three knives, two nylon throw lines, and forty feet of braided nylon climbing rope. My ditty bag contained tools, headlamps and flashlights, gadgets, duct tape, and repair materials. I carried two first-aid kits, with drugs, splints, and dressings supplied by my doctor. My books barely fit inside two cardboard packing boxes.

The canoes appeared in good shape after the road ordeal. The older one was the first design marketed by the Mad River Canoe company, of Waitsfield, Vermont, in the early 1970s, after the company's founder, designer Jim Henry, had won a couple of national downriver titles with a fiberglass prototype. It was called the Malecite, after a tribe of the St. John and St. Croix river watersheds in Maine.

It weighed fifty-five pounds, virtually nothing to someone who had broken his teeth on eighty-five-pound aluminum Grummans. For seven years I had paddled it on Adirondack and Canadian lakes and rivers almost every day, three seasons a year, in every imaginable condition. It was fast, though not racing fast by today's standards, and not quite deep and capacious enough for big-water or whitewater expeditioning. I brought it for the flats below Tenosique. Its low profile, flat keel and sheer line made it peerless in windy conditions, and it had a solo center seat in the event that I ran out of paddling partners before the end of the trip.

The workhorse of the trip would be a two-person whitewater design called the Freedom, a newish model built by Mad River from Royalex, a durable foam-plastic laminate. For the Freedom, Mad River had slightly modified an existing model, the Explorer, increasing the amount of rocker and flaring the ends. The result was a craft tough enough for an extended journey that included demanding whitewater and rugged conditions.

I had seen one lying beside a float plane on a Quebec river, outfitted for whitewater with kneepads, thigh straps, and flotation bags fore and aft. Heavy-duty vinyl reinforced it at the gunwales and decks, rather than the company's trademark ash and butternut. I could tell it would shed waves and turn quickly in technical rapids. Its only obvious drawback was its heft—about eighty pounds, outfitted—and inevitably it would be sluggish in flat water, both compromises I could live with.

For now, all I needed was a place to store the boats, off the ground and out of reach. I followed the winding paths and footbridges back to the champa. Panchan's clientele wafted in and out of the common area in holiday spirits, most of them sarong-wrapped or bare-chested. On the second floor a number ate breakfast, drank coffee, and smoked at long mahogany tables. A sitar played a slow morning raga on a portable tape deck. Rainwater dripped from the shiny leaves of epiphytic philodendrons whose vines spiraled around the trees surrounding the champa.

I walked up the stairs and into the kitchen and ran squarely into Moises Morales standing at the stove cooking eggs. Ah, Chris, he said, feliz año nuevo, and gave me a warm abrazo with the spatula still in one hand.

He asked if I would join him for breakfast. I sat at the kitchen table while he busied himself at the stove and the local Chol women who normally did the cooking stood patiently to the side. One of the helpers, an American woman named Michelle, poured me a cup of coffee.

Did you feel the earthquake yesterday morning? Moises said, joining me at the table and placing before me a plate of eggs scrambled with chiles and onions.

I had, but thought I had imagined it. No one else had mentioned it.

It happened so early, he said, putting down his fork and smiling, faunlike. Everybody was so drunk from the festivities they probably never felt it. He waved his hand dismissively.

We slathered our eggs with habanero sauce and ate in silence. Rakshita had told him about my trip, which he thought a good idea, though dangerous. Bandits had been robbing rafters, he said, which I knew. As we discussed my plan, a succession of Dutch and German supermodel clones, guests of Panchan, wearing extremely short lederhosen, halter tops, and hiking boots, came flouncing in from the café bearing New Year's greetings and glasses of wine for a toast. One by one they approached with their rippling midriffs, pierced navels, and glorious bosoms and enclosed Moises in long-armed embraces. They towered over him and pressed his face to their chests. He kissed each more or less chastely on the cheek and returned their abrazos, smiling from ear to ear. We all stood and toasted the new year and world peace, they with their breakfast wine, I with my coffee.

Rakshita and Michelle raised their glasses. Water ran in the sink and over the weirs downstairs. The sitar droned on the tape deck. The Europeans' operatic pulchritude contrasted with the modest beauty of the Maya women, who held aloft their own juice glasses of wine to a year they had every reason to hope would be an improvement over the last. All seemed aware that among the Maya New Year's is a perilous time, that all temporal watersheds carry the potential for derangement, for time coming loose from its moorings, and that the Zapatistas had chosen it for their uprising precisely for its cosmic significance.

Observances, therefore, should be made with the utmost care. Hubris was punished as decisively here as among the most archaic Hellenes.

When the observance passed, our eggs and conversation finished, I stored the boats atop the art deco baño at Moises's suggestion. There they would be visible from the kitchen, he pointed out, and out of reach of the curious.

In 1974 Moises had hosted at Panchan an informal symposium of young and established Mayanists, including archaeologists, epigraphers, and art historians, which later came to be called the Primera Mesa Redonda de Palenque, or the First Palenque Round Table. Today the Mesa Redonda is an exalted forum, but the first amounted to little more than a bunch of longhairs and a couple of old-timers meeting for drinks. It included prodigies like seventeen-year-old Peter Mathews of Australia and a young art historian from the United States named Linda Schele, who were feverish with ideas and aching to overthrow prevailing dogmas.

They discussed advances in the decipherment of Maya hieroglyphics, which had languished in theoretical limbo until Tatiana Prouskouriakoff and a Russian named Yuri Knorosov had jump-started it in the fifties and sixties. Out of the blue Moises suggested that the missing link scholars were seeking—the connection of sign to sound—lay all around them, in the nearby Chol communities of Tula and Tumbala, whose people, he believed, descended from the agricultural yeoman classes of ancient Palenque.

He said the rulers of classical Palenque probably spoke an early version of Chol. Seizing the moment and a sixteenth-century Chol-Spanish dictionary, the scholars were able to match certain words and syllables with various glyphs and glyph elements prevalent at Palenque. Thus they arrived at the name Pacal, "Shield," for Palenque's celebrated eighth-century ruler, and began composing a genealogy of kingship from the city's founding to its fall in 799. From that conference, an intellectual watershed, proceeded an unabated flood of advances.

A small industry grew up around the Mesa Redonda scholars. Their discoveries proliferated and their reputations flourished. Only Moises gradually fell from grace with his peers. Lacking degrees, he saw his papers go unpublished. His ideas, which continued to be prescient and original, many thought amateurish and poorly conceived. His temper and confrontational manner in an already contentious field alienated many, and his relations with the hierarchical nabobs of INAH, the Mexican archaeological agency, that had issued his license to guide in the ruin, grew strained.

With Palenque's townies, the perennial boosters and backslappers who control all tourist burgs, he was forever at loggerheads. They thought him too solicitous of Indians. In 1968, following the student massacre in Mexico City, he was imprisoned temporarily, ostensibly for ringleading a band of looters, but actually for his outspoken leftist politics. When the forests around the village began vanishing he immediately agitated for a national park to protect the ruin, a proposal that came to pass, though on a smaller scale than he had called for. Local developers noted angrily that the park bordered Panchan. Moises received anunciados, or death threats, and armed himself, more than once repelling intruders in the night.

Now he had mellowed. Past seventy, he looked slim and fit. (Archaeologist Michael Coe said he resembled the Peruvian novelist Mario Vargas Llosa. I would add with elements of Israeli leader Simon Peres.) He had received the valkyries' tribute with an air of benign patronage and entitlement, like a Conradian jungle lord. (Palenque's widows and divorcées, and various graduate students, had pungent observations about him in this regard.) With time he had outlasted enemies and his own mistakes. His ten children had grown; the hotel thrived.

Michael Coe had acknowledged his contributions in the book *Breaking the Maya Code,* a chronicle of the glyph decipherment published in 1994. Moises took speaking engagements in the United States and Europe. The roster of celebrities and foreign leaders he had guided read like a who's who of twentieth-century diplomacy and popular culture. His relations with INAH had improved, and he had grown to accept the fact that his greatest accomplishment, the one that would affect the course of Maya studies in years to come, had been the transmission of that fire for the Maya, for Chiapas, and for Palenque which burned in him to the young, many of whom evolved into prominent Mayanists.

At Panchan, Moises put to practice principles of sound land use he had held and espoused for years, and that were no more complicated than landscape architect Ian McHarg's old doctrine of "listening to the land." When I first met him he had spread his arms to encompass his grounds, the Michol, his plantings of mahogany and cedar, and declared that when he died he wanted to be surrounded by trees.

Panchan now sustained a dozen cabañas holding two double rooms each, scattered over fifty acres of forest. At the rear of the property, a second two-story champa, campground, and café catered to mochileros (backpackers) and other vagabonds. Rates were reasonable, to say the least. He had cut almost no healthy trees to accomplish this. The sound of running water ran through the property. The measure of his philosophy's success was the success of Panchan. Open less than a year, the hotel had few vacancies.

I was prepared to view Panchan critically, to note, for instance, that matters of sewage treatment were handled with a benign, characteristically Mexican indifference. I had Rakshita's word, at least, that thought was being given to the problem, a consequence of the hotel's unforeseen success.

My cabaña stood in a small glade beside the Michol and the cylindrical "temple" where Rakshita held yoga and meditation sessions. A tiny feeder spilled into the Michol over a series of weirs. One of the largest bromelias I had ever seen sprouted from the crotch of a many-buttressed mahogany at least eight feet in diameter standing on the opposite bank. The silence was nearly complete, except for running water, flycatchers flitting through the understory, and the mochileros' muffled drumming coming from the woods.

The room was small and spare, with a concrete floor and a back door leading to a solar-heated shower stall. Screened windows reached from near the floor to the ceiling, letting in light and air. The porch was wide and had a comfortable bench, and the small cedar table inside was large enough to hold my laptop and a book. It was a quiet, comfortable, and modest base. Best of all, it was under the forest canopy, away from the village's noise and sprawl.

ONE EVENING I met Scott Davis, one of the pioneers of commercial rafting in Chiapas, at Las Tinajas, the unofficial paddlers' mecca in the village. Scott had outfitted my first trip in '89. A guide, David Kashinski, joined us.

Scott and David had just arrived from Belize. We sat across from each other at a sidewalk table. They drank Coronas in the enveloping heat, I drank lemonade. Inside, the television played a *Baywatch* rerun dubbed in Spanish.

Not yet forty, Scott had run motor rigs on the Grand Canyon for twenty years. In looks, mannerisms, and speech he resembled a lot of river guides I had known. It made me presume a kind of kinship, but I flattered myself. He was immersed in rivers and river knowledge in a way that I—who had been dreamy, and always observing myself in the role of a river guide—had never been.

They had been ambushed and robbed just below Budsilhá Falls in March 1994, the year of the Zapatista uprising. Scott brought it up when I mentioned I was going all the way to the gulf, but in his friendly, laconic way declined to discuss the experience.

To fill the void we told stories: the hell trip, the rescue, the solved problem, the celebrity customer. They poured out of him, and I told a few myself, surprised at the things I had done once and forgotten. Within the space of two Coronas he loosened up, bringing the conversation around to the ambush on his own, obliquely, the way you might line up for a rapid. Once he was committed, he had to finish.

It was a private trip, he began. A group of European friends, adventurers like himself. They had wrapped up a caving expedition and decided to make the five-day float from Corozal to Tenosique, with stops at Yaxchilan and Piedras Negras, before flying home.

Scott's commercial season had ended, but his partner was still afield on a separate trip. Until he got back, Scott had nothing to do but hang around Palenque.

At the last minute, he decided to accompany the cavers.

The party dawdled at Yaxchilan and Piedras Negras and the big playa across from El Cayo. Another outfit, Far Flung Adventures, followed a day behind. Far Flung had three rafts carrying a party of middle-aged and elderly birders and amateur Mayanists, a typical one for the Usumacinta. Some years as many as six outfits worked the river.

Scott had stayed friendly with the rebel officer we had first met at Piedras Negras. In 1993 the officer warned him about "bad men" in the area, not connected to the insurgency. They had guns, he said, and Scott should avoid Piedras Negras from then on. Scott thanked him, though he had no intention of staying away from the ruin's pristine beaches, old-growth forests, and unadulterated ruins. Fugitives and criminals had hidden along the river at least as far back as the 1890s, when Teobert Maler complained of smugglers and other unsavory characters.

That's the kind of place it was, marginal, "fluid," in more ways than one.

Yet all that season would-be pirates accosted Scott's trips, running along the riverbank waving rifles and calling, We want to rob you! He was an old Chiapas hand by then, inured to casual threats, and he knew that one way to avoid being robbed was to ignore them.

Far Flung caught up with them at Piedras Negras. Scott's party packed and left early on the morning of the second day to get a head start. At Budsilhá they swam in the pools and dove from the ledges. In the early afternoon they rounded a large bend to the northwest. Not far downstream they would enter San José Canyon, with its thousand-foot limestone walls, tricky narrow channel, and class 3 rapids and whirlpools.

Scott paused at this point. The waiter, who knew him, brought our dinners: tlacoyas for him and David, enchiladas suizas for me, in Tinajas's usual enormous portions, with more lemonade and Corona. An otherwise healthy dog stood by our table holding up a paw and begging for scraps. A few doors down you could hear the electric organ of the evangelical church warming up. European women from the hostel across the street strolled by wearing flimsy halter tops. A typical evening in Palenque at the hour of the paseo. The waiter left and Scott continued.

When he saw the men in masks and they waved him over from the Guatemala side, he ignored them, as he had all winter. His boats were spread out at that point, with a raft and two kayakers, including David Kashinski, lagging behind. Somewhere upstream, Far Flung followed with its party of seniors.

He saw the front right tube deflate before he heard the shot. One man fell in the water before Scott realized they were under fire. He asked the man what he was doing falling overboard and the man told him, I'm shot. Three more shots followed. One of the women fell on the floor of the raft, shot in the arm, the hand, and the side.

The others pulled in upstream on the Mexican side. Scott told the uninjured man to apply pressure to the woman's arm and he helped the man in the water back into the boat. The man's wound was superficial. He signaled to the attackers and rowed to the Guatemalan shore while blood pooled in the floor of the boat.

The bandits watched in ski masks and sunglasses while Scott rowed his boat of wounded to the Guatemalan shore. They carried beat-up .22 and .222 caliber rifles. They said they were Zapatistas and ordered him to call down the other boaters, who watched from the opposite shore, upstream. He climbed out onto the jagged limestone boulders that line the shore at lower water levels and refused to call down the other boats, insisting on handling the medical emergency first. They threatened to kill everybody if he continued to resist. There were four of them, two men in their twenties and two in their forties, obviously poor and uneducated. Scott told them he would call down the other raft and kayakers if they would let him leave in ten minutes. They could take everything they wanted except boats. They wanted a boat.

At that point a Mexican military helicopter hovered unaccountably overhead. The attackers ran into the woods. Scott tried to signal the chopper with a hand mirror, but the chopper moved slowly upstream. The men came out of the woods. Scott called down the other boats from across the river. When they arrived he told them to unload everything: personal and kitchen equipment, everything. They would leave in five minutes. As they offloaded the stuff, the chopper returned and hovered again. Again the bandits retreated under the forest canopy. (You could see the sun glinting off their shades, David Kashinski said.) It gave the paddlers just enough time to get away.

The encounter lasted about forty-five minutes. They ran in the dark through San José Canyon and over the ledge drop at Boca de

Cerro, observing silence. David Kashinski got out at Francisco Madero to borrow a vehicle and meet them in Tenosique. They reached the takeout at 1:30 A.M. Scott walked to the road and flagged down a bus. By two-thirty they reached Tenosique, where they roused a clinic and the military. At the clinic, the wounded woman, one of Europe's best cavers, walked off the bus under her own power, to Scott's relief. David Kashinski met them with a truck. They reached Palenque around four-thirty.

I handed the dog a scrap of unfinished enchilada. Scott said he would shun that stretch of the river until the bandits left or were captured. The previous year, he said, a Mexican outfit, Mexico Verde, had also been ambushed and there were numerous unconfirmed reports of private trips which had been robbed and suffered physical and sexual assault.

Scott told his story to the tourist board in Mexico City, in vain. He spoke to the military commander in Tenosique, who said the chopper had been on a routine patrol. The pilot had seen them on the shore, but Scott had failed to give the "international distress signal," so the pilot continued upstream to check out Far Flung, whom he had seen from the air. Scott complained that the bandits not only had robbed his friends and his equipment, but had robbed him and other outfits of a livelihood, along with a large percentage of the economy of Palenque and nearby communities. The commander shrugged.

This year only Mexico Verde, a company owned by a young hotshot from Guadalajara, Mauricio Morales (no relation to Moises), had booked trips below Yaxchilan. He added that a Guatemalan rafting company, Maya Expeditions, had been contracted to supply a new archaeological dig starting up at Piedras Negras in March. The dig was the first since the peace accord in December. In fact, it was the first dig at Piedras Negras since the 1930s. It remained to be seen, Scott said, whether the bandits were still operating downstream and what effect they would have on the dig.

He strongly suggested I give the place a wide berth.

That would be hard if I kept to my plan, even though I knew from experience that plans amounted to little in the republic's outer darknesses.

Perhaps the bandits had moved on, now that the political struggle had subsided, David suggested. Nobody actually believed they were Zapatistas, in any case.

Scott added, A lot of contraband is going down that river. Every night darkened boats head downstream past Yaxchilan. They could be carrying refugees, guns, artifacts, illegal timber and hides. They are definitely moving drugs. It could mean that the bad guys at Budsilhá are more than bandits, that they are operating under protection. You should be as careful about who you talk to as where you go canoeing.

We paid the check and walked a block up to the zócalo, the dog with the sore paw following us. We sat beneath the box-trimmed trees with their white-painted trunks while couples and families, gringas, and sullen young men circumambulated, and boys threw lit firecrackers at our feet. Hundreds of grackles chattered in the trees, almost drowning out the blasters. After a few minutes we parted, Scott and David for their rancho outside town, I for Panchan. We agreed to stay in touch. Scott told me not to worry. Everything would work out, he said.

OVER THE NEXT three weeks I met three more people with knowledge of conditions along my route. The first, Mauricio Morales, ran the outfit Mexico Verde and told of being ambushed in San José Canyon the previous year. His story differed from Scott's only in that no one had been shot, and one of his crew, a Chiapas-based American named Machete Jim, had been relieved by the bandits of at least fifteen thousand dollars in cash.

Morales and his middle-class rafting customers from Mexico City were dining at Panchan prior to his first Usumacinta trip of the season. For safety, Morales told me, he had hired an armed guard for the trip, who would dress as a tourist. At Francisco Madero he would leave off his customers and take on five similarly disguised federales, at his own expense, with whom he would enter the suspected bandit stronghold, a village in San José Canyon. He didn't know what would go down, but it might be "very bad," he said, making the sign of a pistol with his thumb and forefinger.

Around the same time I talked to Morales, Tammy Ridenour, the American whose Guatemala-based outfit, Maya Expeditions, would supply the dig at Piedras Negras, breezed though her first Usumacinta trip of the year. When it was over we met on the patio at the hotel Maya Tulipanes, in Palenque. Attacks were down, she insisted. (Great news!) She anticipated no further problems and would fulfill her contract with the dig.

In the off-season she guided physicians from Doctors Without Borders to remote Guatemalan Maya villages. On this trip she had hiked into one of the Communities Prospering in Resistance (CPRs) near Piedras Negras, which served as the social base of the former insurgency. The village council told her they were interested in becoming official guardians at the ruin and the new national park, perhaps setting up a small concession at El Desempeño to sell handcrafts to rafters. She spent about an hour with them and delivered a letter from Stephen Houston, one of the archaeologists leading the dig, mentioning the possibility of jobs in the ruin.

They were a mixed lot of Latinos and Indians, bitter about their forty-year exile from society, but enthusiastic about peace and committed to living responsibly in the forest. They suffered botflies, leishmaniasis, and the usual snakebites, but no malaria. They felt the bandit activity reflected badly on them, but the bandits left them alone. Any punitive action was up to the governments. The council would meet with her again in six weeks, to talk more about getting involved in rafting and the dig.

The third person I met was Fernando Ochoa, who had helped majority Zapatista communities on Laguna Miramar, in the Montes

Azules reserve, resolve boundary issues and plan for wilderness-style community ecotourism.

All agreed that my goal of a continuous descent appeared viable, though risky. We were scheduled to leave in three weeks, embarking from Tecojá, near El Real and the bridge on the Santa Cruz, where I would join Scott Davis on a raft trip for the first five, noncanoeable days. Then I would transfer to the Freedom at La Sultana, a Zapatista village and Mexican military outpost, where Josh Lowry, Scott's head guide, would accompany me in a kayak on the class 3 lower Jatate.

By phone I had persuaded Todd Kelsey, of Stony Creek in the Adirondacks, to join me in the bow *below* the Jatate, after he finished a project he was working on and could grab a flight. I had failed to find a bow partner for the lower Jatate, however, and Lowry, kayaking in Chile, had yet to show his face in Palenque.

Three

D E L T A A N D P O R T A G E

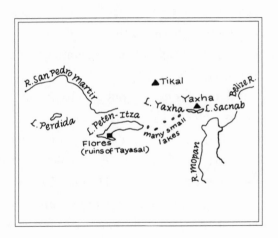

A MONG GREAT MESOAMERICANISTS J. ERIC THOMPSON, MORE THAN
most, recognized the importance of rivers and canoes to ancient
and contemporary Maya. Thompson, whose imprimatur made and
broke doctoral theses, traveled Belize rivers by dugout in the twenties
and thirties, when a vestigial canoe trade still existed, and absorbed
the lore from his boatmen. Drawing on that experience, plus sources
like Scholes and Roys's magisterial *The Maya Chontal Indians of Acalan-
Tixchel,* Thompson sketched out ancient trade routes that circled and

crisscrossed the Yucatán peninsula and extended as far east and south as the Guatemalan highlands and Honduras.

The main coastal route circled the Yucatán peninsula and paralleled the Caribbean and gulf coasts. The interior corridors hewed primarily to the Usumacinta and its affluents, plus a number of smaller rivers draining into the Caribbean and the gulf. A critical route traversing the peninsula's broad southern base used Belizean rivers, a string of lakes and ponds traversing northern Peten, and the Río San Pedro Mártir, an Usumacinta tributary, to close the great circle. A separate portage route branched off at Lake Peten-Itza, to the Pasión, and thence down the Usumacinta.

The great city of Tikal commanded the longest portion of the inland route separating these drainages in northern Peten, as Palenque did the narrow divide between the Usumacinta and the Grijalva tributaries, and Toniná the height of land separating the Grijalva headwaters from the Río Jatate.

Thompson got things wrong, of course, a hazard in any discipline where you have so little to go on. He confused Acalan ("Land of Canoes"), a murky Chontal zone east of the delta, at the headwaters of the Candelaria River, with the nebulous region of snaking tributaries along the Pasión and Chixoy rivers. More important, he rejected the paradigm-smashing theories of Knorosov and Prouskouriakoff, setting back the decipherment for decades. But his maps made clear that only by taking into account the cayuco's properties and the necessity of portages could you interpret the whole cloth of the Maya region. Geography revealed itself to the canoeist's eye.

Thompson postulated the existence of a classical people he called putun, wide-ranging canoe traders of uncertain ethnicity, analogous to Scholes and Roys's Chontals, whose existence had been deduced from anomalous ceramics scattered around the Usumacinta basin— stackable clayware for conserving space on long voyages, for instance. He borrowed the term from the Maya books of *Chilam Balam,* which used it when referring to Chontalpecans. The putun appeared to be implicated in the demise of several polities, and may have given rise to the Itza, whose extravagant postclassic cities in Yucatán, like Chichen Itza, emulated those of their classical forebears. The Quiche Maya of the Guatemalan highlands, interestingly, also claimed descent from people who had ascended the Usumacinta by canoe from a "Place of Reeds" in the Chontalpa.

The putun built cities of adobe on the stone-poor Chontalpa, burning oyster shells for lime. They left no extensive inscriptions and seem to have participated only peripherally in the literate flowering of the classical period. Instead, we know them by the testimony of other groups, and by the widely scattered, distinctive evidence of their trading.

Yet geography placed them at the center of the classical universe. Their long-distance trade networks held together the Maya world and fostered the impression of a pan-Mesoamerican identity—an identity that underlay, or transcended, according to Mayanist Nancy Fairiss, the region's overwhelming diversity. We may imagine them as somewhat outlandish and cosmopolitan, and, according to the art of the Chontalpa, possibly of indiscriminate sexual tastes—like colonial era seamen, at home anywhere, but exotic to the natives. Thompson, who couldn't resist an opportunity to draw a comparison between the Maya and Mediterranean antiquity, called the putun "the Phoenicians of Mesoamerica."

Evidence hints that putun traders may have controlled more than one city on the upper Usumacinta during the classical era. They may also have contributed to the internecine wars of the late classic period and to the downfall of the classical Maya culture itself. When Chontals—putuns—of the late postclassic period confronted Spanish invaders at the mouth of the Usumacinta, the only interest they shared with the invaders was trade.

EUROPEAN CONTACT CAME in 1517, when Cuba's governor, Diego Velásquez, heard news of frequent landings by canoeborne traders from the west, who claimed their crossing had taken six days. Velásquez wrote of the landings to Ferdinand and Isabella, then mounted a questionably legal trade expedition (according to colonial protocol), sending Francisco Hernández de Córdoba west with three ships. A storm blew the expedition off course, and it soon fetched up on the northeastern tip of the Yucatán peninsula. On March 4 the ships anchored off a large town set back from the coast.

Bernal Díaz recorded the voyage, as he did nearly every stage of the conquest, like an Extremaduran Zelig. "We saw ten large canoes, called piraguas, full of Indians from the town, approaching us with oars and sails," Díaz wrote. "The canoes were large ones made like hollow troughs cleverly cut from huge single logs, and many of them would carry forty Indians." The mention of sails is curious, and by "oars" Díaz of course meant paddles. The two are still confused around the upper Usumacinta basin, called remos, oars, in some areas, and cañaletes, or paddles, in others. We will call them paddles, for they were then and are today handled facing forward from a kneeling, sitting, or standing position, with the paddle unattached to the hull.

The Indians came aboard and examined the Spanish brigantines with as much interest as the Spanish took in their canoes. They returned the next day and invited their visitors ashore. Córdoba's men reluctantly followed the Maya cacique to the village, but before they got far a rain of arrows fell on them from behind some hills. Both sides, according to Díaz, lost fifteen men, and the Spaniards captured two Maya, dubbed Julian and Melchior, whom they took back to Cuba to learn Spanish and serve as translators. The Spaniards made it back to their boats and continued westward along the peninsula's northern coast.

They turned south along the shallow western coast for two weeks, as far as Campeche. Low on water, the men rowed inshore to the town, situated on a natural harbor, as it is today. Priests came out of the temples, their hair matted with blood, making suggestive homoerotic gestures. They fumigated the Spaniards with copal and ordered them to leave. Still smarting from their recent wounds, the Spaniards retreated with enough water for six days.

When they weighed anchor a norte struck. Nortes, three-day winter storms characteristic of the southern gulf, pound the delta especially hard. This one, according to Díaz, blew for four days, breaking two anchor cables.

When the wind dropped they spied Champotón, a Chontal town located on the northeastern edge of the delta, surrounded by milpas and water holes. They anchored offshore and rowed over the breakers with their water casks. When they landed, "many squadrons" of Indians approached, outfitted for combat. They painted their faces black or rust red on one side and white on the other. They wore cotton armor to their knees, and carried bows and arrows and two-handed wooden broadswords with obsidian blades. Green and gold feathered headdress plumes bobbed on their heads.

The Spaniards kept watch through the night. In the morning the Indians rained stones and arrows on the Spanish soldiers, wounding eighty (so says Díaz) on the first volley. Fifty soldiers died or were captured. All were wounded and Díaz himself took three arrows, one through the ribs. Córdoba received ten spear and arrow wounds. The Spaniards escaped in their boats while the Indians waded after them, firing arrows and spears and wounding many more.

The expedition stopped again farther down the coast, pulling into a creek that was surely the first Spanish contact with the Usumacinta delta. They called the creek Estero de las Lagartos, for the many "alligators" that lived in it. They filled up with the brackish creek water, and this time bore away for Florida, where they lost more men to Calusa Indians. Córdoba's ships finally wallowed into Havana Harbor, the men barely alive but pumping desperately to keep their leaking craft afloat. Ten days later Córdoba died.

The expedition failed, except to confirm reports of promising lands to the west. Within months Velásquez dragooned his nephew,

Juan de Grijalva, into commanding a better-equipped effort. Along with Grijalva traveled three future conquerors of ignoble repute: Alonso de Avila, Francisco de Montejo (the eventual conqueror of Yucatán and Tabasco), and Pedro de Alvarado, who defeated the Quiche Maya at Quezaltenango, in Guatemala. It also included, once again, the chronicler Díaz.

Grijalva's 1518 expedition was undoubtedly the first to directly identify and navigate the lower Grijalva and Usumacinta rivers. The expedition landed at Cozumel, then retraced the course of Córdoba's expedition. At Champotón, Grijalva ordered a landing to avenge his predecessor. This time small cannons drove back the Indians and they disappeared in the maize fields and swamps surrounding the town.

They held Champotón for three days. Soon after reembarking, the Spanish ships came to "what appeared to be the mouth of a very rapid river, very broad and open," in Díaz's words. "But it was not a river as we had thought it to be but it was a very good harbor, and we called it the Boca de Términos." They took soundings and made charts of the bay, finding empty buildings—"oratories"—onshore. "[They] were merely those belonging to traders and hunters who put into the port when passing in their canoes and made sacrifices there," Díaz says. In them they were horrified to find incense burners depicting men with erect phalli engaged in anal intercourse and masturbation. They killed ten deer and many rabbits. After three days they continued along the coast until they came to the mouth of the Río Tabasco, which they renamed the Grijalva.

A town called Potonchan, one of the Chontalpa's neutral trading ports, stood at the river mouth. Waves broke on a sandbar just offshore, so the expedition anchored two deep-drafted vessels and proceeded in two smaller ships and landing craft into the river. Nearing the town, they heard Indians chopping trees to block the channel. The men got out, according to Díaz, "at a point of land where some palm trees were growing," to see fifty canoes approaching. "Many other canoes full of warriors were lying in the creeks, and they kept a little way off as though they did not dare approach as did the first fleet." As the ranks formed, the captured translators called out, telling the Indians not to be afraid and holding up strands of green glass beads to trade.

Again the Spaniards stood watch through the night. The next day thirty Indians paddled downriver and joined them under the palms at the river's mouth, including the chief of Potonchan. They brought roast fish, turkeys and curassows, tropical fruit called zapote, or mamey, and tortillas—possibly the first European experience of the region's staple maize flatbread. Priests fumigated the voyagers with copal from incensarios. The Maya gave them small golden tchotchkes, little ducks and lizards, not worth much, and pointed west, repeating over and over, "Colua. Mexico." That's where the gold could be found—"sun-shit" they called it, still the name Lacandons use for money. The Chontals valued other minerals, notably jade, or "first infinite grace." Gold to them may have seemed a rare indulgence, difficult to extract, the kind of ostentatious gewgaw Mexicas liked. The Spaniards gave them glass beads and iron tools and continued along the coast.

Grijalva made his way to Cuba after sailing as far north as the Río Panuco, where fleets of canoes attacked him near the present site of Tampico. When the expedition returned to Cuba, Velásquez saw the magnitude of wealth and power that could be his, especially if he got there ahead of other Spaniards. Immediately he began assembling another expedition, this one at least nominally approved to establish a colony.

Hernán Cortés received the command despite a reputation for duplicity. The fleet ran downwind to Cozumel, a putun transshipment point and pilgrimage destination, where Cortés first displayed his skill for cajolery, flattery, threats, and forced conversion in Indian relations. He sacked the oracle of Ixchel, a goddess of the moon, weaving, and sex, and erected in its place a shrine to the Virgin. Cozumel also witnessed one of the numerous instances of synchronicity that haunt the conquest narrative. There, the Franciscan friar Alonzo de Aguilar, blown off course years before, shipwrecked and enslaved by the Maya, was brought from the mainland by canoe in exchange for glass beads. Aguilar became the linguistic rock upon which all subsequent success depended, for Aguilar spoke the language of the Chontals. He became the first link not only to the Maya, but later to the Nahuatl-speaking Aztecs of the interior.

After three weeks at Cozumel, Cortés and his ships rounded the peninsula and landed at the mouth of the Usumacinta, on March 12, 1519. Once again they anchored off the sandbar and made camp on the "Cape of the Palms," as Díaz now called their narrow spit. Once again the citizens of Potonchan confronted them. "The river, the banks and the mangrove thickets were swarming with Indians," Díaz reflected six decades later. He estimated the town contained twelve thousand warriors, many from other towns in the delta confederacy, determined to fight and avenge the taunting they had received from neighboring towns for trading gold knickknacks the previous year. When the chiefs approached them in canoes and told them to leave, Aguilar begged for appeasement and trade. This time the Potonchanecs wanted none of it. They granted the Spaniards' request to spend the night on the sandbar but told them to leave in the morning.

At first light Cortés sent a hundred men around the town by a small trail, ordering them to attack from their side when they heard shooting. An armada of Chontal canoes soon appeared. For the first time on Mesoamerican soil, the Indians heard the requerimiento read to them, a bizarre legal document ordering the Indians to accept Christ and the sovereignty of Spain. If they refused, the document absolved the conquerors of guilt in their deaths. The Indians responded with a deluge of arrows. The invaders fought back, forcing the Indians up against the log barricades they had erected around the town. The Spaniards pulled down the barricades and fought in the streets. At that point the pincer company arrived, and the Indians fled.

The town had been abandoned in the night. Cortés occupied its central plaza, which had a palace and three temples. In the middle of the plaza stood a great ceiba, the Yax-Cheel-Cab, or First Tree of the World, with its characteristic spreading crown. He drew his sword and made three slashes in its trunk as a sign of possession. He then claimed the land for Charles V of Spain (Ferdinand and Isabella had died), rather than Velásquez, an act that rankled the soldiers and haunted Cortés for the rest of his life. The Maya priests shuddered at the raising of the cross—to them an emblem of their world tree and the fulfillment of a prophecy.

In the following days Cortés led his soldiers in the battle of Centla, fought amid the delta's savannas and tangled mangrove channels. It included the first major cavalry charge on the mainland, during which the Indians fled in fear from the horses. As every schoolchild learns, the Indians supposedly regarded the horse and rider as a single, fire-breathing, Centaur-like being. Other mythic events occurred. The Spaniards marveled at the Indians' willingness to impale themselves on the Spaniards' swords while attempting to take captives for sacrifice. After the battle the Spaniards used Indian fat to cauterize their wounds.

Most significantly, perhaps, the defeated Indians gave Cortés, along with food and gold, a gift of twenty young women, supposedly because they felt sorry that the Spaniards had no women to make tortillas for them. Among these was the young woman the Spaniards knew as Doña Marina, La Malinche to generations of Mexicans: a Nahuatl- and Maya-speaking slave from Coatzacoalcos, up the coast, who became the second link in the chain of translation, and Córtes's mistress. The chain began in Spanish, was translated into Maya by Aguilar, then into Nahuatl by Malinche, who eventually became fluent in Spanish as well.

On Palm Sunday, 1519, with the Chontal gold reserves apparently exhausted, Cortés organized a grand masque of Christian worship. Following the Mass, the soldiers paraded through the town to the river, where dozens of dugout canoes escorted them downriver to their ships.

Five years later Cortés returned to the Chontalpa, this time by land, and struggled his way east across the Usumacinta's lower reaches by canoe and on foot, on his way to quell a rebellion in Honduras. In his custody traveled Cuautémoc, the renegade prince and nephew of the fallen Aztec emperor Moctezuma. In the process he and his troops navigated the Usumacinta upstream by canoe before cutting across the vast wetlands east of Tenosique.

It would be another twenty years before Europeans traveled the river upstream from this point and learned of its riches and the recalcitrant, fierce Indians of its headwaters.

Within decades the newcomers' Spanish- and African-Maya offspring (children of colonists and their slaves) ran the coastal canoe trade. Descendants of the Chontals carried on a remnant inland trade under the aegis of regional cofradia sects, the secret societies that kept alive preconquest religious traditions under the guise of Christian guilds, through the eighteenth century. The native population plummeted 90 percent due to disease.

The Chontalpa remained panethnic. African slaves abandoned by British privateers and logwood cutters formed enclaves on the delta's bayous, mingling their blood with mestizos and Indians and contributing to the region one of its most lasting cultural archetypes, the marimba. Some villages remained Chontal-speaking into the nineteenth century.

The delta's natural petroleum seeps have long since been tapped by the government monopoly, Pemex. Nodding oil pumps share the savannas with long-horned zebu cattle, and at night the burn-off towers of gas wells flare across the landscape like eerie sacrificial incensarios. Boats shuttle workers of mestizo, Indian, and African blood back and forth from Frontera, located across the river from the site of Potonchan, to oil rigs anchored in the gulf, dodging the boats of the republic's largest fishing fleet. The Usumacinta, as yet undammed, annually disgorges the surplus waters of Peten, the Cuchumatans, the Chiapas highlands, and the Lacandon rain forest over the low, flat plain, replenishing the delta's intricate aquatic system and sending snakes into the houses of the riberos and riberos to their canoes. These are the same low-volume cayucos of the ancestors, raw slivers of mahogany or tropical cedar, paddled standing with long heavy cañaletes. They share the waters of the lower Usumacinta with thatched lanchas carrying produce and contraband, and the speed-boats of oil-rich teenagers from nearby Villahermosa, the capital of Tabasco.

ABOVE TENOSIQUE THE Usumacinta's wild basin remained terra incognita long after the surrounding highlands and the delta were conquered and resettled. The river supposedly divided the colonial entities of Chiapas and Guatemala, but few Europeans had actually explored it.

After Mexico separated from Spain in 1824, it quarreled with its former fellow colony, Guatemala, over the river itself. Until then Chiapas had been administered as a Guatemalan province, despite its closer alignment with Mexico. Mexico annexed it, then left it oddly alone, never exerting much control over the selva's eastern zone and the upper Usumacinta. It was the frontier: El Desierto de Soledad, "the Desert of Solitude." (Tabasco—the Chontalpa—formed the wealthy western zone.)

The Usumacinta—the fluid, unimportant border between the former colonial entities—eventually assumed the utmost importance. Lumbermen, called madereros, moved upstream from Tenosique as hardwoods ran out along the lower river, working both shores without regard to nationality. By the 1870s numerous small lumber camps, monterías, had been established along the Lacantun, the upper Usumacinta, and the Pasión by businesses from Tabasco and Peten.

The madereros agreed among themselves that everything east of the Lacantun below the mouth of the Ixcan, and everything south of

Yaxchilan along the Usumacinta, belonged to the Peten companies. Everything north and west belonged to Tabasco. Still, according to the Belgian historian Jan de Vos, Chiapas failed to assert administrative control over the frontier.

Between 1882 and 1895, territorial disputes escalated among five of the richest Tabasqueño companies along the Lacantun, the Tzendales (a Lacantun tributary), and the upper Usumacinta. The conflict polluted relations between the two countries, causing the dictator Porfirio Díaz to consider declaring war against his weaker neighbor. Instead, in 1895, he exerted pressure to extend the border to its present terminus at La Línea, expanding Mexican dominance east from the Lacantun to the Chixoy. Afterward he allocated control over all the forested lowlands, in return for ample tribute, to ten foreign corporations, and the area east of the Lacantun to a Spanish nobleman, the Marqués de Comillas. The giveaway inaugurated what de Vos termed the Golden Age of Mahogany, and for the next fifty years shaped relations along the river.

The river remained an unruly no-man's-land inhabited by political refugees, fugitives, and foreign adventurers. Not until archaeologists began excavating Yaxchilan in the seventies did it attract much attention in Mexico City.

ON HIS 1525 march to Honduras, Cortés skirted the river's upper reaches and more or less paralleled the transpeninsular canoe route, demonstrating in the process why the route worked so much better by water. Acala (Chontal) Indians, to whom the route was second nature, provided his map.

Leading four hundred Spanish soldiers and three thousand central Mexican Indians, he left behind the Usumacinta and foundered and mucked his way across a region of prodigious wetlands and forests. To cross one huge marsh, soldiers and Indians built a bridge of poles thrust into the soft bottom, lashed with stringers and crosspieces, while the whole company proceeded slowly along as the bridge went up in front of them. Morley called the march the "greatest" military expedition in history.

A week later the expedition stumbled out of the forest onto Lake Peten-Itza. Standing on the lakeshore, wrote Díaz (along for the ride as usual), they could see the "white temples, turrets and houses of a town called Tayasal" glistening in the distance.

Tayasal possessed all the elements of postclassic Maya society: temple pyramids, hereditary kingship, bloodletting, human sacrifice, a powerful priesthood, a sacred ceiba on the plaza, and glyph writing. Its people were Itzas who had moved south from Yucatan following the declines of the great postclassic cities of Chichen Itza and Mayapán. As Itzas they may have descended from putun traders of the classic era, and hence inherited a long history of canoe dependence.

Tayasal's king, Can-Ek, told Cortés that "many traders traveled between his lands and the coast" and that he heard the news from both ends. He said people from Tabasco had passed through recently and told him of a white conqueror's huge canoes, and of the battle of Centla and its fire-breathing horses. Cortés confessed he was the same conqueror of whom the Tabascan Indians had spoken. They exchanged gifts and Can-Ek rather easily agreed to be converted, at least for the duration of the visit. He then offered to show Cortés the overland route south to Neto, in Honduras, from the opposite shore.

"He asked me," Cortés wrote to Charles V, "to come with him in a canoe, and visit his town and his house, where I would see him burn his idols and might order a cross to be made for him. I, therefore, in order to please him, though much against the wishes of my men, boarded one of his canoes with more than twenty men, most of whom were crossbowmen, and went to his town, where we passed all that day in recreation."

In the evening he took a canoe back to shore and spent the night with his men. The next day they departed for the Río Dulce and the coast, leaving behind a lame horse that later Spaniards found the Indians worshiping, in effigy form, as a god named Tzimin Chac.

LAKE PETEN-ITZA, THE largest body of water on the transpeninsular traverse, lies at the far eastern extent of the Usumacinta watershed, beyond a low barrier of karst, in a catchment basin with no outlet except through the porous limestone bedrock. You can easily visualize it dribbling and seeping into the Usumacinta's essence by way of the low-lying bajos (wetlands) feeding the Río San Pedro Mártir, just west of the uplands, or south to the Pasión via a network of capillary streams. Farther east everything flows to the Caribbean.

Fifteen miles long and as wide as eight miles, Peten-Itza commanded the high point of the ancient trade route bridging the wide southern neck of the Yucatán. The ruin of Tayasal, located on a small island (petén) in the lake, shows signs of continuous occupation since preclassic times. Before the rise of Tikal, a few miles north, it probably dominated the southern link of the circumpeninsular canoe trade. Today the town of Flores occupies the site.

I left Palenque and drove to Antigua, the old colonial city in the Guatemalan highlands, then flew to Flores. A taxi carried me from the airport through San Pedro, Flores's noisy edge-city, a chaotic, unpaved commercial strip of electronics stores and bodegas. Across the water Flores looked medieval, a jumble of tile- and metal-roofed adobe and cinder-block houses, and newish hotels, rising out of the bay to a low summit three hundred yards offshore. Beyond it a long peninsula blocked the view of the main lake, except for a glimpse of open water just beyond the point. A causeway connected Flores to San Pedro.

The taxi dropped me at a sprawling plaza fronting the shoreline across the causeway. I shouldered my portage pack and began following directions through the labyrinthine streets to the Wildlife Conservation Society offices.

Dry season had come early to Peten, as it had for more than a decade, and a fine oatmeal-colored dust coated the cars, the wandering livestock, the people. In front of the cathedral on the island's summit, a marimba band played and women sold peeled fruit and ices. The WCS office and apartment lay just off the plaza. The narrow lane was about fifteen feet wide, freshly paved with cobbles, and sloped steeply to the water. At the lower end a dozen cayucos rocked in the low waves. Following a cycle nobody claimed to understand, the lake level had been rising for years, inundating piers, the bottom floors of shoreline buildings, and the island's lowest ring road.

I stepped into the office as Roan McNab, the WCS representative, emerged from his bedroom, a thirty-two-year-old retriever-like Floridian with whom I felt an immediate rapport. An accomplished raconteur, McNab portrayed Flores in broad strokes as a remote bureaupolis of competing and cooperating nongovernmental organizations and government agencies feeling and bumbling their way through the confusing issues created by the month-old peace. It was a long way in perceptual and cognitive terms from the highland capital, and an exciting, if uncertain, time to work in Peten.

He had just hiked for two weeks around the rain forest of the Maya Biosphere Reserve to the north—by far the largest and least populated protected area of Mesoamerica—scouting for wildlife and meeting harvesters of xate, a low ornamental palm, and chicle, tree sap used in chewing gum, interviewing them about their hunting practices and the species and numbers of animals they saw or killed.

His mission was to analyze hunting pressures in the Uaxactún catchment basin, a sparsely settled, forested area with important early classic ruins just north of Tikal, in the reserve's multiple-use zone. Uaxactún's population, estimated at more than 650, had grown steadily, through immigration and local births. Consequently, legal and illegal hunting had increased both inside Tikal National Park and on the fringes, along with the usual xate cutting, timber rustling, and artifact looting: all more or less legitimate (if frowned upon) means of survival in the multiple-use zone, but not in the park.

A lot of hunters supplied local restaurants with game. Venison gourmets visited Uaxactún for roast tepescuintle, braised brocket deer chops (venado), and curassow mole. "They sit in the restaurants and say, I want my crax rubra [curassow]," Roan said, adding that much of the meat came from Tikal. He had persuaded four restaurants to buy game from local commercial growers and to stop buying from hunters. He just needed to find a way to give the hunters something back for limiting their take, and he had pinned his hopes on tourism.

The fluid political and economic situation at once made easier and complicated his task. Under the peace, settlements like Uaxactún had become eligible for incorporation, which included representation in regional government, and for a concession to harvest certain forest products. Both meant owning a share in the currently optimistic national future, but they had to pay a $140,000 incorporation fee. To raise the cash, many settlements turned to their only marketable resource: timber. Meanwhile, corporations and NGOs were pressuring towns in the multiple-use zone to devise "sustainable" management plans for their forest lands.

The area had been studied hardly at all and Roan feared that a lot of the plans were being implemented without a clear understanding of what a timber economy would cost biologically. Uaxactún, for example, lay along a biological corridor connecting Tikal with the larger national parks and biotopes to the north: El Mirador, Dos Lagunas, Río Azul, and Calakmul, in Mexico. With that connection broken, even "sustainably," Tikal would be reduced to a biological island. The continuous canopy needed to be maintained.

Roan wanted the town to pay the fee through tourism, rather than lumbering, and keep the corridor intact. Community infrastructure could help its people make that choice. On top of the concession fee, he suggested, another $360,000 would provide a family planning clinic, a tepescuintle farm, a chicken farm, a xate plantation, a campsite and cooperative hotel. He hoped to encourage a large environmental organization in the United States to donate that money in return for protecting critical habitat.

Villagers trusted him, he said, because he respected their frontier way of life and wanted compatible forest communities to stay viable. He saw no reason why people in the adjacent multiple-use and buffer zones shouldn't harvest xate and chicle, even within the park at certain seasons, or hunt for subsistence outside the park and under strict regulations.

We drank coffee while Roan spoke with increasing passion about his subjects, jumping freely from Spanish to English, to Spanglish, and from the subjects of Tikal and Uaxactún to his long hikes in the selva. His father taught zoology at the University of Florida, his mother was Brazilian. Between the ages of fourteen and twenty-one he had tagged sea turtles at WCS's project at El Tortuguero, in Costa Rica. One summer he had wandered on his own through the forest counting howler monkeys and recording their behaviors, living in a shack with the project's mulatta cook (a minor scandal) and fishing for snook and tarpon.

WCS, understandably focused on habitat preservation, had come under fire from economic development advocates as a den of "parquistas" uncaring about the needs of the indigenous and rural poor. Roan represented a more comprehensive approach within the organization. I was gratified to have found a bona fide conservationist who shared my belief that the idea of wilderness—a place where "natural processes of nature are maximized," in Gary Snyder's phrase—didn't preclude the voluntary presence of indigenous or otherwise compatible communities. Their collective memories stored the record of human consciousness in the western hemisphere, just as the biota stores the record of biological evolution; and their continued dependence on viable primary ecosystems would help ensure their habitat's survival. It wasn't a question of whether people lived in wild places, but of how they lived there.

I had lived a version of the idea—humans and wild nature coexisting side by side—in the Adirondacks, where the Adirondack Park had been established in the aftermath of the apocalyptic logging and forest fires of the 1870s and 1880s. The Adirondacks still had summer hordes and acid precipitation from midwestern coal plants. Its people did without numerous amenities, and they argued a lot. But it remained the most successful refuge of beauty, wildness, and primal satisfactions that I knew of. With more programs like Roan's, the Usumacinta basin might enjoy a similar recovery.

After we had abused caffeine for hours, he suggested eating at the local NGO hangout around the corner. After that he had to split, he said, to visit his girlfriend, Sarita, who lived in San Miguel, the village on the peninsula opposite Flores. It depended on whether he could borrow a cayuco from his neighbor next door.

Tomorrow, he said, we would rise at dawn to walk some WCS study sections in the park, then catch the morning bird flights from atop Tikal's Temple II.

I left my pack on the bed in the storage room where I would sleep and we stepped out into the fading light. The painted fronts and metal roofs of the houses descended cubistically to the waterfront, alternating tones of pale sulfur, aquamarine, rose, terra-cotta, and the antacid color of limedust that coated everything. Children swam around the beached cayucos at the foot of the lane. The ubiquitous grackles squawked and gibbered and marimbas tinkled in the distance.

While Roan importuned his neighbor I walked down the lane to the water. The heat had cooled and the dust settled, making everything lush and beautiful. It was "rush hour" for the residents of San Miguel, a mile across the strait and inaccessible by road. Archaeologists had uncovered extensive ruins out there. Cayucos passed back and forth, making calm, unhurried, and silent commutes home from work or back for the fiesta that seemed to be under way. Coots and grebes dabbled among them, along with "recreational" paddlers drifting in the cool of the evening.

At least a dozen cayucos lay ranked at the water's edge, of varying lengths and designs: long, narrow, low-volume boats for the open lake; short, wide-beamed craft for heavy loads and stability. Many had a good deal of rocker carved into the ends. Some were painted—yellow, blue and red predominating—or bore epithets like Nothing Is Worse painted on their hulls. A couple were cut off at the stern, with flat transoms for outboards. None had the raked elegance of the Usumacinta boats. They all seemed weathered, old, cracked, and patched with sheet metal.

While I admired the boats a boy deftly sculled and poled his cayuco up to the landing and nudged his bow in among the hulls. He wedged it as close to shore as he could, hopped across the boats, and pulled his bow onto dry land. Then he slung his long paddle over his shoulder and walked off toward the plaza.

Simultaneously three women, each with a small child, walked down the lane. The women wore thin cotton print dresses and high heels, and carried plastic bags filled with groceries. One of them bore a heavy mahogany paddle over her shoulder.

They kept talking while they separated their sky blue sixteen-foot cayuco from the others. When they had it afloat, the women kicked off their heels and clambered across the hulls. One of them held the boat steady for the others. Once aboard, they shifted their cargo and weight around carelessly and without apparent concern, nearly capsizing. They talked while the oldest of the women, thirtyish and somewhat a looker, took her place astern with the paddle (long and narrow, with a faint, bell-shaped flare for a blade), another of them bailed with a coffee can, and the third arranged the children and the groceries to trim the boat and keep them dry, respectively.

With all in order, they turned the boat slowly toward the open water, the paddler making wide sweeps and prying, and the woman in the bow, the one who had tended the children, fending off the other boats with a pole. The cayuco lacked seats, as most do, and all the passengers perched on the gunwales. The paddler hung her right butt cheek over the gunwale and swept and ruddered the long paddle powerfully to break the inertia of the heavy load. Slowly, very slowly, she accelerated into the open water. She had strong shoulders and must have had powerful wrists, for she used a perfect J-stroke, rolling her wrists and ruddering the heavy blade outward at the end of the stroke in one graceful motion. The canoe continued that way for twenty minutes, the women conversing uninterruptedly. Except for the grackles and the marimbas, the evening was so silent (not an outboard or a jet ski in sight) that I could hear them going at it almost all the way to San Miguel, where they disembarked on a beach in the low evening light, put their heels back on, and carried their groceries and their children up a hill out of sight.

THINGS HAD GOTTEN so bad, according to Roan, that legal settlers in the multiple-use zone were poaching game and extractive crops inside Tikal, taking advantage of budget cuts and administrative corruption. Since the last election, the number of park guards had gone from eighty to thirty-five. Perimeter patrols went from twelve men once a week to maybe one a month, with one to three men. Guards' salaries had been reduced and they hadn't been paid in months. Poachers profited from the reduced patrols. Undermanned and unpaid, the guards who remained were afraid to patrol farther than one kilometer from the ruin. Consequently, wildlife swarmed around the ruin at the center of the park. Everything beyond that was fair game.

Worse, Roan contended, Mexico and Guatemala planned a new road from Campeche south to Flores which would follow the same route through Uaxactún and Tikal as Roan's proposed wildlife corridor.

We were driving east in the WCS pickup, past the military campo and the usual lowland mix of ranchos, milpas, and ravaged forest patches. Just past the campo Roan pointed to a vermilion flycatcher perched on a fence post.

We turned north at El Rescate, at the eastern end of Peten-Itza. Nearby, I had read, the ruin of Ixlú bore signs of late classic putun domination. The lake extended westward under a flat sheen of haze, and steep hills lined the northern shore. Immediately the road climbed gently and we reached the park gate.

Beyond the gate, the forest closed in on either side. In the deep, primal timber, the temperature dropped ten degrees. Rounding a bend, we saw a tyra—a sort of neotropical fisher or wolverine—lope across the road twenty yards ahead of us. A minute later an oropendola's nest fell from a tall, epiphyte-laden ceiba, and we pulled to the side of the road. The oropendolas' deep, stockinglike nests festooned the tree's bare limbs.

Roan stepped off the pavement. He said, This is where you see really big barbas amarillas (fer-de-lance, the ubiquitous and deadly viper of Central America). They hang out under oropendola colonies to eat the rodents that come to eat the shit and the fallen babies. Roan parted the brush under the tree and revealed a few fallen nests and empty eggshells already eaten by snakes or rats. Overhead the Montezuma oropendolas hopped nervously from branch to branch, tearing out and dropping old nests and emitting their distinctive gurgling call. Bits of leaves and nest rained down from the canopy.

Another half mile down the road we parked and followed an old transect line into the woods. Within a hundred yards the heavy timber muffled the sound of sporadic traffic on the road. Low palms grew thick in the understory and strangler figs filtered the light. You could sense the low murmur of the big tropical woods, the deep pedal tone of wildness. You knew archetypes stirred just beyond the range of your senses: tapirs, kinkajous, white-lipped peccaries, cougars, barbas amarillas, jaguars—stuff that could eat you. It felt deserted and teeming at the same time.

We heard toucans, gnatcatchers, parrots. Roan's expert eyes picked up various signs: large fallen epiphytes dislodged by feeding kinkajous or anteaters, and places where xate had been cut for seed and chicozapotes had been slashed for chicle sap. If poachers came for these things, he said, they certainly hunted while they were here. A trained and adequately paid corps of guards would make it that much harder for them.

After we left the woods we parked and hiked toward Tikal's north acropolis. Crested guans perched tamely, and coatimundis foraged in the low growth, unperturbed by our presence. Roan spotted an ivory-billed woodpecker and we watched it for a while before circling around the palace and crossing the deserted plaza of the north acropolis. Another trail led us past a couple of pyramids to Temple II, one of the highest pyramids in Mesoamerica.

We climbed the steep steps and scrambled up to a ledge that circled the temple a hundred feet above the canopy. Rounding the west-facing rear of the temple, we found comfortable positions on the ledge. Below, the canopy teemed with birds. Roan recited a catalogue encompassing laughing and bat falcons, various euphonias and tinamous, honey creepers, mealy and white-fronted parrots, red, gray, and white tityras, tanagers, motmots, violaceous trogons, and a yellow-fronted woodpecker that resembled a yellow-bellied sapsucker. We saw yellow and magnolia warblers, migrants from the northeastern woodlands. Roan's survey of North American migrants around Uaxactún had uncovered at least twenty songbird and wetland species, including thrushes, vireos, herons, and grebes, three kinds of flycatchers, and sixteen kinds of warblers.

To the west, north, and east, the canopy extended unbroken to the horizon. To the north, it ran to Uaxactún, twelve miles away, and beyond that across the Maya Biosphere Reserve four hundred kilometers to the heart of the Yucatán peninsula. It was the largest roadless wilderness and the richest biological resource between the Amazon and Yellowstone.

Piedras Negras lay fifty miles west by a direct compass line. The intervening canopy, if left standing, would connect Tikal biologically to the Montes Azules reserve in Chiapas through a biological corridor being established by a wildlife biologist named Ignacio March, of Ecosur in San Cristóbal, and a critical link in the proposed corridor to run the length of Central America. To the north, it would keep Tikal linked to the big country north of Uaxactún, with its deep gene pool of megafauna.

The sun climbed. We reveled in the empty expanse, made it an object of desire, me and the anthropology student with a zoology background. The younger man, with all the force of his longing, felt toward wilderness as I did: that it had people in it. The conflict for Mesoamerica's forest dwellers, we felt, was one of expectations: a life of modest but deep rewards in a natural setting, against one driven by the development-and-appliances model promulgated by international aid agencies.

I told him how surprised and pleased it made me to find someone with his wit and passion working to resolve those forces.

He scoffed, and said that nothing good would happen in the selva until people benefited from conservation.

We dangled our legs and scanned the canopy until the sun drove the birds into the shade and our water ran out. We stood to leave, then loitered on the northeast corner of the temple with all Tikal spread out below. The eastern view looked beyond the ruin over an extensive wetland, thousands of acres of bajos and aguadas (water-holes) percolating through the rotten limestone toward Peten-Itza and Belize. It seemed on the way to nowhere, yet Tikal controlled the circumpeninsular portage, and the overland route south from the Yucatán. It ruled the smaller towns around Peten-Itza and the lake chains to the east by 378, when it won a decisive and influential war of conquest over Uaxactún, its older and smaller neighbor.

The forest pattern would have looked different then than it did now, the wetlands filled with canals, raised beds, fish and crocodiles, cayucos and workers, the surroundings cleared and covered with gardens and milpas. In the aguadas and bajos, the lakes, creeks, and rivers, the shamans would have discerned the Black Road, the watery path through the sky to the Otherworld. Those waters would have centered the universe. At any given moment the people who stood on this spot knew where they were relative to the known world, and the infinite extent of their relations.

THE NEXT DAY I visited the local Nature Conservancy's offices, where I talked to John Beavers and Mike Lara, who were helping CONAP, Guatemala's environmental agency, establish a new 2,358 square mile national park along the Usumacinta and in the adjacent Sierra Lacandon. Beavers, the project coordinator, voiced concern about the lack of communication between CONAP and CONAI, the archaeological agency, over the dig at Piedras Negras. Lara said he knew the members of the resistance community at El Desempeño, had walked in and visited them more than once. He confirmed Tammy Ridenour's report that they wanted to continue living sustainably in the selva and participate in the park as guards and workers. We agreed to meet at the field station near Piedras Negras sometime in late February, when I planned to arrive there by canoe, to take a hike and visit the community.

That evening a local basketball tournament played to a large and enthusiastic crowd on a court across from the church, at the island's summit. The teams were better than you might have expected, a mixture of young hotshots and slower, more mature passers and playmakers. The guard play was especially crisp, and the proximity of the church and ball court mimicked the temple–ball court relationship of classic and postclassic cities, even in the way the game resembled known aspects of the ancient game pelota, in which two teams wearing pads tried to score points against each other with a hard rubber ball, sometimes by forcing it through an elevated ring. Ball courts themselves were considered portals to the Otherworld, and the play imitated the life-over-death struggle of the Hero Twins. At the end of some ritual games, the losers—captives of the sponsoring ruler— would be killed.

Here the historical echoes were impossible to ignore, though no one, to my knowledge, would be sacrificed at the end.

The next evening I paddled Roan across the strait in his neighbor's cayuco so he could pay Sarita a formal visit. I sat on the gunwale maintaining a slow, rhythmic J-stroke with the unwieldy paddle. The boat was stable and tracked well, but it turned like an oil tanker. We beached it at the landing and walked up the hill through a warren of pedestrian lanes.

Sarita Hernández lived with her sisters, her mother, and her aging father, Julian, in a well-kept house improvised out of cinder block and sheet metal. Roan sat in the parlor, munching dulces and suavely charming three generations of Hernández women, while I waited on the patio with Don Julian by the light of an oil lamp.

The old man had immigrated to Peten from Mexico in the 1950s to harvest chicle for Wrigley. He had small lesions on the cartilage of one ear and the septum of his nose, contracted while sleeping in the jungle when the mosquito that transmits leishmaniasis was abroad. The disease was common among chicleros, and incurable, except by expensive and painful treatments unavailable in Peten.

To make conversation I asked him if the paddle I had carried up from the water was made of caoba, mahogany. Sí, he said. There was less and less caoba to build cayucos, he said. As the material ran out, cayucos had become fewer and more expensive. Now old used boats brought prices you wouldn't have paid for new ones ten years ago.

As we paddled home, the muted lights of Flores sparkled dimly across the water, outlining the dome of the island, and the little hooded grebes scattered invisibly before us in the dark.

ON MY LAST day Roan drove us to the ruin of Yaxha with a friend of his, a Peace Corps volunteer named Doug Schaefer, a soft-spoken North Dakota Quaker and the best birder I had ever met.

We left late, driving east from Peten-Itza for an hour and a half over the road toward Belize, through small villages with minimalist tiendas, kids on mules, women carrying ollas on their heads, and evangelist churches with miniature steeples and names like the Holy Wounds, Church of the Crucified One, their perfectly incongruous sloping lawns mowed and trimmed like Church of Christ grounds in suburbs of Omaha or Hattiesburg. To our left, the canopy extended north, to the right a depressing spectacle of unfettered clearing and farming. Running late, Roan attacked the cratered and furrowed road, throwing us around in the cab like rag dolls. From time to time we saw one of the lakes or ponds of the transpeninsular route lying to the left of the road.

Eventually trees crowded the road and we turned left down a narrow track to a shaded checkpoint with water on either side. Two soldiers guarded the checkpoint with Galils beside a sturdy bunker of earthworks and log pickets surmounted by a machine gun. Doug said that a couple of months earlier a recently discovered tomb had been cleaned out by looters, probably an inside job engineered by sacked military officers or government archaeology workers.

Surprised to have visitors, the soldiers swung open the wooden gate and waved us through. We drove across a causeway connecting Lake Yaxha ("Blue-Green Water"), the larger body on the west, and Sacnab ("Clear or White Lake"), names that Maler believed predated the arrival of Spain.

Across the causeway the road tunneled through the old growth before ending at a deserted parking lot under arching trees. A trail led from an unfinished visitors' center to the lake. As soon as we got out of the truck, Doug started naming birdcalls. We walked through the semicleared main plaza under leafy vaults, collared aracaris (a kind of toucan) flitting in the canopy. Mossy tumuli lay under centuries of accumulated earth and vegetation. A few eroded stelae rested beneath corrugated plastic or metal roofs to protect them from acid rain.

I wandered, rapt, while Doug and Roan followed a howler monkey they had sighted overhead. A thin trail undulated irresistibly over a high forested berm, and I followed it, watchful for snakes. Beyond, the trail entered a zone of silence broken only by the howler's slow, solo groaning.

The trail carried me through another partly cleared plaza, past other faded and acid-darkened stelas, to a pyramid about 150 feet high, surmounted by a ruined temple. On the right side the earth had been stripped from the pyramid, revealing gleaming limestone masonry; to the left, soft, grassy earth. I mounted a stairway of rickety wooden scaffolding and split-log treads. Slowly the lakes came in view, and to the north the great green wilderness of the Maya Biosphere Reserve.

I sat on the temple's summit without a thought for Roan or Doug. The sun set over the lake chain, a more continuous system of small creeks and ponds than I had seen on any map, sprawling to fill a shallow depression between low heights. Geography had preserved the ancient continuities.

To the east behind me, the headwaters of the Belize, Sarstoon, and Mojo rivers rose just out of sight, running to the Caribbean. The geographical and historical connection was as clear, unambiguous, and fated as the Champlain-Hudson corridor of home. The route followed the lakes directly below, visible from the temple for eight or ten miles. It was easy to imagine laceworks of canals and raised agricultural beds in the low-lying margins and intervening wetlands, and the creeks and wetlands separating larger waters canalized for navigability, all visible from here.

The sun settled lower. I stared at the lakes' nickel-colored sheen and concentrated on my breathing. Sunlit flocks of emerald green mealy parrots flew squawking over the trees below. Nearby, the lone howler continued his lamentation, modulating short fragments of commentary with longer, more lyrical passages that resonated in the canopy. I stayed that way a long time, until Doug and Roan joined me and we watched the great blood orange of the sun slowly descend and extinguish itself in the chain of waters.

four

THE DIVIDE

THOMPSON ASSUMED, LIKE MOST MAYANISTS, THAT THE PUTUN AND
other trading peoples followed the Usumacinta upstream when
bypassing the transpeninsular route toward the highlands, then simply reversed direction on their return. They portaged San José
Canyon, just above Tenosique, he believed, and the swift water below
Yaxchilan in both directions, where the average current speed is
eight miles an hour depending on seasonal water levels. The theory
overlooked how slow and difficult it remained to travel upstream

above Yaxchilan. Rainy-season floods render it nearly impossible for muscle-powered craft.

The theory nagged at me vaguely from a canoeing point of view until I talked to Ron Canter, an amateur Mayanist, intrepid paddler, and cartographer for the National Oceanographic and Atmospheric Administration. Canter believed that a closer look at the region's geography suggested that by ascending the Tulijá, portaging to the Jatate, and continuing downstream to the mouths of other highland tributaries, travelers and traders from the littoral would have avoided a strenuous upstream passage on the Usumacinta and the canyon portage on trails undoubtedly controlled by Piedras Negras and Yaxchilan. Even better, they would have been able to travel in a loop between the littoral and the highlands.

The alternative only made sense, Canter said. In the northeastern United States many aboriginal routes took advantage of slow-moving waters in one direction and fast-moving waters in the other: one river upstream, the other—after portaging across the watershed—back down. A loop. The entire northeastern geography—tribal and inter-tribal hunting and trapping territories, political spheres of influence—had been parceled out according to the location of watersheds, and watersheds shaped native cosmovisions long before ecologists suggested using them as the basic unit for managing ecosystems.

Canter had studied North American and Mesoamerican precontact trade routes as a founding member of Native Trails Inc., a small paddlers' organization, and had helped identify, document, and preserve hundreds of them. He had never canoed either the Usumacinta or the Jatate, but he had mapped them and many other Mesoamerican routes using firsthand reports, existing maps and satellite imagery, colonial sources, expedition journals, and various scholarly works. With his Native Trails colleagues he had traveled and mapped about two thirds of the rivers and coastal waters of Belize for a guidebook.

From their studies and travels, Canter and the core members of Native Trails had arrived at two general principles: that native canoe travelers followed paths of least resistance; and that, when going out and returning, they avoided covering the same ground twice. That meant that wherever possible they traveled a loop. The connecting links were usually the sea or a lake system at one or both ends.

Canter arrived at the Tulijá-Jatate theory simply by poring over maps, reading, and talking to paddlers. No one else could tell him where the heads of navigation lay, where the land and water routes joined. Few archaeologists knew how rivers shaped Mesoamericans' mental maps, how a portage trail might fit the terrain, or even how fast and efficient a cargo canoe might be.

He had explored the lake chains of Yaxha and run the adjacent Chiquibiu and Mopan rivers into Belize (beautiful class 2 and 3 runs through limestone gorges), where the proximity of headwaters encouraged the navigation of circular routes from the coast. Mid-sized ruins clustered at or near the heads of navigation, close enough to combine control of the route with the proximity of decent farmland. Portage trails in Belize, he found, occupied the same kinds of terrain as they did in Maine.

The Tulijá-Jatate route, Canter felt, had obvious advantages for delta traders. They could sidestep, at least on the upstream leg, the stranglehold Piedras Negras and Yaxchilan surely exerted on the river. As in the case of the circumpeninsular trade and the infamous triangle trade of the colonial Atlantic—in which ships carried slaves, molasses, and rum, respectively, from Africa to the Caribbean, New England, and back to England—they could maximize their geographical coverage on a given voyage, arriving at the ripe markets of the Chontalpa, Yaxchilan, and Piedras Negras on the swift downstream leg, laden with goods from the widest possible area.

The route explained why Olmec artifacts appear in the remote Jatate corridor, previously unrecognized as a highway from the gulf. It explained the siting of Toniná, the farthest western and one of the highest cities of the classical period, located on the divide between the watersheds. Toniná's art and architecture bore odd motifs of a decidedly non-Mayan character, sparer and less baroque than Palenque's, which some scholars attributed to central Mexican influences. It had captured the king of its vastly more powerful neighbor, Palenque, in 711, and claimed the latest recorded classical inscription, the equivalent of 909 C.E. The putun, of course, would have coveted its strategic location.

Before I left for Mexico, Canter and some of his colleagues visited me during a scouting trip from their homes near Washington, D.C., to the Adirondacks. Canter was in his forties and almost pathologically self-effacing. His friends, however—while Canter visited the car or used our shower—told stories of elaborate and ambitious trips he had planned, forced marches across the unlikeliest of watersheds just to travel a loop and avoid returning the way they came.

Canter carried a portfolio containing maps and drafts of maps of a bewildering variety, scope, and detail. Some of them showed sections of the proposed 740-mile Northern Forest Canoe Trail, running from the southwestern Adirondacks to northern Maine. Other, larger-scaled maps showed intricate networks of precolonial North American land and water routes. Still others broke down the Mesoamerican trade routes into sections and cross sections. All the maps attested to a sensitivity to the finest grains in the weave of landscape and memory. None of them looked ready for publication; they were works in progress, drafts on the way to the big picture, the bird's-eye, bee's-eye view of the great understanding that would no doubt reveal something essential about our habitation of the hemisphere.

Unfortunately, through no fault of his own, Canter's information on the Jatate was cursory and incomplete. The river had seldom been run all the way in historical times. He doubted the navigability of the river's Colorado Canyon, where it entered the Lacantun, and directed me to a book called *Secret of the Forest,* by the archaeologist Wolfgang Cordan. When Cordan ran the Jatate in the 1960s, Canter said, he and his guides had carried their equipment around Cañón Colorado on a portage trail river left. Then they launched their cayucos unmanned through the gorge and fished them out at the end.

The route remained problematic for Canter from the point of view of trade. Traveling up the Tulijá, crossing on foot through mountain valleys past Toniná, and paddling down the Jatate would have been faster and easier than the long climb up the Usu against the current, he said, but the extent and severity of whitewater on the lower Jatate might determine the theory's validity.

At the kitchen table we took out my copy of Frans Blom's 1953 map of the Lacandon forest. There was Toniná commanding the upper Jatate valley, near the high point of Canter's proposed portage. A trail—now the road to the Maya villages in the cañadas, and the route of the ancient portage—followed the Jatate downstream to the north until it cut southeast, paralleling the river west of Las Tazas Canyon. A string of small ruins: Delicios, Chapayal, Xoc, and Dolores, guarded the route. A small ruin also guarded the mouth of the Río Tzaconejá.

Downstream, the trail ran out (today a rough road has extended it to San Quintín), replaced by the Jatate and rapids named El Mico, Bodegas, Paso Soledad, Contreras. (Naming implied an intimacy with their idiosyncrasies only paddlers would be likely to possess.) To a canoeist the route made sense. The only question was how far downstream the traders had carried their goods before they returned to the water, the extent of the whitewater, and their skills at navigating it.

Common wisdom assumes their skills and equipment were lacking in that regard, though ample contrary evidence exists. Inscriptions tell us Piedras Negras received frequent royal visits by canoe from Yaxchilan, requiring the navigation of the Anaite and other less difficult rapids. According to Maler, Tenosique prohibited log drivers from running San José Canyon at the turn of the century after a spate of drownings, probably in high water. That they ran it at all suggests most of them made it.

Nobody disputes that North American Indians ran rapids. The Crees' birch-bark crooked canoe, with its extreme rocker, and the Inuit kayak speak for themselves. Whitewater accounts enliven Jesuit and fur trade annals. In 1897 a Mohawk known only as "Pierre," from Kanewake, near Montreal, accompanied the Tyrrell brothers on their trek from Toronto across the northern Barrens for the Canadian Geographic Society. Pierre had earned their attention, wrote J. W. Tyrrell, by "running the Lachine Rapids [in the St. Lawrence River at Montreal] on Christmas Day, out of sheer bravado." Having rafted the Lachine Rapids—and once was enough—I can confirm the bravado of that feat. Mohawks also ran the last log drives on the wild upper Hudson.

In Maine, Thoreau's Penobscot guide, Joe Polis, ran a nineteen-foot bark canoe through the steep rapids of Webster Stream while Thoreau and Channing followed along shore. Thoreau likened it to "navigating a thunderspout." "At such times," he wrote, "[Polis] would step into the canoe, take up his paddle, and, with an air of mystery, start off, looking far downstream, and keeping his own counsel, as if absorbing all the intelligence of the forest and stream unto himself. I sometimes detected a little fun in his face. . . ."

Amazonian Indians voyage by dugout for months on end, on rivers broken by frequent and severe whitewater. Anybody who travels such routes routinely will eventually refuse to portage *every* rapid. Over time travelers gain skill at navigating whitewater, and their boat designs evolve appropriately. Inevitably, some take pleasure from running rapids safely and elegantly.

Moises had showed me an old photograph taken by Robert Bruce in a coffee-table book, showing two young Lacandons standing in a cayuco on Lake Naha. I had seen the Lacandons' dugouts. Unlike those tublike canoes, the one in Bruce's photo had a good deal of rocker and a high bow and stern. You could have run it through San Jose Canyon at average water levels with little or no problem if you knew what you were doing.

In 1928, on the trail from Tenosique to Ocosingo, Blom and his student, Webster McBryde, found themselves stranded on the bank of the flooded Río Santo Domingo, a secondary tributary of the Usumacinta that rises near a cluster of small lakes in the Lacandon homeland.

Swimming his pack animals across the torrent, Blom almost drowned in a "souse hole," or hydraulic. With their provisions running low and darkness approaching, the men felt pressed to reach their destination at a nearby coffee finca. While they deliberated onshore, a family of Lacandons paddled down the rapids in two cayucos.

Blom waved them over and bargained with the headman in Tzeltal for a ferry across the river. The others rummaged freely through the camp equipment, taking whatever they found. Eventually they struck a deal for some machetes. McBryde's account of the crossing bears a striking resemblance to Thoreau's.

"It was an unusual picture," McBryde wrote, "weird and beautiful, which presented itself as we crossed the river in the twilight; the long canoes shooting gracefully through the rapids, with one of the men in either end and working his paddle rhythmically, long hair and loose robes flowing together as he bobbed in sudden vigorous jerks. We were about mid-stream when a flock of macaws, eleven pairs, passed overhead, their long plumage redder than ever in the light of the setting sun."

I RETURNED TO Palenque from Flores, settled in at Panchan, and set about finding a bow partner. A couple of prospects fizzled. Then Susan Prins, who oversaw the operation of the palapas and camp- ground at the rear of Panchan, introduced me to her husband, Alonso Mendes. Susan had noticed a parking sticker on my car from her Vermont alma mater, Middlebury College, where the couple had met as students. I told her my fiancée worked in the college's administra- tion, and we talked for a while, commenting on the odd vectors of coincidence connecting Palenque and the Champlain valley.

Later I joined them in their cabaña in the selva, where I chatted with Alonso, discovering he was a painter and sometime jungle guide of Polish-American Jewish and Tzeltal Maya heritage. His mother, an American artist named Frances Toporek, had worked as a research assistant for Frans Blom, and later for the Harvard Chiapas Project, in San Cristóbal. More recently, she operated the city's only Chinese restaurant and acted as a doyenne of the local arts community. His father, Alonso Mendes Ton, was a headman and former president of Tenejapa, one of the municipalities in the hills surrounding San Cristóbal, and an expert in the complex system of Tzeltal plant classification. In the sixties Mendes Ton had advised the anthropologists and ethnobotanists who produced the massive work *Principles of Tzeltal Plant Classification,* and they had dedicated it to him.

As a child Alonso accompanied the scholars and Indian collaborators of the Harvard project on field trips, collecting specimens and generally helping, and absorbing Maya culture from dual perspectives. When the time came, the Harvard scholars encouraged his artistic development and saw to his prep school and college education in the states.

He stood in both worlds, the gringo and the Indian, but his passion for his father's people, both ancient and contemporary, expressed itself most visibly in his personality. He was in his early thirties, soft-spoken and unassuming. Black hair fell in a shock over his forehead, framing wide, sad brown eyes. He knew of Blom's activity along the Jatate, of the Zapatista entrenchment in the river's canyons, and the region's remote, off-limits mystique. He grasped my purpose intuitively, without explanation, and when I told him I needed a bow partner he volunteered immediately. He spoke Spanish, English, and Tzeltal. Best of all, he was massively built across the chest and shoulders and carried about 10 percent body fat.

Two days later we drove to the Río Nututún, a small feeder to the Chacamax outside Palenque. We carried the Freedom upstream a few hundred yards and practiced turning in and out of eddies in the low-volume runs between a series of aquamarine pools. The river tumbled out of the green scrofulous hills behind the ruin, clear and cool and hemmed by low-hanging, bromelia-decked chicozapotes, but the current was too weak to prepare us for the turbulence of the Jatate. After practicing, we swam in the pools and ran the easy class 2's back to the highway, following the pencil-thin line of current, weaving among the rocks under the bridge beside the Hotel Nututún.

Alonso and Susan had a two-year-old son, Xun (pronounced *Shoon*, Tzeltal for John), who ruled Panchan like a benevolent despot. Moises doted on him.

After Alonso and I arranged to meet at La Sultana, Alonso took Xun to see his grandmother in San Cristóbal for a few days. Moises used their absence to object to Alonso's joining me. Alonso was a father, he said. His days of exploring in the jungle were past. Moises neglected to mention the ten children he had left at home back in the sixties, when *he* had guided in the jungle.

He kept cornering me. Whereas before he had applauded my idea of a grand descent, suddenly he saw it as foolhardy and self-destructive. He questioned Alonso's fearlessness and invoked Charles Frey, the gringo draft evader and protobeatnik who explored the selva during World War II, married a Lacandon woman, and drowned in a hydraulic on the Lacanjá in 1952. He insisted that after guiding in the jungle for twenty years, he knew what could happen. I assured him as gently as I could that I knew a good deal more about running rapids than Frey had, and thought I could handle most emergencies that didn't include guns. He managed nevertheless to aggravate one of my worst fears—high water.

Suddenly rising water levels haunt wilderness paddlers. They are common all over the Usumacinta, where the uplands suffer from deforestation and development, while the midlands are relatively intact. Silt from eroded, overgrazed hillsides in Alta Verapaz, Guatemala, for instance, precipitates in the delta, two hundred miles downstream, clogging shipping lanes and rerouting channels through farmland. Runoffs from heavy rain, unmoderated by forest cover, cause unpredictable flooding in the tributaries. Distant rains can produce flood conditions even when you've had nothing but clear skies.

A few evenings before I left for Agua Azul and the Jatate, Moises wandered over to Susan's café for his evening beer, joining a group of us at one of the small metal tables. He told of searching for ruins in the hills behind Panchan with Mayanists Linda Schele and Peter Mathews when a sudden rain flooded the upper Nututún and its feeder creeks. Coming back, they forded a couple of rushing capillaries as darkness approached, but when they reached the Nututún it was a torrent. One of them nearly drowned trying to swim it, and they made their way slowly downstream in the dark, fearful of snakes and of slipping into the river from atop the high bank.

He ordered another beer. In 1963, he went on, he had guided six junior diplomats, men and women visiting Palenque from Mexico City, to the ruins of Bonampak. In those days Bonampak was a three-day hike from Palenque, rather than a two-hour drive. One of his customers was a former U.S. Olympic swimmer, another a French legionnaire of some kind, but all were fit and in their twenties. After the first day out it rained hard, so they turned back. Soon they found the way blocked by floodwaters on one of the many streams they had forded the day before.

Moises decided to follow high ground paralleling the Río Tinieblas (twilight, darkness), which runs north from the vicinity of Naha into the Chacamax east of Palenque. The rain fell harder. They reached the Tinieblas at the headquarters of a remote logging operation that stood at the head of a canyon. Normally the logs were floated down the upper Tinieblas and its tributaries to this point, piling against a boom made from thirty-kilo chainlinks stretched across the river. From the boom a steam-powered crane would lift the logs onto a gravity-driven rail system that bypassed the canyon, and carry them to the mill at Chancala. You might have found such a system in the Adirondacks or Pacific Northwest seventy-five years ago.

A cribwork bridge spanned the river. At the halfway point stood the office from which the engineer, "a big shot," directed the operation. As everywhere rivers float timber, the logs' release from upstream had to be coordinated so they wouldn't pile up and overload the boom. Crews from Ocosingo, Palenque, and Tenosique, in competition with each other, cut trees and piled them at headers on the banks upstream. On a predetermined schedule coffer dams were opened and the logs floated down to the boom on the "bubble" (the surge), where they were lifted onto the rail line. But the rain had flooded the rivers so fast that the waters swept the separate stacks of timber into the river simultaneously. By nightfall, when Moises and his party arrived on the scene, logs had piled against the boom in an enormous jam.

The water kept rising and logs continued to pile against the boom. If the chain snapped, the logs would either jam at the head of the canyon, backing up the Tinieblas and washing out the operation, or be reduced to splinters in the canyon. A crowd watched from the bridge as the chief engineer sent a boat carrying five or six men under huge generator-powered spotlights to add chainlinks to the boom and reduce the pressure. Logs kept piling on the jam, stretching the boom. People on the bridge screamed to the men in the boat to return to shore, but it was too late. In a rush the boom snapped and a groundswell of mahogany logs and brown floodwater roared down the canyon, carrying the men in the boat along with it. All were lost. Distraught, the chief engineer walked onto the bridge and shot himself in the glare of the spotlights. His body fell from the bridge and vanished in the canyon.

Moises and his party waited at the montería for five days, but it kept raining and the flood didn't abate. Finally Moises led them out along the south bank, through the wet forest. They encountered numerous flooded side canyons where he had to talk his young and by now seriously bush-fatigued charges out of rash acts like swimming a torrent or jumping a wide crevasse, choosing instead the slow progress of leading them around the headwaters of the tributaries. He devised tests to demonstrate the impossibility of their athletic schemes: having them attempt to jump a seemingly narrow but safe distance, or tying a log to a rope and trying to retrieve it from the maw of a hydraulic to show them the force of the water. (They couldn't.)

Some faltered but Moises showed them no mercy. Don't contaminate me! he told one of them. If your things down below (cojones, balls) are in the right place, God will take care of you. If you give up, he will kill you.

After eleven days, five without food, they emerged at Chancala. The sawmill's black sawyer met them, astounded they had survived. Moises told him they made it because they exercised judgment and they didn't freeze.

I HAD FEARED high water unnaturally, so naturally it came to pass. On our first morning after leaving Palenque, the falls at Agua Azul roared in my dreams. My feet lay in a puddle in a corner of the tent I had borrowed for the trip: a diaphanous two-pound Moss, twenty years old, which needed patching but which compressed into a space-saving cylinder about the size of a loaf of bread. During the night the intermittent downpours had found a pinhole in the seam along the ridgeline, planting a persistent drip at thirty-second intervals in the approximate center of my forehead.

I crawled from the nylon chrysalis shortly after dawn and walked to the falls a hundred yards away. A chocolate-colored froth thundered over the travertine dams and the side channels that paralleled the main river, past the makeshift stalls that catered to tourists bused in daily from San Cristóbal and Palenque. The torrent had quadrupled in volume overnight, washing hundreds of tons of thin topsoil out of the upstream milpas and cut-lands for deposition downstream. It was a small watershed with a quick response time. In the last couple of hours the rain had slackened and the waters begun receding as fast as they had risen. Grass and shrubs lay flat along the side channels and on the mid-river islands, and water lines showed on rocks four or five inches above the current level. Farther upstream Tzeltal women drew water from the eddies in buckets.

I viewed the runoff from three or four persepctives. One of them had to do with the fair apportionment of electrical power in rural Chiapas.

Two weeks earlier, when I was with Roan McNab in Flores, Ernesto Zedillo, Mexico's president, had withdrawn the San Andrés peace accords, the agreements reached the previous year between the government and the Zapatista rebels, and talks collapsed. For the past week the main road connecting Palenque and San Cristóbal had been blocked at four or five places, including Agua Azul, by Indians demanding that the state electrical authority restore service to their remote communities and reduce recently quadrupled rates.

The previous day, when we reached the intersection leading to the falls, cars, buses, and camionetas—small pickup trucks outfitted with benches for local transit—were backed up in either direction, waiting for the vote on whether a toll would be charged that day and how much it would cost. A few hundred campesinos, all men, milled in the intersection, talking in small groups and manning spiked boards attached to pull cords, which lay in the road to discourage drivers from running the roadblock. Scott got out and patiently but persistently negotiated our passage down the canyon road to the falls, while Indians thrust through the windows of our van mimeographed handouts listing the offenses against native communities.

The handouts said the communities would leave their electric bills unpaid until the state utility lowered its rates. Twenty percent of Mexico's electricity, and 45 percent of its hydro power, they complained, flowed from plants in Chiapas (the Grijalva drainage), whose reservoirs displaced campesinos and flooded farmland. The exponential rate increases, they said, were part of the so-called low-intensity war, a strategy of harassment tied to the stalled peace talks between the federal government and the EZLN, the Zapatista Army of

National Liberation. (Before the Zapatista uprising in 1994, few if any rural communities had electricity. Electrification was one of the first government sops to curb the rebellion.) The handouts further demanded the release of campesinos imprisoned as a result of the protests so far, and, as always, the removal of the Mexican army from rural native communities.

The Maya, historically, have an affinity for falls, rapids, and whirlpools, places that embody, like caves and mountain summits, portals to the Otherworld. Lacandons lived at Agua Azul in colonial and postcolonial times. The farthest downstream of the three-mile series of falls marked the upstream terminus of trade routes from the delta to the highlands. In the years after the 1910–17 revolution, a finca at Agua Azul had produced cacao and coffee under a series of Swiss, German, and Mexican landowners. Presidente Luis Echeverría entertained Fidel Castro there.

Tzeltal and Chol Indians had "invaded" the land around Agua Azul only in the last couple of decades under constitutional land-reform provisions. Their appeal for official ejido—commune—status had been stalled in court ever since. In the meantime they lived by the falls, washing and drawing water and fish from the river, cutting and burning milpas in the surrounding mountains and forests. Recently, tourists and concessions had brought in more income than traditional agriculture. Some of the community's more forward-looking citizens were concerned that overuse and deforestation might kill the newly gilded goose: the nacreous blue braids and travertine falls of Agua Azul. They had begun to think about the long term, but the old ways persisted.

I stared at the flood. By 1992 the big dams proposed for the Usumacinta had been defeated—for now at least—but rural areas of the state were crying for power. Zapatistas had even been heard to favor the big dam projects and the jobs they would provide, apparently forgetting the dislocations and other humiliations invariably suffered by the peasants as a result of such massive projects. Yet here was all this water, in arid Mexico.

In San Cristóbal, on my way to Guatemala, I had read a once-secret report, compiled in the eighties, which outlined hydro development plans for the entire Usumacinta watershed. The report pinpointed sixteen potential damsites from Boca de Cerro, near Tenosique, to Las Tazas on the Jatate, and two in Guatemala. When news of the plan finally leaked out, four sites had been slated for construction by the nineties. Their shared output was projected to approach 2,890 megawatts, enormous for its time. The dams would have cost from $2 to $3.7 million, in 1982 dollars. Five hundred square miles would have been flooded and 320 river miles would have been altered, including everything on the Usumacinta above Boca de Cerro and half the Pasión, flooding the ruins of Aguateca and Altar de Sacrificios, and much of the Lacantun and Jatate.

The potential ecological and archaeological losses were mind-boggling. A well-coordinated outcry drew attention to the project, and to the river, but economic considerations such as the added cost of transmission to distant markets quashed it ultimately.

Oddly, nobody I talked to mentioned the possibility of small, economical "run of the river" hydro plants for communities in the selva, the kind that wouldn't require huge dams, wouldn't result in siltation, evaporation, habitat loss, or lost tourist dollars. The government and agencies like USAID and the World Bank smiled on the massive projects, it seemed.

With a different kind of aid, the people of Agua Azul might have had their tourists and their hydro, too. Instead, government-controlled energy was being used to manipulate them and other remote communities to smashingly negative effect, aggravating hostilities previously restrained by the relatively good-faith dealings of their leaders.

I wandered back to camp, where David Kashinski cooked huevos mexicanos at the propane stove. The paying customers milled around in rain gear drinking coffee or hanging their tents to dry. Scott said— holding a coffee cup away from his body and bending to inhale the first hot sip—rumor had it that no vehicle would be allowed to pass through the bloqueo until the power came on. Restaurants and craft stalls fronting the falls were closed. If this were true, the one-day practice run we had planned on the nearby Río Shumuljá would be imperiled, along with our impending departure for the Jatate.

We took our time drying equipment and drinking coffee. By ten-thirty the water had receded. The only thing to do was give it a try. We loaded the boats on Scott's four-wheel-drive pickup, climbed aboard the combi, and drove up the canyon to the intersection.

Traffic backed up in three directions and a crowd bigger than yesterday's clogged the crossroad. A long string of pickups and combis awaited the disposition of the day's cobro, or toll. I climbed from the van and followed Scott into the mob. Steam evaporated off the elephant-ear ferns at the jungle's edge, and fragrances of rot, exhaust, and yellow guanacaste blossoms scented the air. Hard-bitten campesinos wearing white cotton and traditional palm sombreros, rakishly creased, mingled with the modish young protesters in NBA gimme caps, jeans, and sneakers. Despite the chaos, the men had specific roles handing out information sheets, manning the spiked boards at either end of the intersection, participating in discussions.

A radio blared incomprehensibly through the feedback of crackling speakers. The only woman in sight, a well-dressed Ladina from one of the campesino unions supporting the blockade counseled strenuously in favor of exacting a toll and allowing traffic to flow. The dialogue took place in simultaneous Spanish and Tzeltal. She argued a shutdown would only attract the military, who last week cleared out five blockades on the road, wounding and possibly killing an undetermined number of campesinos and imprisoning others. (Details were hard to come by. Reliable information didn't exist.)

While I listened to the woman, Scott emerged from the rabble. It was all right, he said. We could leave. He only hoped we'd be able to get through when we returned that evening.

The crowd parted before us, the protesters' faces passive and unreadable. When we turned right, toward Ocosingo, the men pulled away the spiked board and stood aside.

The clouds burned off, the temperature climbed. After twenty minutes we took a right onto a dirt road that wound for twelve kilometers through a small aldea, and continued for half an hour past mixed forest and milpa, with glimpses of jagged karst ridges and narrow canyons. After a while we came along a clear stream running into the Río Shumuljá, a Tulijá tributary that itself receives the waters of the Agua Azul.

We launched our boats from a high bridge and drifted uneventfully for the first couple of miles through flats and over washed-out class 2's, through the beautiful valley draining to the Tulijá. Jungle and milpa steamed on either side. A green agami heron flushed downstream ahead of us. The scene was pastoral, with mixed forest, recovering and bearing milpas on the valley floor, and patches of forest on the ridges. Little question of lost wilderness here, where Mayas had farmed, traded, and lived continuously since the classical period.

You could imagine ancient cayucos plying the river at lower water, the low-volume boats of local farmers and the larger trade canoes of the outlandish putun. Classical pottery shards indicated extensive farming had run all the way up the drainage, and that the milperos had paid tribute to Palenque. Moises believed the upper Tulijá had absorbed the commoners who abandoned Palenque at the time of its collapse. The elites, he believed—in typical contrast to accepted wisdom—moved to the Usumacinta to escape the commoners' wrath and evolved into the culturally conservative Chol Lacandons, predecessors of the contemporary tribe, but of different linguistic stock. This made sense to me, though archaeologists considered it one of Moises's unsupported inventions.

Other pottery evidence indicated the putun themselves may have caused the city's downfall, or at least moved in and occupied the site after the conflicts of the period had wreaked their havoc.

I meant to judge the upstream navigability of the Shumuljá, one of the Canter trade route's important links on the upper Tulijá. The farther we traveled downstream, however, the less possible that judgment became. The current pushed us along at a good clip, running high and brown with silt. Nobody would be paddling upstream that day.

We made it down one difficult rapid, though a boat flipped in the high water. Downstream we passed under the fifty-foot cataract where the Agua Azul plunges into the Shumuljá. Beyond that, only flats and easy ledge-drops remained, many washed out by high water. At lower levels, it would have been easy for crews of ancient traders to line or carry loaded or unloaded cayucos over the obstructions, then paddle up the intervening slow currents.

In the late afternoon we took out below a swift rapid in the shade of ceibas forming an arch over the river, the green Tulijá valley spread out below us, and returned safely to Agua Azul.

Before dinner I talked to one of the white-cotton-and-sombrero hardcases at the falls, an old-timer. He leaned against a tree with his arms folded, watching the bathing beauties. A delegation had petitioned the governor in Tuxtla Guttiérez, he said. They had agreed to stop the roadblocks and lift the toll after being assured that power would be returned. He shrugged. If the deal wasn't honored by tomorrow, twenty thousand Indians from all of the highland municipalities would take to the road and close it down. They would be aided, he boasted, by the EZLN.

In the morning we packed for the Jatate but the combi from Ocosingo that was supposed to meet us failed to appear. We got in the combi that brought us from Palenque and drove toward the cruce. From the numbers at the roadblock and the current of barely suppressed rage, it looked like the deal had fallen through. The road was closed and public transportation boycotted. Not even the camionetas, which carried the campesinos from their homes to their milpas, or to market and home again, were operating.

Scott and Raul Roca, his assistant from Palenque, waded into the roil of humanity searching for anybody in charge. I followed them.

Beneath the incomprehensible loudspeakers the Latina union rep pleaded for moderation. The hard-liners told her they had acted in good faith yesterday by lifting the cobro, and they were duped. They took a show of hands and the old-timers carried the issue: nothing moved.

Scott returned to the combi. He had arranged for his own truck to pass, and persuaded one of the headmen to let an idled camioneta carry us as far as Ocosingo. From there another, unembargoed camioneta would take us to the Jatate.

We shouldered our packs and transferred them from our combi to the hired camioneta. About six of us climbed into the bed of the camioneta under hundreds of hostile eyes as Scott waded back into the crowd to work out details. A man approached and began arguing with David Kashinski, demanding money. Over the heads of the Indians I could see Scott returning, swaggering through the group of protesters, a determined solitary figure amid an angry, yet oddly timid, throng. He wore nylon shorts and a T-shirt, flip-flops, and shades, his hair red and disheveled, his mustache long enough to catch the foam out of a beer can. He towered over them at five ten.

He listened and argued with the man in Spanish accented with an Arizona drawl. No, señor, that's *not* what we agreed. Okay then, let's go back and talk to the *other* jefe. They both disappeared. In a few minutes they returned. Everything was fixed, Scott said, and left. Our driver started his camioneta and we watched as Scott's truck, carrying kayaks on its rack and all our rafts and equipment under its cap, slowly parted the crowd and passed through the blockade.

The driver followed. The crowd parted for us once more, but the faces were more hostile than ever. Then the driver stopped. They wouldn't remove the studded board from the road. A swarm of angry faces surrounded the truck. The driver, paid in advance, parked.

We got out and carried our packs through the crowd on foot, nodding and wishing the Indians good luck. Scott, we assumed, would be waiting for us just beyond the crowd, out of sight. But when we got there the road was empty. The sun had cleared the mountain rims. We headed for the shade of some tall acacias just around the first bend. Behind us, one of the daily buses from Palenque to Tuxtla, the state capital, moved slowly through the crowd—the woman from the union must have won her case. We jogged out of sight around the bend. When the bus appeared we flagged it down and climbed aboard.

We rode in the back with the Indian women and children, most of them evangelistas or PRIistas, the men off in the milpas or keeping a low profile while the current disruption played itself out. We watched the road for Scott, but Scott had vanished. David said we'd catch up to him at the zócalo in Ocosingo.

The bus crawled upward over the fractured landscape, out of the bananas and into the pines, roughly following the route of Ron Canter's ancient trade portage. The light turned blazing and unsubtle, the mildewy funk of the lowland rains dissipated. Two hours out of Agua Azul, the bus descended again toward the head of the Jatate valley, a fertile enclave girdled by guerrilla-ridden cordilleras, and the headwaters of the Usumacinta. Below shone the red-tiled roofs of Ocosingo. We had crossed the divide.

SIXTEENTH-CENTURY FRIARS FOUNDED Ocosingo as a collection center for converted Tzeltal-speaking forest dwellers. It evolved into a market town overseen by absentee Spanish landowners, who benefited from a debt-peonage system that provided free Maya labor on the ranches, plantations, and monterías of the hinterlands. Now it was the seat of Mexico's geographically largest and farthest-flung municipality. Racial divisions were clear and sharply drawn. Ladino cowboys, oil workers, and state security police patrolled in pickups while Indian men and women in traje carried produce down from the outlying aldeas on their backs, bound for the bustling market at the lower end of town.

The name meant "Place of Pines" in Nahuatl. The climate of the tierra templada—the transition zone between the piney woods and the lowland rain forests around three thousand feet—and the setting at the valley's head were exquisite, the sierras Lívingston and Corralchen extending southeastward framing a natural highway to the lowlands. Toniná stood in the ranchlands nearby, where it provided the paving stones for Ocosingo's streets.

The valley captivated early gringo visitors. In the twenties Traven adopted Ocosingo and lodged often at a "restaurant" run by a Ladina madam of wide experience and education, befriending the Indians in her employ. From there Traven launched muleback forays to the Jatate and the Usumacinta, pursuing various freelance opportunities of both a scholarly and literary nature. When he died in Mexico City in 1969, his ashes were flown to Ocosingo and scattered from a plane over the waters of the upper Jatate.

The bus let us off on the chaotic commercial strip on the highway outside town. We shouldered our packs and started walking.

We found Scott at the zócalo, surprised by our story. He said a white camioneta like ours had been right behind him when he left the roadblock. We huddled in the meager shade of the zócalo, under the box-trimmed trees with their whitewashed trunks, waiting for the next camioneta to pick us up. Nothing moved but the television in a bar across the street—Ocosingo still had power. Some of the raft customers and guide trainees wandered off to shop in the stores fronting the plaza, or to drink in the bar. The rest waited under the trees.

Carnival rides lay packed in crates on the plaza's southeast corner, near the sixteenth-century church that had been strafed during the battle on January 2, 1994, suspected of harboring Zapatista snipers. You could easily imagine the plaza as a battleground. It had just the right scale for some overheated human drama: slightly canted and smaller than you'd think, no more than a hundred yards from end to end, and some lesser though aesthetically proportionate distance across, with a church, colonnaded hotel, shops, and municipal building. The roofs bristled with antennae and radio dishes.

At the upper end the municipal building sported a new coat of pale lavender on its upper balcony and facade. A plywood barrier obscured the lower floor. I crossed the empty expanse in front of the municipal building under the hot glare, passed the bust of Benito Juárez, the republic's nineteenth-century Zapotec president, and peeked behind the plywood barrier.

The windows had been replaced, but dozens of bullet holes scarred the stucco, each with an aureole of peeled plaster left over from the Zapatista attack on the state security police. The seguridades, a ragtag troop of Latino and indigenous thugs recruited from poor rural towns, were vilified by Zapatistas above the federal government, the army, or the PRI. They harassed Indians with petty arrests for drunkenness and minor or imagined offenses when convenient to vested interests, and protected and sometimes joined the guardias blancas, the freelance pistoleros who effected violent dislocations of Indians from occupied or otherwise disputed lands at the behest of the landed elite, often with only the shadiest of justifications or none at all.

For these reasons the barracks were a prime Zapatista objective, second only to the army barracks and prison outside San Cristóbal, and attacked with perhaps the most personal zeal. From the front of the building you could easily imagine the rebel troops, masked and unmasked, moving up out of the canyons in the truck beds with their assortment of unmatched and insufficient arms, then continuing farther up from the market through the narrow streets and taking positions on the rooftops and the doorways of the storefronts and hammering the barracks with rifle fire.

They caught the drunken security forces off guard and held the town for two days. It was a bold move, and the bloodiest fighting of the war, occasioning foolishness, bravery, and brutal, arbitrary retribution after the tide turned. It became the rebels' worst defeat when the air force arrived before the withdrawal order; their commanders left them too long on the plaza, and the army cut off their retreat. Dozens were pinned in the market and wiped out—a stupid, unnecessary loss that Marcos had acknowledged as a blunder.

An ugly new office building adorned the northwest corner of the plaza, housing the federal human rights commission, the sole eyesore in an otherwise pristine colonial setting.

We left town in a three-vehicle caravan and followed the paved road for an hour, past the turn for Toniná to the first crossing of the Jatate, where we stopped for lunch. The road was paved as far as a fork a few miles past the bridge. The right fork skirted the upper canyons and followed the ancient portage trail, the one we had perused on Blom's map, to La Sultana, where the Río Tzaconejá met the Jatate. That way the canoe traders carried their wares overland from the Tulijá to the Jatate and upper Usumacinta, and that way lay the heartland of Zapatismo.

Our camioneta took the left fork, however, under the looming ridgeline of the Sierra Lívingston. The road turned to dirt and followed a series of wide switchbacks over the spare pasturelands to the very base of the sierra. The truck lurched through clouds of dust and we clung to the steel-pipe canopy frame for dear life, all except Josh Lowry, Scott's head guide, who rode in the cab with the driver. Fortunately, we had been supplied with a cooler of Tecates, bottled water, and refrescos, and our thirsts were prodigious. The conversation picked up despite the lurching of the truck. The signs of civilized, semi-industrialized Mexico fell behind.

In the midst of the talk Raul Roca informed me, apropos of nothing, that Mauricio Morales's trip on the Usumacinta had been ambushed at Budsilhá, despite all his precautions and Tammy Ridenour's earlier safe passage. They had been fired on with AK-47s just downstream from the falls, and Machete Jim had escaped to the Guatemalan side. Mauricio's bodyguard had never gotten a shot off, never even pulled his gun, and the bandits had roughed up Mauricio's cook, a woman and a friend of Raul's, pretty badly. Machete Jim wandered into Palenque three days later. Raul thought the bandits had purchased the AKs with some of the fifteen grand they had scored off Jim the previous year.

The truck stopped on a high switchback under the Lívingstons. I walked as far away from it as I could, far enough that my fellows' unceasing jabber faded in the wind. It had been a long day. Raul's revelations and the increasing proximity of our put-in brought on a sense of dread surrounding all the possible disasters I could imagine, including high water, deportation (my two-week visa for Chiapas had expired), painful injury, confusion, and snakebite.

Dust filtered the coppery afternoon light flooding down the Jatate valley. My urine stream beaded on the road dust. Off to my left the view fell sharply in progressive stages toward the lower Jatate and the canyons of las cañadas, dramatic enough to spike the juices of the most jaded topophiliac, its blue ranges crumpled and folded like the sheet of paper Cortés threw on the table in front of Carlos V to describe the Mexican landscape. Down there, where the clear green Jatate would carry me within ten days, lay the Montes Azules reserve, the last stand of the largest tropical rain forest north of the Amazon and the forbidding haunt of recalcitrant Mayas going back to the seventeenth century.

Here, however, the forest was nowhere to be seen. On the spine of the Lívingstons, up where the trees were fairly thick, you could see individual pines bowing in the wind. In the foreground a solitary jacal stood amid stingy pasturage, overlooking the Jatate's narrow upper gorge. Banana fronds twisted in the breeze.

In the twenties Frans Blom had found a cave up there containing an idol, incense burners, and signs of recent veneration, and had climbed through unbroken pine forests to reach it. Now the slopes were domesticated, scrub pasturage with traceries of stock trails and sparse timber near the summits. Pale, overgrazed grama grass carpeted the valley floor where people my age remembered shady galleries of mahogany and ceiba mixed with longleaf ocote pines. Spindly cecropia and acacia scrub grew in the watercourses. Despite the devastation, it reminded me of a post I had read on the Aztlan listserv, written by the anthropologist Robert Carlsen, concerning the cosmovision of Mayas on Lake Atitlán, in the nearby Guatemalan highlands.

"The World, you see, is the biggest idol of all," Carlsen wrote. "This god, typically referred to in the anthropological literature as Dios Mundo, is understood by the cofrades (the secret religious brotherhoods of Santiago Atitlán) to literally be the face of an ancestral deity. It is telling that in Tz'utujil, the local Mayan language, the word for world is ruchiliew, which literally means 'face of the land.'"

The contours of the land, the arc and curve of the topography, with the extraordinary heights, distant ranges, and crepuscular canyons; the light, filtered by dust; and the silence created the impression of some hieratic space where earth met heaven, like the Fertile Crescent, Tibet, Attica. Perhaps dehydration and fatigue conditioned my perception. But it was impossible not to imagine that events of consequence had occurred here, even though they lay far outside the historical grid studied by norteamericanos, and that we stood on the edge of some profoundly significant geography.

It made the magnitude of habitat loss and the intractability of the political standoff that much harder to digest. It also seemed to make the effort at some sort of preservation that much more desirable. The borders of a special protected zone for the watershed would not be that hard to discern, even to a nonscientist. From the west, you could see, it would begin just about . . . here.

We rounded the point of the Lívingstons in a shower of green and gold light. Around the bend a deeper, wilder valley opened up, and beyond that a further concatenation of misty ranges. The road snaked across the valley floor toward another pass. By the time we crossed into the next valley, sunset flooded the canyons and ignited a pair of limestone summits overlooking the Jatate.

The truck rolled down a rocky track past the site of San José El Real, headquarters of the old Bulnes latifundio. We pulled to the side and all dismounted from the truck again. There was the Santa Cruz bridge, where I had first imagined my descent five years earlier. Josh stood on it and gazed into the river just as I had then. The water was silky and opaline and smelled rich and oxygenated. It purled over a sharp drop just upstream, then compressed into a chute between lime-stone walls. I stood beside him holding open Blom's 1953 map, watching the clear greenish water surging over a drop into the chute below.

Josh, who had arrived from Chile just days before our departure, would accompany Alonso and me on the lower Jatate. We stared at the rapid in silence, moving from one side to the other for perspective, comparing routes, a couple of river bums observing a time-honored ritual.

We looked over Blom's map, a remarkably accurate and evocative one considering the instruments and skills at his disposal, and traced our route over the next two weeks and the courses of other rivers as yet undescended by anybody we knew.

Soon we heard engines coming down the rutted track to our rear. A Humvee rounded the bend by the El Real entrance and bumped down the hill on its high tires over the boulders and gullies toward the bridge, bound for its base at San Pedro downstream. It was painted matte olive drab, with a machine gun mounted in the short-bed manned by a helmeted and flak-jacketed Indian. Behind it followed a matte olive deuce-and-a-half carrying a squad of soldiers accoutred in up-to-the-minute U.S. government issue earmarked for the War on Drugs, not Indians. We squeezed to the side of the bridge to let them pass. The truck slowed. The soldiers—Zapotecs, Mixtecs, and Nahuas from Oaxaca and central Mexico—looked through the slats of the truck and returned our waves.

On the passenger side of the cab an officer looked up from the orders or the map he was reading. He had European features and a Latin-lover mustache. Inside the rolled-up window his face passed a foot from mine. Our eyes met. We waved.

five

THE HEADWATERS

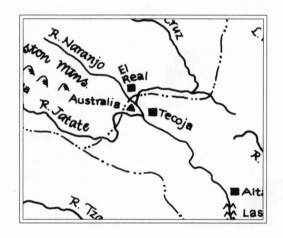

IN CLASSICAL ART, TWO GODS PICTURED AS CANOEISTS ACCOMPANIED
travelers on both actual and metaphysical journeys. Mayanists
know them as the stingray and jaguar gods, or the paddler gods. The
stingray god, who paddles in the stern of the cosmic cayuco, wears
through his septum the barbed tail-spine from the eponymous winged
fish of the gulf's tidal flats and inlets. The spines, among the most
revered objects of trade between the coast and highlands, were used
in ritual bloodletting to pierce earlobes, arms, and penises, inducing

altered states and calling forth ancestors. Sometimes the stingray paddler wears a headdress resembling the xoc, a mythological fish.

The jaguar paddler wears a spotted hide, signifying the transformational role of shamans, a direct link to the formative period and many
indigenous religions in the jaguar's range.

Both gods, their features aged, paddle the souls of the dead to the
Otherworld and the cosmic canoe—the Milky Way—across the sky. As
the galaxy pivots overhead like a giant compass needle, each position of
the needle commemorates a different episode of cosmogenesis. In its
horizontal east-west phase the smear of stars represents the path of the
sun across the sky, the route of Itzamna/First Father to the place of creation, and the cosmic canoe itself, the path and the vehicle as one. As
the constellation swivels, following the earth's movement, the bow of
the canoe dips below the horizon and reenters the underworld, carrying its sacred passengers back to Xibalba.

When approximately perpendicular to the horizon, the Milky Way
becomes the axis mundi, the giant ceiba that holds up the sky, with a
crocodile (earth, underworld) at its roots and a sacred bird (transcendence, prophecy) in its canopy, the unifying center column of the vertically oriented cosmos.

Finally the galaxy shrinks to the edge of the night sky, leaving a star-
less void near the constellation known in both Maya and Western
astrologies as the Scorpion, a vacuum euphoniously termed the "White-
Bone-Snake," the "Black Transformer," or the "Black Dreamplace." It is
the path to the Otherworld, the portal opened by the passage of the cosmic canoe. It declares that night skies and bodies of water are one and
the same. The path to the Otherworld follows through each.

The analogy is clear to anyone who has floated in a canoe on a
windless starry night.

Archaeologist David Freidel explained it to me this way: At night
the cosmos inverts itself, so that what was below is raised above. To
reach the sky, like First Father, or the Hero Twins of the *Popol Vuh,*
who played the ball game with the Lords of Death in the Otherworld

and defeated them, you had to get on the "escalator down," which is the Watery Path. The Watery Path would carry you directly into the sky. That is, it would transform you from flesh into spirit, from stasis into flux. Once you were on water, you stayed on water, straight to transcendence.

Metaphorically the Watery Path turns up in numerous works of classical art. At Palenque, for instance, a carving over a subterranean chamber shows the young Maize God, or First Father, diving underwater. On his famous sarcophagus lid, the dead Pacal falls backward down the roots of the world tree, the inscription reading, "He entered the road [i.e., the path]." Cave paintings from the classical period exist in Belize and Yucatán which can only be reached along underground streams.

The most illustrative of these works are the scenes incised on a set of human thigh bones from a tomb at Tikal, depicting the paddler gods conducting ruler Hasaw-Ka'an-K'awil's ornate life-canoe to the Otherworld, accompanied by a monkey, a parrot, a dog, and an iguana.

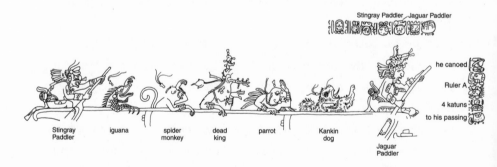

One bone shows the "guide"—in this case the jaguar paddler—executing the commonest stroke for steering a canoe, the pry, while the bow tips steeply into the Otherworld.

The stern of the large canoe towers over the passengers' heads. The bow—equally high, presumably—is already obscured by the canoe's plunge downward, the stern rising at an angle behind.

Decorative carvings adorn the canoe's gunwales and peaks, like the huge ocean-going dugouts of the Pacific Northwest. The paddlers may be standing or kneeling, but the boat appears deep enough amidships that competent vogas could safely navigate it through most class 2 or 3 rapids. Given enough paddlers, they could even maneuver it in fairly technical sections by backpaddling.

You view the scenes from three angles, the largest and most comprehensive from the side, with the cayuco level and traveling from left to right, and the paddler gods and crew members shown in detail.

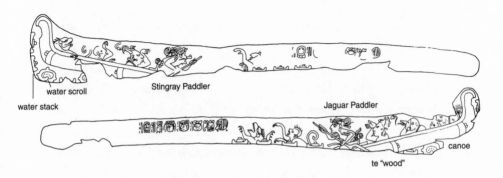

water scroll

water stack

Stingray Paddler

Jaguar Paddler

canoe

te "wood"

THE OTHER TWO angles show similar though mirror-image versions of the canoe diving into the Otherworld. The crew members thrash helplessly as the bow submerges. (The iguana wears an ambiguous expression, possibly of delight.) Having moved to a position amidships, the paddler pries with his cañalete, poised and braced, as the boat follows his guidance into the abyss. His attitude, the angle of the canoe in its plunge, the expressions on the faces of the parrot, dog, iguana, and monkey, suggest a moment familiar to anybody who paddles whitewater: the instant of suspension at the lip of a falls, wave, or hydraulic, when the boat tips, the steersman corrects the angle one last time, and everything hovers on the brink of success or failure.

The scenes take place on at least two planes: one metaphorical, a portrayal of Hasaw Ka'an K'awil's journey to the Otherworld; the other astronomical, a model of the actual Milky Way dipping under the horizon. Additionally, as many canoeists will tell you, it shows a boat entering a precipitous rapid.

The inscription reads: "He canoed four katuns [eighty years] to his passing." The glyph for "He canoed" is rendered thus: 🖼. .

Any place or geographic feature that embodied these events and concepts would have been culturally esteemed. Surely the act of negotiating any such metaphorical or concrete passage would have occasioned appropriate changes in the traveler as well.

THE FIRST SECTION of our descent—about twenty miles—began and ended at the heads of narrow canyons peppered with caves and springs, portals within portals; doorways, wormholes, from one world to the other. Unexcavated ruins, contemporary settlements, and current sites of veneration clustered about them.

Everything reflected the cosmos above and below: the twin peaks at the valley's head; the caves, springs, and constricted passages at either end; the river, the cayucos plying the river, features that bespoke fluidity. Here at the headwaters, the invisible world still manifested itself in the physical landscape, despite the recently imposed distortions of roads and rebellion.

Near the bridge stood the old hacienda El Real, at the head of a canyon, where the upstream waters dropped off steeply. Small ruins dotted the vicinity, and Tzeltal Mayas had lived there historically. At the mouth of the canyon, where the Santa Cruz joined the Jatate, another ruin stood on the point of the confluence, across from the more recent ruin of the hacienda Tecojá, where we camped.

El Real and Tecojá stood on one of the oldest trails to the selva—to Tenosique, Bonampak, Yaxchilan, Naha. Gonzalo de Ovalle in 1586 took it to quell the Chol-speaking Lacandons of Lake Lacam-Tun, today called Miramar, deep in the Jatate valley.

Later came the nineteenth-century mahogany barons, chaingangs of Mayas indentured for petty offenses and debts who cut the trees, and gatherers of chicozapote sap for chewing gum. They were followed by the anthropologists and ethnographers on foot and muleback, pilgrims of a different stripe who sought in the stories and customs of the turn-of-the-century Lacandons echoes of the *Popol Vuh* and the classical Mayas' primal religion, like cosmic radiation left over from the big bang, some defining spiritual base for the western hemisphere: Maler, Seler, Soustelle, Tozzer; Ret Marut, a.k.a. B. Traven; Frans and Trudi Blom; Robert Bruce, Wolfgang Cordan, and beat Charles Frey; midwestern missionaries from the Summer Institute of Linguistics, Latter-Day Saints, Seventh-Day Adventists, Jehovah's Witnesses. Here, in these canyons and forests, in this watershed, all were certain, something explanatory and unexampled had occurred. Something that tied it all together, that emerged from the shapes of the land.

Among them, Wolfgang Cordan explored the Jatate valley and made a successful partial descent in the early sixties, which he recorded in *Secret of the Forest*. Like Teobert Maler, who hoped to find Lacandons still using hieroglyphics, Cordan searched for carved dates to help him fix the classical "fall," hoping to stumble on undiscovered ruins in the process. "This long stretch of two hundred miles," Cordan wrote, "measured from El Real to the junction of the Lacantun with the Usumacinta, is very inadequately mapped and archaeologically a *terra incognita*." It is little better known today.

Cordan came to the selva after World War II and had a checkered career, taking an Indian "wife" and quarreling with Blom over scholarly territory. He wrote that a certain Juan Ballinas attempted to run the Jatate in the 1880s, while trying to figure out how to drive logs to Tenosique, and eventually completed a partial descent after two failures. Cordan followed the upper valley on foot from El Real to San Quintín, where he and his men built cayucos and successfully navigated as far as an old montería on the Usumacinta named Agua Azul (a common place name in the region). He carried a Bolex movie camera to record the trip but conveniently lost it overboard somewhere along the way, which may explain certain discrepancies in his account.

Ballinas remained at El Real even after Carnuto and Quintín Bulnes settled there, patriarchs of the family who controlled the Jatate for the next fifty years. The first Bulneses emigrated from Asturias, in Spain, during the Hapsburg Maximilian's anachronistic occupation of Mexico in the 1870s. By the time Juárez became president they owned coastal and river steamers in Veracruz, cotton mills, and coffee-roasting plants. In 1876 they helped finance Porfirio Díaz's military coup, instituting the prototype of the Latin American dictatorship. In return, Díaz gave them everything between the Río Jatate and the Usumacinta, a territory of 150 by 40 miles, tax free.

Carnuto and Quintín Bulnes eventually occupied the grant and carved out territories supplying food, hardware, and liquor to monterías. Carnuto took two days crossing the mountains and forests from Ocosingo. At the Santa Cruz, which he mistook for the Jatate, he found Ballinas already settled at El Real, and built his house across the river using stones from a nearby ruin. Quintín followed the left bank downstream and found "inexhaustible" timber resources along the Jatate and Perlas rivers. Where they joined he established the montería San Quintín.

Nobody knew the grant's exact borders. In *Trozas,* one of his six Jungle Novels, Traven wrote, "Two jungle streams . . . met there and flowed as one, winding a long way through jungle and bush and finally joining the great Uskumacinta [*sic*] River. Whether it was a matter of winding for a hundred or two hundred or even four hundred kilometers was something nobody knew, because distances were never measured; nobody had time for it or even wanted to do it. No one was interested in scientific research, still less did anyone care about the beauties of nature"—sentiments widespread today, though to a lesser degree.

The enormous tract supported Tzeltals already residing there under previous, though obsolete, tenure understandings, and other Indians indentured to the monterías. Yucatec-speaking Lacandons occupied the lakes around Naha and Miramar. Latinos and highland Mayas alike regarded the unconverted Lacandons as cannibals, calling them Caribes, after the reputed man-eaters of the Antilles, and confusing them with Chol-speaking Indians of the same name, the ones raided by Ovalle and eventually eradicated in the 1690s.

Díaz liquidated Mexico's resources and industries, selling railroad concessions to the British, mines to the Americans, coffee plantations to the Germans. Three million acres in the Usumacinta watershed went to four speculators from Mexico City and a Spanish nobleman, the Marqués de Comillas, whose name still attaches to a huge corner of the drainage east of the Lacantun. The sale divided mitosis-like among a dozen or so corporations and individuals. For the first time, the Usumacinta wilderness was parceled and deeded, setting the stage for one of the most successful and brutal forced-labor rackets in postcolonial history.

The lumbermen, or madereros, desperate for workers and with easy access to a poor and uneducated labor pool, conscripted Indians by two or three methods, called enganche. The commonest method involved loaning money to Maya villagers during fiestas. While the Indians got drunk they were signed to contracts to work off debts higher than they had incurred and that they couldn't pay. Any petty crime or unpaid debt could land them in the camps as well, and Indians often willingly bartered their labor in return for cash advances to pay for medical fees or a funeral, or to purchase livestock. Some monterías were more humane than others, and willing conscripts gambled they could work off their debt and return home in a reasonable amount of time—reasonable to them, at least.

The unlucky recruits were press-ganged into two- or three-week forced marches though the bush, overseen by the labor contractors and their merciless armed goons, called capatazes. At the monterías the conscripts joined three-man teams charged with grueling production quotas. The huge old-growth trees had to be felled, limbed out, cut into sections, and hauled to the riverbank. The company charged for food and every item necessary for their work: machetes, axes, clothes, footwear. Payment was in scrip, worthless anywhere except in the company stores or the bars and brothels that grew up around the camps, so the contracts were often extended rather than redeemed. Escapes occurred, though most of those who didn't die of snakebite or starvation were found and returned within days.

Traven's jungle—or caoba—cycle chronicled the system thoroughly, relentlessly, though debt peonage had been banned for a decade by the time he got there. Traven's information came from his guide, Amador Paniagua, who had spent years in the camps, and from the Indians and hacendados of El Real and Tecojá. At both houses he was welcome to write and study while coming and going from the forest.

Traven had fomented a short-lived Soviet-style republic of students and anarchists in Munich, coinciding with the Russian Revolution. When it fell he escaped to Chicago on a tramp steamer and made his way to Mexico, traveling in Chiapas under the name Torsvan, one of many aliases he took in exile. In the postrevolutionary republic of the nascent PRI, he witnessed the worst excesses of unchecked capital, and he documented them zealously.

He valued the civilized trappings the Bulneses cultivated in the wilderness, and the Bulneses themselves as friends, but made no bones about where his sympathies lay. In *The General from the Jungle,* the last novel of the cycle, he tells of Indians overthrowing their capatazes at the first signs of revolution and liberating the neighboring monterías. The climactic battle takes place between the rebels and government troops protecting a place clearly modeled on the lands and ranches of El Real and Tecojá.

Events relating to the revolution did occur around El Real and Tecojá, but not as recounted by Traven. In 1914 the Carranza government canceled the Indians' debts, then expelled them from the haciendas. Ironically the Bulneses had been among the humane madereros, voluntarily liberating their Indians and giving them back their lands in 1910. The family fled for Yucatán, nevertheless. While a unit from Tabasco, the Usumacinta Brigade, emancipated some monterías between 1913 and 1915, the revolution had a fitful and incomplete history in Chiapas. The selva was too remote for the new laws to be enforced, and labor infractions continued until well after a revolutionary state government was elected in 1924.

Eventually the Bulneses returned. The new patron, Enrique, Carnuto's U.S.-educated son, found the house standing at Tecojá, where the Santa Cruz joins the Jatate, but the cattle were gone and the pastures grown in. Corrupt government timber managers, low stumpage prices, and overcutting had devastated the valley. Enrique sold San Quintín and rebuilt the ranch. He and Alejandro, his son, were the refined dons who entertained Traven and the Mayanists who soon streamed through on their way to the jungle.

When Traven's novels appeared in the 1930s, many of the ranchers he had befriended took umbrage and denounced him. All except Enrique and Alejandro, with whom he continued to correspond from Mexico City.

Enrique Bulnes died in 1937. The family sold off its holdings to pay its debts. The children went native, the son Manuel taking multiple Indian wives and moving across the Santa Cruz from El Real to San "Carnuto," where he acted as adviser and Latino jefe of the valley's native population. Eventually another Asturian immigrant, José Tarrano, married Enrique's widow and rebuilt the ranch.

We pitched our tents outside the ruined casa at the mouth of the Santa Cruz. The last bars of sunlight cleaved the Jatate's upper canyon and struck the twin limestone summits of Chaxalat ("Naked Art Thou," in Cordan's translation), rising two thousand feet from the valley floor across the river. The full moon rose in the notch of the adjacent Santa Cruz canyon.

The air had moderated; it felt high and remote. The river's bouquet drifted up the bank, and the little rapid that emptied into the Jatate made a restful background murmur. It seemed as much a separate universe as a separate watershed.

I wandered around the casa while the guides made dinner and some of the customers sought relief in tequila. I couldn't tell how long it had been since anyone lived there, but the spread seemed salvageable by a hardworking back-to-the-lander with good carpentry skills. A massive royal palm and equally massive ceiba covered with bromelias dominated the foreyard. A wall built of stones possibly salvaged from the nearby ruin surrounded the courtyard. Bougainvillea grew wild from the roof gutters, and ragged, untended roses bloomed.

Mayas had inhabited the spot for centuries, long before Spanish merchants and gringo academics came along. Now the land fell within the ejido grant of the neighboring village. The local Tzeltals had by and large migrated from the highlands no earlier than the sixties, but it was not unthinkable that among them were some whose families had lived here as far back as the postclassic period and beyond.

Recent political reversals had given it back to them, but memories of oppression persisted. The doors and windows were shuttered. Bullet holes pocked the outside wall, crazing the adobe's plaster finish, and the drips from spray-painted letters "EZLN" ran over the holes.

I sat among the pillars of the colonnade, which I remembered from photographs in *Tribes and Temples,* absorbing the scene as deeply as I could. Overhead the peaks held the sun's last rays. The moon climbed higher in the notch upstream. Chachalacas and grackles made their distinctive rackets in the trees nearby and goatsuckers darted at the edge of invisibility.

Already I felt overwhelmed by history, a despair for wild beauty, and a suspicion that all was lost. Like Traven, always on the lookout for the uncontacted tribe or extant classical city, we—some of us—are forever searching for the world that existed or vanished just before we could remember, before we arrived. This, despite voluminous commentary to the contrary, is hardly a specious instinct. Rather, what could be more human, the longing for the better world, the truer place?

IN THE MORNING we drove back to El Real and lowered the boats from the bridge to the limestone shelf beside the chute we scouted the evening before. We cast off and drifted down the slot between the vertical walls, strung out in a line of five kayaks and two rafts. At Tecojá, seven kilometers downstream, David Kashinski outfitted the equipment raft for the days ahead. We would meet him for lunch and continue down the Jatate.

Immediately below us, translucent waves kicked up at the top of a constricted passage. Josh ran it in his kayak without scouting, vanished in the chute, and we followed at his signal, taking the initial drop at a slight angle to avoid hitting the wall at the bottom. We bounced off the wall and kept paddling while Scott shouted commands through the remainder of the long, swift chute, the raft clearing the sides by inches.

We entered a canyon not much wider than the chute, the river gliding flat but swiftly in the penumbral light. High walls leaned in overhead, the trees joining their limbs in an arch—a monkey could have crossed from one side to the other without taking air. Twenty, thirty feet up the high waters of countless rainy seasons had scooped and sculpted the limestone in wide swirls.

We drifted through the cool shadows. Water seeped down the walls, creating sun-dappled gardens of dangling mosses and ferns, epiphytic cacti, bromelias and orchids. In the shade at the base of the walls, xate grew in dense profusion. Whiskey bottles and Styrofoam coffee cups turned in the eddies, thrown off the bridge upstream by soldiers or oil-truck drivers from the well near Naha.

Half a kilometer later the river broke over a drop at the mouth of the canyon. For the rest of the morning we ran a series of class 2 to 4 rapids, scouting and planning our routes down to the minutest paddle stroke. In the river's low volume the kayaks did fine, as canoes would have, but the bigger, less maneuverable rafts needed another hundred cubic feet per second to ease their passage. We hit rocks on every run. On most we performed at least one complete one-eighty, a stern-first maneuver, and a deliberate carom off a boulder or a wall.

Scott fell out when the stern of the raft flipped upward at the bottom of a sharp drop and catapulted him out. He managed to hold on to the boat while I called commands and we fished him in, but he took a hard blow to his leg from a rock. I had my first swim near the top of a long class 2, when the boat came to a hard dead stop against a rock and I, daydreaming, kept on going.

Soon the casa's tile roof appeared, set slightly back from the river on its little rise, the crown of the dooryard ceiba towering over it. At midstream a boy up to his knees peered into the clear riffles, fishing with a gigging spear unlike any I had seen before. As we approached he looked up and waded to shore as if yielding way for us.

We pulled to shore and grounded the boats. At the landing, David had set up lunch and we began making sandwiches while he inflated the equipment raft and lashed the aluminum oar-frame to it with nylon straps. While we milled about, a contingent of neighboring ejido elders came down to see us off. They wore jeans and smiles, their arms folded on their bellies, and they smoked and talked about the country and the weather like farmers everywhere. They took an intense interest in the boats, bouncing on the inflated hulls and slapping the tubes.

Three of them sat in one boat while they conferred with Scott on the condition of the peace (they were for it—their power was off, but they were too busy and too far from the roadblocks to participate in the protests), and the possibilities of a future partnership in the boating enterprise. The uprising had kept Scott off the Jatate for two years and they were glad to see him back. They agreed it was in the best interest of the resource itself—the Jatate—and the long-term success of rafting in Chiapas that they devise means for the community to benefit from the growing numbers of kayakers and rafters they all believed would follow. They discussed training Maya kids as raft guides and developing Tecojá as a headquarters and crafts emporium. Scott suggested charging fees as a first step, then creating a system for staggering launches and regulating camping and waste removal in the big canyon downstream.

They gave the trip their blessing, going around shaking hands and wishing us buen viaje, buena suerte.

Those guys started the rebellion in this valley, Scott said. They're pretty much your typical Zapatistas, easygoing, polite, helpful. Why doesn't somebody write about them?

The boy who had been fishing and two of his friends were sitting on the equipment raft. Scott offered to carry them a couple of hours downstream to San Pedro, their village. David placed the boys three abreast atop a cooler immediately forward of his rowing position, where they examined the rigging and watched the packing operation. They had been fishing for macabil, one of the most plentiful out of the drainage's seventy or so endemic species of fish. (There were about 150 overall.) The fishing was good, they said, and showed me their weapon, a kind of atlatl, or spear-thrower, that instead threw a barbed coat hanger powered by a length of surgical tubing.

Finally we shoved off and ran the short set down to the confluence, the elders waving their ball caps farewell.

The Santa Cruz joined the Jatate in a slowly rotating eddy, the Jatate slightly bigger, a deeper shade of green fading to pale aqua in the shallows. The shore sloped gently to the water shaded by tamarinds and the odd chicozapote. As we floated past the confluence I looked for the ruin called Australia, which Blom had mapped in 1928, but from the river I could see no sign of its earth-and-forest-hidden mounds, nor the large mahogany grove he called the grandest he had ever seen.

Blom failed to date the site, and I could find no records of it that did, but Australia was probably a small ceremonial center serving a scattered rural populace, especially in the amorphous, polyglot era immediately preceding the Spanish conquest.

It stood, effectively, at the head of navigation for the upper river, a region rich with portals—caves, springs, confluences—controlling travel and trade in the hidden valley that extended from Tecojá to the head of the Las Tazas Canyon, thirty-five kilometers downstream. In classical times it would also have commanded the overland route from Toniná to Bonampak, Yaxchilan, Piedras Negras, and points east, and to Pochutla, a postclassic island town on nearby Lake Ocotal Grande.

For those thirty-five kilometers the river presented no navigational obstacles, even for cayucos. We drifted through a succession of easy riffles and small rapids separated by long flats. Chaxalat loomed overhead. In the daylight you could see game and foot trails tracking the sparse monte (scrub forest) on its heights, good habitat for snakes and the ubiquitous brown jays, but little else. A few pines grew spikily from the rocky summits.

The river glided over pale gravel, about fifty yards wide. A bad road followed the river on the left, well back from shore. Trees screened the riparian milpas from our sight, but there were frequent breaks at fords or crossing places where people washed themselves or their horses, standing in the water or lounging onshore. Dark men in bikini briefs hunted for snails in the shallows or tended fish traps. Women soaped their breasts and waved languidly as we passed, and the boys on David's boat shouted greetings to those they knew.

Paddlers ferried cayucos from one bank to the other, or poled up riffles, keeping to the eddies. Other cayucos floated in the shallows near shore, tied to trees. They varied in design, none resembling the low-volume craft I had seen three hundred miles downstream on the Usumacinta, nor were they as elegant. Most were deep-bodied, long and flat-keeled, and patched with sheet metal or plywood—cargo craft. Some, however, showed the influence of fast currents and easy rapids, with high ends and abrupt sheerlines. A few had rocker carved into the ends, for maneuverability and riding over waves.

In the distance the ranges paralleling the river veered toward and away from the shore, alternately constricting or expanding the valley floor. You could see new and recovering (abandoned) milpa climbing steep, once-forested slopes. Mist still clung to a few crests, as if tangled in the deeply green old growth that stood there. New England had looked like this at the brink of the industrial revolution, the valleys planted, the once-lush mountainsides nude, and the panther and wolf gone from the territory.

We camped on a gravel bar inside a wide bend where densely

wooded ranges crowded the river, anticipating the canyon we would come to by noon tomorrow.

I walked across the baseball-sized stones to wash up, the tents in their gaudy nylon hues composed erratically over the bar. The Jatate curved clear and cool in its bed, and black-capped swallows sheered and dipped over the water. I had wiped my face and zipped up my bag when Josh, who had pitched his tent near the water, pointed toward the cobbles of the gravel bar.

Resting among the stones, nearly invisible in its camouflage, squatted a toad identical to any North American garden toad, only five times as big. Big as a rabbit, in fact. Its size and the enlarged parotid glands along its head showed it to be a member of the grand species of the genus Bufo, Bufo marinus, the largest of the so-called "true" toads. When disturbed, marinus emitted a milky alkaloid from its glands that could cause pain, nausea, and a narcotic effect strong enough to render dogs "hypertensive, convulsive, and catatonic."

According to bulletin number 160 of the Smithsonian Institution, "Large individuals of B. Marinus may have a body of nine inches and a mouth large enough to swallow small birds, but insects constitute the major portion of their food." The toad is found all over the tropics, recently appearing in Hawaii, Florida, and Australia, with dubious consequences for habitat and native species. Its relative, B. alvarius, of the American southwest and northern Mexico, also emits toxic secretions.

Alvarius gained notoriety in 1994 when police arrested a California couple for possessing a hallucinogen containing the serotonin analog 5-MeO-DMT, which they had purportedly extracted from the toad's alkaloid secretions, dried, and smoked. A brain chemical, serotonin produces feelings of well-being. The man, a forty-one-year-old teacher, told drug agents that he got so high from smoking the extract that he could "hear electrons jumping orbitals in his molecules." Some people had tried alvarius secretions as an aphrodisiac: one couple reportedly died after ingesting a potion made to be rubbed on the genitals.

Marinus bones have turned up in Olmec burials, terminal classic

Maya graves at Seibal, along the transpeninsular route, and in late post-classic burials at Cozumel, spanning twenty-five hundred years. In Olmec graves the bones sometimes appear with jade votive objects and miniature canoes, suggesting to some Mesoamericanists that Bufo's active ingredient, bufotenine (5-OH-DMT), also a serotonin analog, may have been one of the components of the hallucinogenic potions taken by ancient Mesoamericans for trance journeys and vision quests.

Anthropologist Kent Reilly is one of them. Olmec travelers of the middle formative period (approximately 700 to 300 B.C.E.) carried the objects of their religious ceremonial complex with them in the forms of vessels resembling toads, toy canoes, and figures crouching on their heels with hands on their knees. The crouching figures were carved of jade, serpentine, or other precious minerals and were shown in various stages of changing shape from human to jaguar.

One jade figure, now in the Princeton Art Museum, shows a ruler (also, typically, the chief shaman of his people) in the crouch, like a toad at rest, a position that scholars believe had yogalike, trance-inducing properties. (Carolyn Tate has written about the four basic postures of Olmec figurines: standing and seated meditation, transformation, and feet-on-head contortionist.) A pattern of incisions on the figure's shaved head represents the skin splitting "to reveal the supernatural figure beneath": a toad sticking its tongue out. Some experts think this pattern portrays the shaman in the process of becoming a toad. Reilly says the imagery merely symbolizes the shaman's transformation, shedding his earthly guise for his journey to the Otherworld.

Other crouching figures and toad chalices show a stripe down the figure's back, representing the "split or tear that develops . . . when the toad"—the living Bufo marinus—"enters a transformational or moulting state," six times a year. During the moult the hide splits along the dorsal and median lines and down the limbs so that the animal can swallow its own shed skin "in a series of slow gulps."

Ultimately, all the toad figures turn into jaguars, the foremost symbol of power. The shamans or kings merely assumed the toad posture and possibly ingested toad fluids to get there. They also snuffed powdered hallucinogens such as tobacco, datura, morning glory seed, and dried mushrooms from the miniature canoes.

According to European folk tradition, Bufo toxins were supposedly associated with shamanic practice and witchcraft. "Toad-licking" reports abound in both Europe and the Americas.

In Mesoamerica, jaguars, toads, and water/Otherworld imagery often appear side by side. Toads and frogs hold up the outdoor altars erected by Maya shamans for rain ceremonies. At Cacaxtla, an anomalous, postclassic ruin in Veracruz, jaguar-spotted toads guard underground passages. It seems unlikely that the imagery relates solely to the animals' earth-related role as portal keepers, and that a culture so attuned to the transformative properties of natural substances would have been unaware that Bufo secretions were hallucinogenic.

Reilly encouraged his fellow Texan, a pharmacist and amateur Mayanist named Mike McBride, to examine marinus secretions for their physiological mechanics and hallucinogenic potential.

McBride encountered considerable negative evidence. In a 1996 paper, ethnobotanist Wade Davis, author of *The Serpent and the Rainbow,* a study of Haiti's Zombie cult, among other books, and alternative medicine proponent Andrew Weil dismissed folk traditions and cast doubt on the Bufo secretion's hallucinogenic properties. They pointed out the substance's difficulty in crossing the blood-brain barrier, and wrote that most of bufotenine's reported effects take place at serotonin receptors in the heart and cardiovascular system, rather than in the brain. They concluded that bufotenine was too physically toxic for effective human use and that the toad bones in Olmec burials may have belonged to alvarius, though alvarius does not appear south of the Sonoran desert.

McBride agrees with Davis and Weil regarding bufotenine's physiological effects. He adds, however, that physiological states like acute hypertension compromise the blood-brain barrier, "allowing drugs with identical characteristics as bufotenine to enter the brain. Not surprisingly, B. marinus poison contains approximately five percent epinephrine (adrenaline)," which causes acute hypertension. With the blood-brain barrier thus compromised, relatively small amounts of bufotenine could cause hallucinations.

McBride adds that serotonin brain receptors responsive to lysergic acid (or LSD), psilocin, and other true hallucinogens respond identically to bufotenine. In neuropharmacological research, bufotenine simulates the action of LSD on those receptors, and experiments show that its effects are identical to those of LSD at high doses. "Mounting evidence" suggests that it attaches as well at the same molecular protein points, triggering the same neurologic responses.

McBride admits that specific proof is lacking, and notes that he has no intention of trying bufotenine himself. He adds, however, that "a very large body of evidence indicates that ancient Mesoamericans often went through extremely toxic pharmacological exercises to gain entrance into the Otherworld." Circumstantial evidence suggests that both canoeing and toads catalyzed transformative experiences, especially among the peoples of the gulf littoral.

The extract may have been dried and smoked, mixed with strong native tobaccos, or consumed in solution with the alcoholic beverage balche. One scholar says Indians fed the extract to ducks, whose livers filtered out the poison, then ate the flesh. McBride, like others, thinks they administered a solution of Bufo toxin and balche anally, through a clyster, usually a gourd, a method that may compromise the blood-brain barrier, and a practice that had widespread use throughout the Americas in speeding intoxication and avoiding the side effects associated with taking some substances orally.

One early Spanish writer observed Huastecs, a Maya-speaking people of Veracruz and Tamaulipas, having pulque, the fermented sap of the agave, "squirted into their breech." Numerous vases depict people giving enemas to others or to themselves, and several conquistadors adopted the practice. Today, Huichol Indians in Nayarit use enemas for taking peyote, to avoid the nausea that accompanies chew-

ing the dried cactus, and certain Amazonian Indians use it for
ayahuasca for the same reason. Curiously, Native Americans employ
the technique solely for inducing trances, while Europeans have historically used it to relieve constipation.

In vase paintings the enema-givers (usually female) often have "non-
Mayan" features, according to a paper, cowritten by Brian Stross, in
volume 2 of Justin Kerr's *Maya Vase Book*. They wear exotic clothing and
a "distinctive net headdress." A characteristic crosshatched jar, with a
narrow neck and wide mouth, contains the enema solution, and a
gourd dipper ladles the liquid into the clyster. A kind of pack frame
still in use carries the large jars of enema liquid, indicating that the
mixture may have come from outside the Maya area, transported and
administered by traveling merchants. It probably contained balche and
one or more of the hallucinogens used in the region.

One series of images in Kerr's *Maya Vase Book* shows a man giving
himself an enema; an adjacent frame shows the narrow-necked jar and
ladle. Three images follow in which the man squats toadlike beside the
jar, morphs dramatically, and finally emerges as a jaguar, following the
same stages outlined by Reilly for Olmec shamanic transformation.

Moises dismissed the question of hallucinogenic enemas as little
more than a faddish topic for dissertations—the flavor of the week,
he called them. He acknowledged that the putun, whose god Ek
Chuah is often portrayed bearing the kind of pack frame associated
with merchants, were especially given to the practice. They may have
introduced it to the upper Usumacinta.

I stood on the gravel bar amid darting swallows. Without question
the toad augured well for our descent, with all its associations, its birth
in water, metamorphosis, and attachment to the land—whatever the
psychotropic effects of its secretions. Everything about it connected it
to the Watery Path, its morphology as allusive as the butterfly's.

Canoeists were amphibious as well—at least as much as Spanish
cavalrymen were four-footed—equally at home on land and water, or
trafficking in the Otherworld. I could see how people might have

thought that as long as canoe travelers kept paddling back and forth between worlds, emulating the stingray and jaguar paddlers and translating their individual experience into something infinite, the world would keep turning and all would be well.

MORNING MIST COVERED the river, rising to treetop level by the time we launched. Gradually the sun burned holes in the gauze and you could see forest-clad ranges with rags of gray cloud tangled around the crests which farther upstream had been scarred by lumbering and burning. The pines gave way to the rich, deep green of primary rain forest—ceiba, cedro, and oak—and you had the feeling of having crossed a line from the transition zone into the blue-green bowl of the lowlands.

Swallows flitted through the fog. Our cold sandaled feet and bare skin warmed as we paddled long stretches of slack water into sunlit openings where you could apprehend the curve of the land in bursts before the mist closed again. Agami and great blue herons stalked the shallows, ospreys swan-dived off their perches, and iridescent green kingfishers chattered on the wing. Maya horsemen sat their mounts in the current, slumped and smoking, waving as we passed.

Late in the morning we rounded a bend near Las Tacitas, river right, miles from a road. The village's school sat in the open on a slight elevation two or three hundred yards from the water, fronting a jagged blue peak. When we entered the wide flat opposite the landing, the school emptied and streams of kids ran down the green slope along shore, yelling and waving. They followed us and called out, Where are you going, how long does it take, are your boats good in the rapidos? At the landing were tied an oversized fiberglass ponga, a motorized craft that looked like a high-ended dory, and many cayucos of a high design consistency and craftsmanship we had not yet seen in the valley. We wished the children buenos días and continued on.

By noon the flanking ranges crowded the shore and agriculture thinned out. We grounded the boats for lunch under a high cliff on the left where the sierras squeezed together into the narrow passage at the head of the canyon.

The river funneled between the high walls and disappeared. Flecks of white spittle marked its plunge off the edge of the known world.

I slathered a tortilla with peanut butter and walked to the rocks at the edge of the water, the edge of the canyon, and stood there with Scott and J.P., a young guide from Flagstaff on his first Chiapas expedition, contemplating the defile.

J.P. smoked. He asked was that the big stuff right down there. Scott said there were two or three class 3's, then you were right into Slaughterhouse (the name of a rapid).

Josh slid down the bank. There was an altar to the river gods against the cliff just up the hill, he said. One end of an old cayuco used to lie beside it, but that was gone now.

J.P. exhaled smoke and looked around. Good place for an altar, he said.

I finished my tortilla and followed the trail up the bank. The altar leaned against the cliff on a narrow bench between the river and the rock face, identical to the ones Maya shamans built in Yucatán. A few feet away a stream gushed like a hydrant from a vent in the cliff face, directly into an eddy. The place was, by any standard, a magnificent portal.

The altar stood in mottled shade, a small structure woven from sticks and maize leaves, leaning against a green Maya cross about four feet tall. It had a platform supported at the corners by pine boughs bent in an arch at the top, mimicking the vault of the heavens. The design was a cosmogram meant to center the universe, gathering and concentrating divine forces as a lens concentrates light. Thirteen sticks stood in the ground in front of it, their tops split to hold candles and smeared with wax. A few feet away cold black ashes lay in a fire ring, along with the bones and feathers of sacrificial chickens, an empty salsa can, an aguardiente bottle. Rain-blackened copal incense and pine resin streaked the cliff face.

The altar was probably used for simple daily observances that accompany births and deaths, yet the location and the recent presence of a votive cayuco reinforced Josh's commonsense interpretation. The stingray and jaguar paddlers would have felt at home here.

The people who built the altar and sacrificed there would have been first-or-second generation immigrants from the highlands, nominally Catholic, probably Zapatista. Protestants tend to wean Indians more thoroughly from pre-Christian practice, though nothing characterizes Maya Christianity better than apostasy. Whoever they were, they would have come here for a seasonal observance, for a simple curing, or, in David Freidel's words, to renew the nurturing bonds between the inhabitants of this world and those of the Otherworld—bonds sorely strained in recent years by war and ecological disaster.

Perhaps the celebrants came to sacrifice when the Milky Way dipped under the horizon and the big cayuco dove into the Otherworld. They might have been conscious only that it was a time to build altars near portals, burn incense, kill chickens, and down a few aguardientes in the woods. Something they always did to remember their ancestors, that had to do with falls, canyons, cayucos. What better place? And by following the Watery Path into the canyon, we joined them in the observance.

No wonder they took such interest in our journey and our boats. We were their surrogates.

Six

THE WATERY PATH

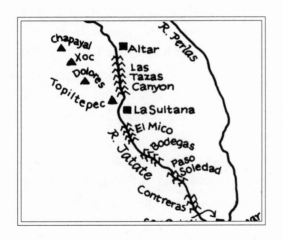

WE RAN SOME NARROW CHUTES TO A CHAIN OF POOLS, A TWILIGHT world nothing like the landscape we left behind. There were cayucos tied in the pools, relatively high-ended, high-volume craft possibly paddled down the chutes at low water, or else lined and swum. The canyon walls left only slippery rims of earth along shore, if that.

The walls framed a narrow cleft three hundred feet overhead and a shadow zone at water level. Water seeped from the decaying karst, streaking the walls with green, orange, and purple bands of algae and oxides. Everywhere up and down these vertical trickles, ferns and pendulant epiphytes sprouted. We drifted in a strange effusion of copper light. Springs gushed out of caves. Beams flickered underneath us in the dark jade pools.

A barrier separated the canyon's sepulchral otherness from the mundane valley of milpas and revolution just upstream, a barrier no less tenuous or irrevocable than the one that separated the fisherman and the fish. Here, cayucos laid claim. Below the pools, however, no claims were in effect. It was possible to say with fair certainty that beyond this point no boat had traveled safely before the canyon's first descent by outfitter Cully Erdman in 1980. Given the canyon's terrain, few people traveled beyond the pools under any circumstance.

Erdman had learned about the Jatate from a freelance river bum and organized the first descent for a segment of ABC's long-running program "American Sportsman." In those days the road from Ocosingo reached only to El Real, Erdman's put-in, and many children in the valley had never seen a gringo. The residents exhibited their natural affinity for riverboaters, but they had no electricity then, no radios, no chainsaws.

The average drop per mile from Las Tacitas to La Sultana is about eighty feet. Once into the thick of the rapids, it increases to at least a hundred feet per mile, twice the average for a class 4 or 5 river. Erdman considered the Jatate right on the edge of runnable.

The party included two expert kayakers, but the camera crew had never paddled rapids harder than class 3. Deep in the canyon, not knowing what lay ahead, they would paddle up to a rapid, scout, and shake their heads in disbelief. They made it, however, taking out at the mouth of the Río Santo Domingo, fifty miles downstream, and hiring mules to carry them to the nearest road, three days away.

We ran some strange little rapids with channels braiding off them, then tied up against rocks well above Slaughterhouse just as clouds closed over and it started to rain. The view downstream fell away into air and the canyon widened, curving outward toward a forested rim invisible above the clouds.

The guides clambered out over the tubes of their rafts, with me scrambling behind. We spread out along the fractured and bizarrely sculpted limestone reefs flanking the rapid, poring over the route in our minds. The waters thundered, sending ionized, highly oxygenated fizz into the air.

It began with a sharp drop into a chute. You had to run directly over a midcurrent rock and through the hydraulic behind it, angled sharply to the right to avoid pinning or flipping against the big slab that divided the chute halfway through. The passable right-hand slot was so narrow that the raft had to be leaned, lifting one tube higher than the other. At the bottom the current curled around another huge rock and slammed into the right-hand wall with a nauseating corkscrew effect.

The customers stood around holding their arms in the chill, sensing the guides' uncertainty, like dogs. I felt the familiar mixture of anticipation, dread, and excitement that comes before running any hard rapid.

David decided to maneuver the ungainly equipment raft through with hundred-foot safety lines tied to both ends. He posted me along shore to make sure the stern line didn't become snagged on one of the jutting limestone breccias like the ones I was standing on.

He pushed the boat over the guide rock and held the stern line. The boat, its oars onshore and its cargo well secured in waterproof bags, washed over the guide rock, through the hole, and up onto the big flat slab, where it stuck. The guides, pulling from opposing angles and at distant ends of the safety lines, managed to slide it off the slab into the right-hand slot, so the current grabbed it with incredible force.

I had already lifted my section of the stern line over a big outcrop, but had absentmindedly remained between the line and the rapid. When the current grabbed the boat, the line snapped tight. A millisecond before this occurred I saw my mistake and its unthinkable consequence—me swimming in Slaughterhouse. At the last possible instant I hit the deck, slipping off the rocky knobs I was balancing on and barking my shins. The line whined over my head, then ricocheted free of David's grip.

The heavy raft halted abrubtly as the line snagged underwater. It lumbered and yawed sickeningly against the line and the force of the river, water pouring over it and out through scuppers in the inflatable self-bailing floor, almost totally submerged in the slot. The river roared like a low-hovering chopper. We watched, helpless, our collective resolve for running Slaughterhouse leaching away in the mounting tension.

The only solution was to cut the line. Scott put on a second life jacket and somehow hooked the boat close enough to jump aboard. He leaned over the stern and sawed the line until it parted. The swamped boat washed up against the wall at the rapid's lower end, as Scott predicted it would, and slid off into calmer water with the guides pulling mightily on the bowline. Nobody complained when we all declined to run Slaughterhouse.

The rest of the afternoon we ran about ten rapids, each formed by calcareous minerals seeping from the earth, precipitating into travertine over the centuries and hardening into low barriers damming the river at regular intervals. The water sculpted wild braids and chutes out of the soft rock, giving the Jatate's rapids their distinctive character.

The rapids followed in quick succession. We ran most of them cleanly, often just paddling to the lip and looking over the edge to scout.

The rain continued. Through breaks in the overcast we caught glimpses of the canyon's true depth, a thousand feet or more, like a mist-shrouded gorge in a T'ang landscape painting. The band of level ground along shore widened. Patches of riparian forest appeared: mixed stands of mahogany, cedro, and zapote that had never seen a chainsaw or felt a chiclero's blade, tall and thick and leaning their canopies over the water. Multiple species of xate grew in unharvested stands. It was an oasis of biological integrity in an otherwise ravaged landscape.

Around four-thirty we washed out of a class 4 rapid onto a long flat between steep walls. We tied up on the right in front of a cave—really a high, wide overhang under the vertical canyon walls, our campsite. The horizon line of the next rapid danced at the far end of the flat.

We slept comfortably on the sand floor under the overhang. Overnight the rain turned into a norte and the river came up about four inches. Normally an exquisite bluish-green, it now ran chalky and opaque.

We delayed cleaning up and packing as long as we could, to the point of boiling water and brewing a second five-gallon pot of coffee. No one wanted to leave our deluxe shelter. While we packed, the overcast parted and unleashed a flood of sunlight through the canyon, but only for a few minutes. Soon it closed and rained again.

With everything packed, we drifted slowly down the flat to the head of the first rapid, Jaguar Falls, pushed along by the rising river. The overcast hung high enough to expose vertical walls composed of bare, rotting karst, off-white and supporting scrub vegetation and epiphytes where they had gained a hold. The rim faded in and out of sight in the clouds, at least five hundred feet above the river level and probably much higher.

Within minutes we grounded on a travertine barrier covered with high grass and sedges. Below lay the single squirrelliest rapid I had ever seen. You could walk out onto the slippery reefs that bordered the drop and examine it microscopically, which everybody did. This consumed half an hour, with all the qualified parties offering suggestions.

A safe run depended on hitting the correct entry point: miss it by as little as six inches to one side or the other and you would be unable to make the next move. The mercurial currents near the verge called for finely calibrated backing and drawing maneuvers. At the last instant, with the boat aligned correctly, you had to power over the lip to gain steerage in the wildly accelerating current.

At that precise point, in the transition between inertia and acceleration, we were compromised by adverse weight-to-power ratios.

Scott put me in the left bow, opposite him in the right rear, so I could drive the boat forward when called for (theoretically), and execute left-hand drawstrokes at his command. That way he could keep prying on his stronger right side and not have to lose steerageway by switching from one side to the other.

We tipped over the edge aligned perfectly, our feet tucked under the tubes. My forward strokes had the apparent effect of running in a dream—none. Yet we managed the necessary move or two, plummeted over a vertical drop into the big wave at the bottom, and washed out into the pool.

Across the pool lay the head of the rapid named Rock Garden, which looked like bulldozers had dumped enormous blocks into the river. Huge trapezoidal boulders sheared from the canyon wall lay everywhere in the channel. No obvious line presented itself, at least not for anything as wide as a raft.

The kayakers in their narrower boats managed to weave their way through. To reduce weight in the rafts, Scott had the customers walk around. Scott, David, and I ran the first raft, pinballing across the drop from one rock to another. Three times the boat stuck to rocks while the downstream force of the river held it fast. We manhandled it back into the water each time, then jumped back in at the last minute. At the end we had gotten the three rafts down an essentially unrunnable rapid without incident.

The subsequent rapids unfolded in a blur of spume, one after another, nameless and named: Candlestick, Rooster Tail, Misty Falls, where I fell out of the boat for the second time on the trip. Few of our runs were pristine—we bounced off walls and boulders, got turned backward, or somebody swam.

With each one we descended deeper into a lost world enveloped in clammy folds of rain and mist. The canyon walls loomed in and out of the murk. We saw neither reptile nor mammal, nor so much as a bird, though the habitat was rich and intact to the eye: unscathed high-canopy forest climbing the more gradual slopes and making shady galleries along shore. Even the travertine islands and reefs supported tiny ecosystems.

The riverbed inclined so steeply you could often see the next two rapids down the slope. In the rain and gloom the surroundings turned monochrome, flat, undifferentiated, so that one rapid merged with the next and the one after that into a single rapid which we scouted and ran over and over. The rhythm of scouting and running became its own purpose and goal. Expectations evaporated. The river kept rising.

We made camp fairly early at the head of a rapid called the Slide, where two boys surprised us fishing with handlines in the opaline eddies and side pools near the mouth of a steep creek. They had a two-pound macabil and said they had lost a bigger one (of course). They wore Zapatista-issue military caps and jungle boots familiar from dozens of news photos and said they had bushwhacked to this point two hours from their home near the canyon rim.

We pitched our tents on the small campsite and ate in the rain. Shortly after dark (about 7 P.M.) I went to bed, where I gobbled ibuprofen and took notes by the light of my headlamp until a dark front passed over me, lowering my eyelids and casting me into a dreamless void.

The river ran noticeably higher in the morning and the rain contin-ued. While we stood around downing second or third cups of coffee, the boys strolled into camp. They had camped a few yards away, on a rock slab by the creek mouth. They wore nylon rucksacks issued to Zapatista fighters back in '94 and paid for with illegally diverted gov-ernment agriculture grants. One of them carried an ancient .22, its short barrel duct-taped to the stock, the other a shoulder bag con-taining a few dozen shoots of young xate to start a vivero, or nursery, at home. They said that by growing the ornamental palms at home they could maintain the wild seed stock longer than if they cut it. (Gringos used the plant to dye dollar bills their distinctive green, locals believed, to explain the value given to this common plant.)

They told us of monkeys, coatimundis, deer, otter, peccary, tapirs, and jaguars inhabiting the canyon. Fewer than four hundred jaguars were supposed to live north of Venezuela, but if the canyon contained as much untrammeled habitat as it seemed to, and as rich a prey base as they assured me it did, it may have provided the cat a safe refuge, as did the adjacent Montes Azules reserve. I thought the boys knew their home territory too intimately, identified with it too closely, to conceive of misrepresenting it.

With the boats loaded, we pushed off and immediately grounded at the head of the Slide. The water had risen considerably, and the rapid, which the previous evening had presented a kind of Platonic ideal of a rapid, had grown into an exaggerated, histrionic version of itself. We scouted for forty-five minutes. Within fifteen, most of the customers had elected to walk around.

It began with an extremely narrow entry guarded by tiny Scyllas and Charybdises, rocks hidden just under the surface which swirled the water into contrary and unreadable currents. Just beyond the edge it mounded into a long sluiceway—the so-called Slide—that was crowned in the center like a road or playing field. On either side the sluiceway fell away into gnashing diagonal waves and hydraulics that at this level looked like they could flip a boat and trap a swimmer.

Rising water magnified the rapid's features. Chief among these were the hydraulics, also known as "souse holes" (or just "holes"), and the eddies, two embodiments of the same hydrological principle.

All fluids under pressure form countercurrents when passing around an obstacle. The stronger the current and the more abrupt the obstacle, the stronger the countercurrent.

Eddies form pockets of calm or upstream flowing water behind rocks and ledges. Paddlers use them to rest on their way down a rapid, or to their advantage while working their way upstream. Hydraulics are like eddies that circulate vertically rather than horizontally. Mild ones are benign, but hydraulics that form behind large rocks or sharp drops in strong currents are the paddler's commonest hazards, dislocating shoulders, flipping boats, and wreaking general havoc. Strong ones can trap bodies and whole rafts, and recirculate them indefinitely, or until the water volume decreases. They sometimes form within waves, and are often indicated by downstream horizon lines that are hard to detect. Most whitewater drownings occur in hydraulics.

For the Slide you had no choice but to nail the entry and ride the crown. When the current passed the crest it accelerated from almost nothing to probably seven or eight miles an hour. A boat would have to hit it gaining speed, and keep paddling hard in the turbulence to stay up and stay straight. One mistake either way and you'd slip off the side and flip. Boat-eating waves and holes that heaped up at the far-off bottom of the rapid would likely pull you in and finish you off after that.

Josh ran flawlessely, but one of the other kayakers flipped near the top. Unable to roll, he held on to his boat and swam to the bottom of the rapid.

J.P. joined our boat, adding power and experience. Scott lined up for the entry. At the critical moment we dug in with our paddles. The boat leaped forward onto the crown, and the world dropped away. We passed through a membrane separating the twentieth century from the timeless dream of Mesoamerica. The crest of the sluice vectored forward and down toward two enormous waves. Hydraulics exploded on either side. Josh waited far below. I turned my head to the left and saw the two Zapatista boys watching us, frozen, expressionless, from the rock slab at the mouth of the creek.

The boat plunged into the first wave, stood straight up, yawed, and we paddled over it into the second, which folded the boat in half ("taco'd" it, in guide parlance), burying us beneath tons of cloudy luminescence and landing a couple of us on the floor. Those of us still paddling dug in, averting a last hydraulic, and washed out into the pool. It was exhilarating and our last clean run of the day.

The rain continued. The walls closed in and the rising water shut off some of the easier routes and carries, forcing us to improvise our way through passages that flooded in milky braids over the now-continuous travertine formations. Everybody swam. The pools between rapids became shorter, and in some we missed the eddy and had to run the next drop blind. Fatigue set in.

In one chute I fell out, trying to lean too far over the gunwale to effect a left-hand draw. It sucked me far ahead of the boat in the rushing flume and slammed me into a ledge. The boat followed, out of control, squashing me against the ledge with all the weight of the boat and the river. I pressed my face to the rock, praying the boat wouldn't become pinned. Then the bulbous tube bounced off the rock, releasing me. Half a dozen hands reached over the tube and I flopped back in, relieved but shaken.

Within minutes we stood at the top of Kayaks Away, where a steep chute led into a swirling vortex, called a remolino, followed by three falls six to eight feet high. The swelling river tore furiously over the cascades. Scott scratched his head and consulted with Josh. The flooding had eliminated the standard route, which at this water level would place you dead center of the remolino.

The only alternative was to put the left tube on the edge of the chute and the other in a thin layer of water that poured over a rubbly, abrasive travertine slide on the right. If enough water flowed over the slide to buoy the raft and you maintained the correct angle, you could just nick the edge of the remolino and power over the first drop.

Josh and two other kayakers went ahead and demonstrated that it could be done in a kayak. With the leverage of his long oars, David nailed the entry in the equipment boat and swooshed around the whirlpool and over the zigzag drops. Scott watched him, then got back in our boat and went over the plan. As we backed and sideslipped for the entry, I worried that what power we did have had been diminished by the beating we had all taken. We would never overcome our inertia going over the edge.

We broke over the lip a hair too far to the right and immediately started skidding on the slide. The force of the current on the left side of the boat pulled the stern around so we were in danger of falling backwards into the whirlpool. Scott called for a left-hand draw to straighten us out. I leaned over the gunwale, but the paddle blade grabbed only an inch of water on the slide. I was stretching farther out toward deeper water when the boat stopped short on the dry slope and catapulted me out.

I skidded down the rough travertine, straight into the vortex, and funneled to the bottom, maybe eight, ten feet deep, maybe more, so deep it was dark. I stayed there a long time, spiraling blindly in the murky, bubbly silence, buffeted like a newspaper in a hurricane. Common wisdom suggests going limp when stuck in a hydraulic, or swimming for the bottom where the countercurrent will expel you. Instead I held my breath and fought toward the light, my only instinct to escape.

I knew I had to breathe soon, saw myself doing it, I was so close to quitting. As the point of surrender approached, I thought, distantly, It *would* be this way, and heard David Freidel's voice reminding me over the phone: "The path to Xibalba is a watery one."

What more direct route to the Otherworld existed? It would have been the ultimate form of belonging, to be subsumed and digested into the landscape through the purification of a watery death.

But I thought, I have to finish. A moment later I popped out long enough to take a breath, hurtled over the surface of another ledge, and stayed down almost as long as the first time. I tired even faster, but the river expelled me, plunged me over the last drop and into the hole at the bottom, where I cycled for another eternity before surfacing in calm water, abraded from the rough limestone and amazed to be alive.

Josh picked me up and let me hang on his kayak while David rowed over in the equipment boat looking worried but relieved. I took a stroke toward his raft and grasped a tube. That was a fucked-up swim, I sputtered, looking up at him from the water and trying, for some reason, to smile.

I had "trav burn," big raw raspberries on one elbow, my knees, and right buttock, and various strains and aches, though I had swallowed little water. One of the adjustment straps on my life jacket had torn. That was it. I shook it off for the moment—we had more rapids to run.

In camp that evening the group demeanor was subdued compared to the last two nights. The guides had put in a serious workday, and there were other wounded.

In my tent, water dripped intermittently through the ridgeline. I read and took notes. When I switched off the headlamp, my mind raced and my body throbbed. Bad songs from the seventies pounded in my head. I turned on the headlamp and read again, the tiny drip making a gentle tattoo on my forehead. Outside, the river's white noise drowned out the sounds of the rain and the few conversations still going on. The next time I turned off the lamp and closed my eyes, I saw myself swirling in the murky, light brown turbulence of the Xibalban night.

I CRAWLED OUT of my tent feeling like I had been in a car wreck. Cold rain poured through the saturated canopy in a steady mass, and charcoal-colored mist shrouded the canyon walls. You couldn't see across the river, now running full and ash-colored, though you could easily apprehend our human origins in water and the high water content of our bodies, and the ephemeral membrane that keeps us from dissolving completely. Nobody lingered over coffee. We rushed through breakfast to make our rendezvous at La Sultana: Scott and his crew with Rachel; Josh and I with Alonso and the Freedom. David Kashinski had asked to join us in a kayak as well—a welcome addition.

Pushing off, Scott told us to keep our feet braced under the tubes and to hold on when we went over a drop. No swimmers today, he said.

I took the hint and went through the first three or four drops gun-shy, grabbing the safety straps a little too soon before we passed the lip and leaning far away from the approaching wave or hole. I was ready to take the stern and be in charge of my own boat, be it canoe or sampan, in rough water or calm. But I also felt as though my dues had been paid, my sacrifice made, and that though the rain continued and I faced high-water canoeing for the next few days, everything would be all right in the end. In any case our runs were uneventful.

The bridge came in view a mile downstream, about two hours after we broke camp, a man-made apparition out of context in the wild canyon. I turned upstream for a look back before we rounded the corner and the canyon passed from sight. Above, the river emerged from its deep cleft and fell in a series of white horizontal lines, one after the other in a gentle curve that swelled at the base like a marble stairway, dizzyingly steep and grand.

We passed a pair of soldiers bathing on the right side of the river, a tarp set up to screen them from the direction of the camp. They expected no traffic on the river and they eyed us sheepishly and suspiciously, soaped up and standing knee deep in an eddy. The first of the soldiers' cabañas appeared on the right, and a single guard walked onto the bridge to watch us.

The concrete bridge spanning the Jatate at La Sultana, strategically one of the most critical junctures in the conflict zone, is little more than fifty yards long. The canyon gradually widens and levels out. The mountain walls continue rising straight up from the shoreline, and the road, such as it is, is carved out of the slopes high above the riverbed. The soldiers' extemporized shelters teeter on the steep slopes of either shore. Downstream the river fans out in braids and low travertine ledges covered with vegetation, toward the mouth of the Río Tzaconejá, flowing in from the west.

The military base was established during the selva's occupation, after the rebellion. The log and earthwork bunkers guarding the bridge's four corners look like something out of the French and Indian wars, only they're mounted with machine guns and protected from the rain by nylon tarps.

On the night of December 31, 1993, camionetas carrying fighters in pasemontanes (ski masks) and holding rifles at port arms rumbled slowly out of the cañada along the ancient portage route for Ocosingo, fifty miles north and west. (Today you can buy models of these trucks on the streets of San Cristóbal, with little masked dolls holding stick guns in their cargo beds.) At least thirteen men from La Sultana died in that fight. A few days later Zapatistas from La Sultana kidnapped the former Chiapas governor, General Absolón Castellanos Domínguez, and held him for two weeks.

Immediately under the bridge we eddied out to the right and grounded on a sloping beach. Two young Indians wearing sharply creased fatigue pants and white T-shirts, sporting dog tags and military haircuts politely asked Scott who the hell we were and what we thought we were doing. Scott explained he had received permission from the brass in Ocosingo to beach and take out here, and that the base commandant had been informed of our arrival. The explanation satisfied them. Right away we started carrying equipment up the steep bank to the road.

The trail wound through the soldiers' compound in the shade. The cabins each housed two to four men. Six-inch logs framed the walls, macheted to a point and notched at the corners exactly like traditional log cabins, with big roof tarps stretched across the ridgepoles. The cabins had lightweight plywood doors fitted with Plexiglas windows, and dirt floors.

White-painted stones from the river lined the walkways. The men had planted xate, cacti, and philodendron ornamentally in little plots in the dooryards, and some had even coaxed a few spindly maize stalks to maturity in the shade. For these Mexicanized Indians, whether they came from the central highlands, Oaxaca, or Veracruz, the plants maintained their aboriginal attachment to the corn cycle, even during wartime.

I held a corner of a raft as we carried it up the bank and came out on the road. Soldiers milled around looking severe and wearing U.S. combat gear: M-16s, flak jackets, boots, helmets. They peered at us over the edges of the bunkers guarding the bridge. Some of the rafters made a fuss over a baby spider monkey one of the soldiers carried on his shoulder. It peered at them with importunate eyes.

Amid the towering equipment and the mass of soldiers, I looked up the road and saw Alonso sauntering toward me wearing blue jeans and a straw cowboy hat. We shook hands and he assured me all the equipment had made the trip from Palenque.

We reconnoitered quickly. We had estimated it would take us six days to reach Pico de Oro, on the Lacantun, the first place after Colorado Canyon served by public transportation. That allowed just enough time for David and Josh to get back for their next job for Scott. On the seventh day I was scheduled to rendezvous with Todd Kelsey at Pico, and Josh needed to be in Palenque to begin a video shoot covering his and Scott's first descent of a highland river called El Chichón, for the Outdoor Life cable network.

We decided it was best not to hang around too long. We had a long way to go, and our welcome could expire any minute.

A major descent still lay before us, but the questions of the Freedom's handling and Alonso's ability remained unresolved. Compared to decked kayaks, which also have the advantage of the Eskimo roll, undecked canoes—open, and with higher volumes and greater surface areas—are riskier craft in whitewater. In our case, Josh and David carried their own tents and minimum personal gear: the Freedom carried all the food and kitchen equipment for four over seven days, plus our own equipment, a total of a hundred pounds or more, not counting our body weight.

When I had picked up the Freedom at the Mad River factory the previous summer, I had little chance to try it out in whitewater. The rivers were too low. Then a summer rain raised the Saranac River a few miles away. My son Noah and I drove the boat over to a short whitewater section of three connected sets half a mile long: an easy class 2 entry; a short, narrow gorge, approaching class 3 at high water; and a class 2 rock garden emptying into Franklin Falls Reservoir.

The river ran high. The Freedom handled well in the entry rapid, though with Noah in the bow at two hundred pounds we shipped water in small waves. In the gorge we plowed through a couple of sizable haystacks and headed for a small eddy, river left. Crossing the current, the Freedom, heavy with water, was stable compared to other canoes, and it turned sharply into the eddy without yawing, both good signs.

While we bailed, however, I decided to ask Mad River to make me a spray cover, a nylon deck that attaches by snaps to the outside of the hull, with skirted cockpits over the bow and stern seats. They carry their own difficulties, and would add another dimension of uncertainty to the endeavor. But they kept out water and I wanted at all costs to avoid scrubbing the trip on account of equipment failure or inadequacy.

On the beach I took my time, packing the canoe for balance and maneuverability, lashing the packs to the D rings on the floor. We wet the yellow spray cover and began fastening it to the metal snaps arrayed along the hull below the gunwales. At the same time, Josh and David got in their kayaks and soldiers watched while they sported in a wave directly under the bridge. The cover fastened, we lashed our spare paddles to the top with Velcro tie-downs. I coiled on the bow and stern lines, and added to the stern a forty-foot length of braided climbing rope. When we finished clipping in water bottles and bailing scoops, we took our places and fitted the spray skirts around our waists.

In the big pool below the bridge we got used to the feel of the boat while I went over the basic rules of thumb, all stuff we had talked about but had practiced only once on the Nututún. Soldiers watched from the bridge and the shore. We paddled to the head of the eddy and pointed the bow into a line of twelve-inch waves; leaned downstream and let the current pull the bow around. The boat straightened and we practiced bracing, holding our paddle blades flat to the water like outriggers to stay upright in the waves. That was it. We waved to the soldiers and paddled toward Josh and David, who waited at the head of the first drop.

The water ran grayish-green, ponderous in its deep, invisible churnings. We paddled back and forth along the face of the rock dam to find a runnable channel, the water pouring over and through it in a sieve of channels and falls. The river disappeared in the thick vegetation growing on the barrier, so you could have taken it for an island.

Eventually we found a chute about three feet wide and five or six feet from top to bottom. The kayakers went ahead, disappearing into the wall of brush and grass, then over the lip. From above we saw their elevated paddle blades waving to us to follow. Alonso and I lined up carefully and powered into the chute. The Freedom tipped over the edge, rode an accelerating slide into a three-foot wave, and we eddied out on the right. It was a small but tricky drop and we had managed it without a hitch.

For the next hour we negotiated a travertine labyrinth, running dozens of chutes and sluices, mostly single falls three to six or eight feet high and only half as wide. For two miles the river fell over terraces held in place by stone rehardened from the molten residue of seashells, with branching walls and channels, making pools and shallow flats where the water would have been pellucid had it not been sullied by rain.

It was a paradise for water people, for bathing, fishing. At lower water levels you could walk from shore to midriver along the travertine dams. Once, I had looked down on these same terraces from the road above and had seen them running clear and blue as lapis, a scene almost too beautiful to absorb.

We entered a rhythm, weaving through the maze, gaining confidence. The Freedom handled perfectly, stable and responsive under its load. Finally we came to the head of a real rapid, a class 4 thunderer that divided around a high island. Josh, who had been gently counseling boldness to prepare us for what lay downstream, suggested running it. If we dumped, he reminded me, he and David would pick us up. I opted instead to carry, wanting to reinforce Alonso's confidence and my own before we tackled anything that big.

We found a landing on the left, at the head of the rapid. While the others prepared lunch I scouted a carry trail, following a narrow track along the bank downstream, then out across some travertine breaks traced with dozens of leaking runnels. The trail followed one of the rock dams to a narrow log bridge across a small channel, then down carved steps to what appeared to be an old log landing. It was an obvious carry trail, long in use—possibly very long. Downstream and around the end of the island I could see the waves of the next rapid.

At the landing, Alonso had broken out the lunch pack and two boys from La Sultana had appeared. One of them wore the Zapatista boots, the other the standard black rubber boots of the country. The canoe and our equipment spellbound them. They turned down our offer of peanut butter on tortillas and listened passively to our plan for running through Colorado Canyon, down the Río Lacantun to the Usumacinta, and all the way to the gulf. I couldn't tell whether they considered this the most obvious idea in the world or the most ridiculous.

In my dry-bag David found a copy of *Rebellion from the Roots,* John Ross's good general history and theory of the New Year's uprising, and showed it to the boys. They pawed over the book, staring at the photos of Marcos, masked fighters in the jungle, civilian dead, Zapatista dead at Ocosingo, the sacking of San Cristóbal's city hall—a gallery of their valley's and its people's dead and condemned, of their cause undertaken for the most utopian and pure if misguided of reasons. Their brothers and fathers had fought in the conflict, and the army occupied their village. In age they would qualify for the next uproar when it came.

We stuffed ourselves, then the boys watched us pack and head out, David and Josh around the island to run the rapid, Alonso and I down the carry trail. I portaged the boat on my shoulders, Adirondack style, balancing it by the yoke at the center thwart. It made me feel self-reliant in a way I had not since we arrived at Agua Azul. At home, after hours on the lakes and rivers of canoe country, you looked for-

ward to stretching your back and legs on the carries. You also anticipated the assurance of utter self-containment the act conferred, the
reminder of your ability to move unfettered through a landscape,
over vast distances.

The exposed limestone had turned slimy in the rain. I stepped
carefully along the path, the seventy-five-pound Freedom on my
shoulders, and inched over the log bridge. When I grounded the boat
at the far end, Josh and David were surfing in the waves just past the
island. Behind me Alonso carried a portage pack, winding his way
down over the grassy water terraces. Watching him, I had that rare,
exquisite feeling of being located in a geography.

The river had compressed into a single channel, squeezing up a
train of standing waves we ran easily. The next drop looked steeper.
Josh suggested we give it a try, once again to prepare for the
inevitable big stuff to come. We ran a powerful chute, made a quick
move, and straightened out for the waves. Alonso braced perfectly,
and the Freedom never flinched as the bow climbed and plunged in
the big haystacks.

At the bottom a major tributary entered on the right that could
only be the Tzaconejá. The smaller river tumbled gently through the
overarching trees from the west, visible for a hundred yards before
vanishing around a bend upstream.

Just inside the mouth the shore sloped gently to the eddy. A level
shelf separated the tree line from the beach. Travertine oozed from
the point where the rivers merged and froze into a ridged and scalloped mass that extended well out into the confluence, a perfect
campsite.

The overcast parted, and strained, muted sunlight fell on our
camp. Alonso went to work with the machete, cutting brush for his
tent site. The job of camp cook fell to me, but Alonso objected when I
set up my stove. He found three good-sized stones and placed them in
a triangle around an existing mound of ashes. Then he used a stick of
resinous wood for tinder and lit a fire. The flame caught; he built it up

by adding dry hardwood branches. I put my grill over the flames and immediately set the water boiling.

I pulled the canoe up, flipped it over, and chopped jalapeños, onions, and cheese on the upturned bottom. While we worked, Alonso sipped from a plastic bottle of posh, the raw cane liquor of the highlands. He'd scored it the week before in San Juan Chamula, outside San Cristóbal, during the Festival of Games, at which posh is a sacrament. He offered the bottle around.

While the chile simmered, I carried the first-aid kit to the water and washed and dressed my abrasions. Bending over the water, I caught a whiff of copal (called pom by the Maya), a few molecules drifting on the air, one of the region's distinct memory-fixing stimuli. It faded and I dismissed it as an olfactory phantom. Then I caught it again, stronger and mixed with the scent of the fire. Perhaps Alonso had tossed half a sheaf of copal nuggets on the fire, the kind like hardened pitch wrapped in dried corn husks, sold in local markets and burned in profuse quantities at the Festival of Games. I twisted around and called, Alonso, you burning copal?

It would be consistent with his drinking posh and his insistence on setting up the three mythic hearth stones, a cultural artifact offered in the spirit of renewal. It would also purify our campsite, and offer thanks for a successful first day afloat. Such practices meant something to Alonso, who had attended the recent festival as more than a tourist.

I sat with my feet in the water, looking behind me. Alonso glanced up from the fire, his expression vaguely addled with fatigue and posh. It's the wood, man, he said. It's copal.

He had inadvertently come upon a good-sized stick of copal wood, one of many resinous woods in the forest, and whittled some shavings to start the fire. They caught so well he added larger pieces from the same long stick. Now it was almost gone. Having realized its value, Alonso said he would save the remaining chunk to kindle fires on the rest of the trip.

Copal is the dried sap from two species of mid-story trees belonging to the genus Bursera; one of them makes a clear, yellowish substance, the other a black and resinous one. To the Maya copal belongs among the sacred substances known as itz, along with milk, tears, semen, sweat, rust, and dripping candle wax, "precious substances that sustain the gods," in Freidel's words, like the sap of the world tree. It is the province of shamans, who symbolically (like sap) ascend the trunk of the world tree to break earthly bonds and perform duties in the Otherworld. They burn it in huge quantities, sending black fragrant plumes heavenward to please the gods and hold the portals open. It accompanies rituals of all kinds. It blackened the cliff face behind the altar at the head of the canyon.

The smoke poured out over the campsite and the rivers. We assumed it had been supplied by "the place," the resident spirit of the confluence, so we could render appropriate offerings. (After a while in the selva, in Mesoamerica generally, you come to accept such things without relinquishing other long-cultivated skepticisms.) We grasped without question or irony that we were participating in the landscape in an atavistic way, and therefore we had received a certain pass and bore an extra burden. Offerings were in order.

I silently let the smoke rise in thanksgiving.

After dinner we separated and spent a few minutes out of each other's immediate company, quietly watching the river or cleaning up around the kitchen. The clouds developed pink and yellow deckling along their edges. Mangrove swallows dipped over the water. A thrush called from deep in the forest, sounding not unlike a veery or wood thrush, but not exactly like one either. The day's last rapid fell thunderously just out of sight.

I sat on the travertine point watching the river, reflecting on my incredible luck in finding Alonso, and having in both Josh and David along for safety and company. (I owed their presence to Scott.) They were the easiest-going and smartest group of river people I had been part of for some time, completely lacking inflated egos and agendas.

Nobody had a thing to prove. Yet it wasn't saccharine, either. You had to watch your step. No episode of brain-lock or clumsiness went unpunished.

I hobbled back to the campsite, where David and Alonso were sipping posh.

I feel like forty miles of bad road, I said.

You look like you belong in the hospital, David said.

Seven

THE CAÑADAS AND

MIRAMAR

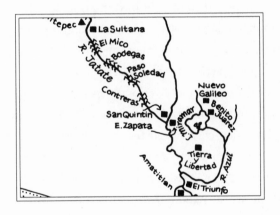

WE HAD LOST CONSIDERABLE ALTITUDE SINCE LAS TACITAS. THE deep canyons of the Jatate and adjacent rivers, the surrounding forbidding mountains, and the suffocating, amorphous forests had made the region we were entering traditionally one of Mexico's most impervious refuges. Threatened wildlife persisted there in viable (though shrinking) populations. Intractable tribes had removed themselves there since before colonial times. Previous and current politi-

cal dissenters had made the region their home. Recently, the full
weight of the Mexican military, industrialization, and globalization
had reduced it in size and effectiveness as a sanctuary, and its communities were hard-pressed, but the region itself retained undeniable
vestiges of a wilderness no-man's-land.

The Olmec had outposts there, probably for trade. In 1928
campesinos showed Traven an image carved on a rock a little ways up
the portage trail from where we were camped at the mouth of the
Tzaconejá. They called it a chac, or generic rain deity. Cordan photographed the carving and published it in *Secret of the Forest*. In 1968
archaeologist Susannah Eckholm visited the site, quickly surveyed the
ruin, and photographed the carving. She supported Blom and Cordan's
belief that an Olmec artist had carved the image, though the site lay
three hundred miles from the Olmec heartland.

The carving depicted an upright bird-man, with talons and a beak—
a common Olmec image of shamanism and kingship. It wore an elaborate headdress, and a padded hip belt for playing the ball game. Under
one arm the figure carried a tablet bearing maize imagery, and looked
east over a karst bottomland riven with springs, sinkholes, and caves.
When Eckholm returned in 1972 to study the site more thoroughly,
the carving had been chiseled off the face of the rock and looted. No
sign of it has ever been found, if indeed it survived its removal.

Eckholm believed an artist from the Olmec homeland on the gulf
had created the work, judging by its excellence. In the ruin—a simple collection of earth-covered mounds with a plaza and ball court—
she discovered potsherds from the San Lorenzo vicinity, a major
Olmec site in the Tuxtlas. She also found late classic, putun-era Maya
ceramics, suggesting a period of continuous use, if not continuous
occupation, beginning with the middle formative period.

Eckholm couldn't account for the carving's presence so far from
the Olmec heartland, and so apparently removed from the recognized Olmec diaspora. She believed, however, that it indicated some
larger Olmec incursion into the upper Usumacinta drainage.

In later, classical times the valley would have fallen under Toniná, with occasional shifts according to the winds of war. Bonampak lay just over the Meseta Agua Escondida, at the Lacanjá headwaters.

When Spain first intruded, small groups of Mayas lived scattered in the immediate vicinity, speaking forms of Chol and Tzeltal and living as forest dwellers. They used bows and arrows, wore feathers in their septums, hunted and practiced sophisticated milpa agriculture, and preserved many practices of their forebears. They took regular pilgrimages to major and minor ruins, offering sacrifices, burning pom, and dancing. They never doubted their descent from the ancient builders in stone.

In 1556 a black man fighting with the Spaniards had been captured and his heart cut out during an attack on nearby Pochutla, on Lake Ocotal Grande. Reports of other blood sacrifices were common. Ritual cannibalism may have followed such occasions, as it did human sacrifice during the classical period. Undoubtedly the Chol Lacandons let their own blood, as their ancestors had, and as the modern Lacandons did (secretly) until the 1950s, to achieve altered states and make sacrifice. The last known human sacrifice occurred in the highlands in 1868.

At Miramar, a few miles downstream and inland from La Sultana, Chol Lacandons lived like classical throwbacks on a small archipelago in mid-lake, while the conquest played itself out in the highlands.

At the same time, a town named Topiltepec occupied "a small peninsula formed by the confluence of the Tzaconejá and Jatate rivers" (our campsite) until 1586, according to Jan de Vos. Contemporary references are scarcer than usual, it disappeared so fast.

In the 1530s Francisco Gil Zapata, a lieutenant under Francisco de Montejo, swept down the Jatate, sacking Lacam-Tun/Miramar nearby and enslaving much of Topiltepec's population. The town survived until fifty years later, when Fernando Ovalle, under ecclesiastical command, transferred its people to Ocosingo. When Ovalle was finished, the selva's small Tzeltal- and Chol-speaking populations had vanished, including those of Pochutla and Topiltepec. Only the Lacandons of Miramar remained.

We don't know exactly who the Indians were who occupied Topiltepec, but they undoubtedly spoke early forms of Chol or Tzeltal and maintained intricate ties with their Chol Lacandon neighbors at Miramar. They also controlled access to the Jatate inferior, and its direct route to both the salt and jade sources of the upper Chixoy and the Motagua river valleys, and to the Pasión, the main Usumacinta, and the gulf.

We have no evidence that Topiltepec maintained trade functions in the colonial era—sixteenth-century sources catalogued mainly slaves and souls, not the material means of daily life. Geography and the imperatives of canoe country, however, suggest it was one of the selva's two important collecting points for trade goods in the terminal classic and postclassic periods.

So does language. The names Topiltepec ("Cane Hill") and Pochutla ("Ceiba Grove") are Nahuatl. De Vos ascribed this to the Toltec incursion from central Mexico in the middle and late classic period. More likely Nahuatl-speaking traders from the gulf controlled both of these towns.

Yucatec-speaking Lacandons, like Chan K'in, late arrivals from Peten in the seventeenth century, occupied the Jatate and Miramar until the late 1960s, when Cordan found a Lacandon named Bor, a member of the extended-family caribal headed by Chan Bor, living at the mouth of the Perlas, downstream from the Tzaconejá.

Chan Bor's original caribal had stood at the mouth of the Lacanjá, sixty or seventy miles downstream, until a band of chicleros attacked it one night, raping his wives and murdering his daughter. Afterward he pulled back to Miramar and the Jatate, recapitulating retreats by colonial and nineteenth-century Lacandons.

In 1950, when the Bloms camped at the mouth of the Perlas, they found Chan Bor and his people nearly starved from drought-induced crop failure and suffering from cultural decay hastened by the encroachments of western culture—specifically in the form of missionaries, highland migrants, and pressure to enter the cash economy. The Bloms mounted a rescue campaign, publicizing the Lacandons' plight and organizing an airlift of supplies.

Ten years earlier, when Mexico had first declared the eastern selva public land, thus ending the reign of the monterías, colonists had begun trickling in. In the 1960s, as land pressures mounted in the highlands, immigration exploded. Despite the age-old animosities between highlanders and Lacandons, Chan Bor and his people had taught the newcomers to San Quintín and the new ejido named Emiliano Zapata, at the mouth of the Perlas, how to survive in the lowlands, and helped them through their first hard years in the jungle.

But Chan Bor's people got relocated north to the Lacanjá headwaters. There they fell under the sway of the Summer Institute of Linguistics, an evangelical mission headquartered in Omaha, and its chief emissary in Chiapas, Phillip Baer. Chan Bor, depressed and deracinated, converted to Christianity, the first to'o'hil to do so, and the first crack in a priestly succession of three thousand years. He mexicanized his name to José Pepe Chan Bor and grew dependent on the missionaries for food, medicine, and consumer goods—becoming a pitiful figure to the traditionalists under Chan K'in, whom he avoided, scuttling into the forest if he met one of them on the trail.

Ironically, one of the first demands during the 1995 peace talks of the migrants' offspring—the Zapatistas—was the construction of new roads into the cañadas. The government obliged readily. Since then the military, and the economic and cultural forces that come with it, had infiltrated the rebel stronghold along roads the Zapatistas themselves had fought for, not bargaining on permanent army residence, patrols, constant harassment.

At San Quintín, barracks were erected to house thousands of soldiers, and a bridge was going up over the Jatate. The bridge and army base had imported skilled Latino workers who needed places to sleep and eat. Indians from San Quintín, La Soledad, Betania, and Emiliano

Zapata, the nearest ejidos, got jobs as laborers. Indian wives and daughters earned cash servicing soldiers and highway workers, a much more dependable source of income than farming or weaving.

Disease, petty crime, depression, alcoholism, child abuse increased, along with oil and uranium exploration, and corporate agriculture. (Hydro development could follow.) The hermetic, forbidding Desert of Solitude now faced the driving wedge of Mexican modernity.

When complete, the bridge would link the road from Ocosingo with the one from Las Margaritas to La Realidad, the Zapatista headquarters a few miles west over the Sierra de la Colmena, uniting the army bases at San Quintín and Guadalupe Tepeyac and effectively bisecting the Zapatista heartland.

Still, the rebels held the jungle, where the army was reluctant to follow. Government ground patrols kept to the villages, the roads, the better-known trails.

ANCIENT TRADERS WOULD no doubt have relaxed at Topiltepec until the floodwaters receded. (Blom's map indicated an unexcavated ruin at the mouth of the Tzaconejá.) We had no such luxury, and launched early on the heavy, brooding current, the overcast scudding and tearing into gray rags.

The Tzaconejá had tripled in volume overnight, almost flooding David's tent where he had pitched it beside the water. For the first few hundred yards the river split down the middle: pearly gray on one side, the opaque yellow of eroded upstream rangelands on the other, then merged into a single café-au-lait stream.

We drifted on the flood, with no idea what to expect. Eddies and remolinos bubbled up out of nowhere. The clouds dissipated. A thousand feet above on the right we could see the road-cut paralleling the river toward San Quintín.

The canyon rose steeply as high as the road, then gradually tilted away toward the ridgetops a thousand feet higher. Cultivation scarred the steep slopes in erratic patterns, but along the ridges the forest was continuous, the green punctuated by dispersed yellow blossoms of guanacaste and the complementary blossoms of lavender cojolites.

Every mile took us deeper into the heart of the cañadas, closer to the Montes Azules reserve and the wild heart of Zapatismo. We ran about a dozen class 3 rapids, mostly short wave trains between swirling pools and flats, passing cultivation along shore and small balsa rafts tied up on the right where someone had crossed to tend a field or hunt. Then the canyon and the channel narrowed again. Small waterfalls poured in from the sides. We lost sight of the road and the higher mountains behind galleries of streamside timber.

Here the "El Rosario" dam would have been built, had the plan gone through. A priority of the secret 1980 survey, El Rosario would have backed up both rivers and inundated 5,570 hectares of canyon and forest, despite rotten karstic substrata that would have heightened the dangers of construction and siphoned off power.

The sun broke out for the first time in a week. We stopped on a beach in a miniature gorge and ate lunch under walls of sculpted limestone topped by flowering epiphtyes and yellow guanacaste blossoms. Afterward we lay out our wet clothes and exposed our wounds and various fungi (we all had athlete's foot) to the healing rays for half an hour.

While we rested Josh changed into his only spare garment, a pair of lightweight cotton trousers. He carried almost no personal equipment, I had noticed, beyond his tent and sleeping bag. He ate dinner out of a Frisbee and used a plastic maple syrup jug for a water bottle.

From his upbringing in remote northwestern Colorado he retained a cowboy's reticence and reluctance to express opinions. You couldn't pin him down without shading your inquiry precisely. Expertise belonged to others, his attitude seemed to say, not to people who traveled the most bewildered rims of the earth and who had glimpsed the magnitudes of human ignorance.

From what I had seen so far, he stood alone as a river pro, his judgments unencumbered by ego and other mental baggage. You imagined he thought you lacking somehow, or had tuned you out, until a comment or anecdote caught his ear and he broke out in a loud and very peculiar laugh that sounded like the call of a mythic bird, or maybe a small dinosaur, a succession of loud "ha!"s that went on longer than you thought appropriate.

He had a curling nose, huge wrists and forearms, and a jutting jaw, like Popeye's; a forty-four-year-old body that gave away nothing; a full, graying beard.

In camp he didn't lift a finger beyond morning coffee duty, something you sensed had more to do with ritual and ensuring a good cup than a desire to help. He pitched his tent off by himself. He spent winters kayaking in Chile, and had a girlfriend somewhere.

I trusted him implicitly.

Within minutes of relaunching we had lined the top half of a difficult, rain-swollen rapid—perhaps the one Blom marked El Mico (spider monkey) or Bodegas; it was hard to tell—and scouted exhaustively before deciding to run the class 4 bottom section. It called for a clean turn into an extremely fast channel, and an upstream ferry all the way across the river to the left. Then we had to swivel the boat downstream and straighten out in time to miss the gaping hydraulic on the right and drive squarely into a powerful wave.

We picked our way down some technical rock gardens and came to the unrunnable Paso Soledad, "Lonely Pass." The carry trail wound over a steep bluff on the right, through snaky-looking abandoned milpa. At the end we separated and examined ourselves for ticks and chiggers, the infamous garrapatas, that frequented places where livestock had recently grazed. They had infested our inner thighs and crotches, their favorite destination. We spent half an hour by ourselves picking off the microscopic vermin before they laid their eggs in our flesh and chilling the inflamed areas with river water.

In the next rapid we dumped when Alonso, still inexperienced, leaned away from, rather than into, a wall on a sharp curve. The current caught our upstream gunwale and threw us over, sweeping us wildly through an S-turn and bouncing us off rocks. I swam to an eddy and clambered out on the left. Downstream David rescued Alonso and towed him to shore, while Josh pushed the turtled but high-floating Freedom to safety. Luckily we all wound up on the same side of the river.

It took me twenty minutes to reach the others, climbing over enormous boulders with razor edges. Hollows gaped under the rocks, perfect habitat for everything venomous. I had to step over logs blindly and reach over boulders without checking my handholds. Fallen trees blocked the way, making me swim or wade around them over jagged irregularities, further bruising my calves and shins.

When I got to the others, Alonso was relieved, shaken, but still willing—a good thing: more bad water lay ahead. We lined the rest of the rapid, and the next, and scouted the one after that. At Josh's insistence we sneaked it on the left, zigzagging through a rock maze in a narrow side channel. After that we ferried and straightened for a wave train that culminated in a broad eddy. We'd survived a swim; the boat and all the equipment were intact; our safety boaters had done their jobs.

The eddy laved a curving beach in the shadow of a high cliff on the right. We'd all had enough and called it a day, pulling up to the beach and just sitting in the boats before marshaling the energy to make camp.

We cooked on a fire Alonso had built with fragrant copal shavings and ate in the time it took the tropical dusk to gather and fade. Parrots chattered overhead, crossing from one side of the river to the other as I washed the dishes at the eddy and the dark settled over us.

In the morning the parrots flew back across the river. We shoved off and lined the first rapid, then had perfect runs in two successive class 4's. In the third, we dumped again. Construction debris had been toppled into the water where the river passed close underneath the road, clogging the easier sneak route near the left shore and mounding the current into a terrifically fast wave train that poured over a ledge. Hydraulics yawned on both sides below the ledge, either of which could hold the swimmer and his boat. The safe channel between them passed over a chute five feet high and about two feet wide.

Paddling furiously, we got the Freedom up on the waves with the boat cocked slightly to the right. The hydraulics boiled and spouted like lava pits. We roared over the chute in a plume of spray, hit the bottom and braced simultaneously, Alonso needing no command: a perfect run. Josh gave us thumbs-up from the eddy.

We had taken on a lot of water. Downstream the river curved back to the left and dropped over another ledge. The route ran far right. I tried to turn the Freedom that way, but it was too heavy. The current pushed us toward the hydraulic. I called for Alonso to draw on the right, to help me turn the boat and ferry to the safe channel, but he drew left. I called louder and he drew harder—on the *left,* again, pulling us straight into the hydraulic. The boat flipped. We washed out and swam. Josh rescued the Freedom, then he and David picked us up.

We got together downstream and bailed out the Freedom. This time Alonso looked shell-shocked. I told him that a lot of novice canoeists confused left and right, especially with some loudmouth bellowing at them in the stern. In every respect he was doing a great job. He didn't care, he said. He was through running rapids. He also said the river was more dangerous and harder than I had let on it would be, an accusation I couldn't refute.

Yet we had made it through the worst of a bad situation without serious injury or equipment loss. Our teamwork kept improving. All that remained was the unknown factor of Colorado Canyon, a day and a half downstream. I apologized, thanked him, reminded him that we had the best possible support crew. Everything would work out.

After half an hour we reached Contreras, the last rapid before Colorado Canyon, a straight, steep wave train with a slightly tricky entry. A boulder fall bordered the rapid on the left, a high wall on the right. We scouted, but Alonso balked. Josh said it was best to get back on the horse sooner rather than later, but Alonso didn't budge. A confrontation would achieve nothing. The rapid was short, so we carried over the boulders.

Below Contreras the river pushed us along through winding flats still high and brown from the Tzaconejá. Right away we came upon children bathing, our first encounter with locals in two and a half days. The mountains retreated from the river. The shores turned pastoral, scrubby with tamarinds, cecropia trees, the ubiquitous brown jays. We passed more bathers and fishers, young men posing like Calvin Klein models in bikini briefs, casting nets or handlines. The river eddied through riffles and deadwaters, and kingfishers flew alongside. About two o'clock we passed the bridge under construction, workers dangling from cranes and scaffolds. They taunted us, and called, "Watch out for the crocodiles, ha-ha-ha," while armed soldiers watched us darkly.

Around us the green ranges of the Sierra del Caribe stretched away to the southeast, beyond Laguna Miramar, four miles east, toward the nucleus of Montes Azules and the wild core of refuge that defended the Chol Lacandons for a century and a half, the traditional practices of the Yucatec Lacandons through the 1960s, and now, rumor had it, harbored Subcomandante Marcos and his trusty laptop.

Soon we heard young female voices and saw women bathing near shore. They said they lived in Emiliano Zapata, at the mouth of the Río Perlas.

Within minutes the Perlas poured strong, clear, and greenish-blue out of the biosphere reserve to the north. We beached on a wide gravel bar and David stayed with the boats while the rest of us walked to Zapata. Some boys carried buckets from the Perlas to wash a colectivo, a communally owned and operated bus that made one of two or three daily trips to Ocosingo and back. They had pulled the bus out onto the gravel fan that extended far into the Jatate to get it close to the water. Bulldozers and loaders had mined the bed, leaving the gravel unnaturally mounded and contorted. It was a beautiful juncture despite the defacement, the Perlas pushing chalky and clear down a narrow channel between high forested banks. You could easily imagine an idyllic jungle homesite there.

Women bathed in the tributary. A man stripped to his briefs and waded across the stream searching for firewood, his pants in one hand and a machete in the other. We walked up the road toward the *centro*, passing groups of women going for water and children just out of school carrying books. Some of the young girls wore skirts and blouses, others traditional embroidered huipiles and cotton skirts. Most were barefoot. All greeted us in a friendly manner.

Near the centro footpaths led off into the bush. Thatched houses stood close together on the grassy lanes, many with ornamental plantings. The zócalo itself was a wide-open area on a slight rise, aesthetically bereft but for its setting within a ring of green mountains. Pigs, mules, and fowl grazed around the crumbling civic center.

There I had camped three weeks earlier, while visiting Miramar, four miles north, and attending an important town meeting at Zapata. It was in the weeks before my departure from Palenque, when I had driven in from Ocosingo with Ron Nigh, an agrarian anthropologist, and outfitter Fernando Ochoa, who was developing a tourist plan for the villages around Lake Miramar.

Beside the basketball court stood the government tienda, a frame building with whitewashed mahogany siding, closed. Electrical wires were strung all over the village on new concrete pylons. A mound of sand, bags of concrete, a mixer, and cement blocks stood idle, attesting to someone's resolve to enact a public work.

We followed the single street to an open tienda and stepped into the stuffy gloom. The proprietress attended us nervously: the electricity was out, she complained, children clinging to her long skirts. She lacked refrigeration or lights. We bought tepid Cokes, sucked them down, and bought more. Then we filled a stuff sack with eggs, cans of salsa and chiles, avocados, pasta, and other odds and ends. The woman apologized for being out of tortillas, but said her neighbor down the street might have some.

We walked back to the corner and hailed the house she had pointed out, a poured-concrete structure with a shaded patio in the rear. The woman came out and invited us to the patio, where she sold us a bag of fresh tortillas big as dinner plates, and a bunch of green plantains that hung from the ramada shading the patio. Men lounged in hammocks out of the sun, complaining of the rate at which their boom box consumed batteries. Beyond the house, past a gully of mixed scrub and milpa, we could see the San Quintín airstrip and the roofs of some military-looking buildings.

The lights from those buildings had burned brightly during the previous nights I had spent with Ochoa and Nigh in darkened Zapata.

We were to attend a meeting where the town's economic future would be discussed. When Fernando Ochoa first started visiting Zapata and Miramar in the early nineties, the four communities of highland immigrants surrounding the lake were locked in long-standing land disputes. The lessons in forest milpa management Chan Bor had taught them had worn off. Bad market-driven agricultural practices had shrunk their arable acreage, but the borders of the ejido grants had never been marked and no reliable maps existed. It didn't help that the four towns spoke distinct Maya languages and that their grants fell within the highly ambiguous boundaries of the Montes Azules reserve.

Fernando had brought satellite photographs of the area to help them mark their borders. The trust he gained thereby helped him arrange an agreement among them to refrain from cutting timber or hunting within a kilometer of the lakeshore, preserving about eighteen thousand acres. The agreement limited watercraft to cayucos and a single cooperative motor launch. In return, Fernando promised to bring to Miramar nature lovers and scientists, rather than disruptive commercial ecotours, who would pay a fee per day for minimum-impact, wilderness-style camping. Within five years the communities would take over the business.

The plan's success hinged partly on Fernando's ability to attract enough people to record a gain. Despite low numbers, so far the agreement held. Populations of monkeys and crocodiles were holding steady or increasing. Soon, Fernando told me, he would try to extend the no-cutting and -hunting agreement to the top of the lake basin.

For his part, Ron Nigh was advising Zapata's farmers how to shift to organic methods and low-impact crops like wild cacao, brown rice, and shade-grown coffee so they could broaden their economic base and become less dependent on corn and coffee monocultures, and the pesticides they required. Such dependencies had haunted them in the past. The community could increase profits enormously, he said, by roasting its own coffee and hulling its own rice, and selling directly to markets in the states and central Mexico. Progress was slow—like all farmers, they were suspicious of change, and no funds existed to ease them through the transition—but Zapata's elders supported the shift.

Nigh said Gruppo Pulsar, a Japanese conglomerate (now part of Seiko), had donated $10 million to manage the biosphere reserve. Some of the money would finance a string of Conservation International ecotourist hostels on the edges of the reserve. The rest was enough to take care of Montes Azules for a long time, building and maintaining trails and campsites, and hiring citizens from the selva communities as guides and guards.

Such programs, Ron suggested, were desirable, but until the forest towns had self-sustaining economies, no amount of "greenmail" would protect the selva. Only strong local economies and family planning would maintain a balance of use and preservation, and those could only follow a secure peace.

In the meantime, Nigh, who grew up on a Nebraska ranch, counseled the villages. It was an uphill battle. Like all farmers, they viewed with skepticism anything and anyone connected with government. That included most *non*governmental organizations. They only keep talking to us, Nigh said, because we go back when we say we're going to go back, and we do what we say we're going to do.

After driving fifty jarring miles from Ocosingo, we had made camp at dusk on the village's grassy plaza, and hired a man named Nicandro to carry our equipment to Miramar in the morning. After dinner we strolled to the village basketball court for the meeting. You couldn't have found a better setting for such an exercise: a wilderness clearing where the Perlas entered the Jatate, mist-shrouded ranges extending in all directions. Non-Zapatistas attended, mostly evangelistas protecting their interests, but no women, it surprised me to see. Suffrage had apparently not extended this far down into the Zapatista rank and file.

The assembly ranged in age from sixteen to forty. Anyone older stood with the speakers. As at all such gatherings, closer attention might have been paid. They sprawled on the court, exhausted from a workday that had begun fourteen hours earlier, or stood in small groups smoking and gossiping. Some of them had clearly been violating the community's alcohol ban. They wore jeans or running shorts, and polyester cowboy shirts or T-shirts. Many wore baseball caps with the visors reversed.

Fernando brought them up to date on the tourist program for Miramar and the search for funding. The application for a federal development grant of three thousand dollars had just been denied, along with all other aid applications from Chiapas. The grant would have purchased a used pickup truck, a composting toilet, and materials to build a second palapa at Miramar and a visitor's center in Zapata. Fernando suggested they could still complete some of the projects if he procured the materials and they supplied the labor. It would be hard to attract tourists and protect the resource, he insisted, without better infrastructure, especially sanitation.

Where are these rich tourists you promised us? some of them

asked, impatient, if not openly hostile. Raise the daily fee! others demanded. For a while the meeting verged on chaos. A young man in a pressed white shirt, black slacks, and a good haircut stood and translated for the non-Spanish speakers. He was the schoolmaster, and reputedly a rebel teniente. You could believe it, he took over the meeting with such easy but firm authority. He called for a vote and it was resolved unanimously. They would provide what Fernando requested.

Consensus governed in the cañadas. Nothing passed until everybody came on board, through persuasion or other forms of pressure. Many decisions took forever, like the San Andrés accords, which had gone unratified for months, or remained unacted upon. The process would not be rushed.

The presidente and village elders spoke after Fernando. By the time Ron Nigh got up it was almost dark. The court lights were out, like the rest of the village's electrical service, and some of the men slept. Ron addressed the group in halting Tzeltal, bringing smiles of appreciation and outright laughter from those still awake. But the discussion grew heated, involving a radical departure from business as usual. The men argued while Ron stood silently and the elders appealed to them to heed his suggestions and begin planning to shift to organic farming methods and diversify their crops. This was a harder future to imagine than fleecing tourists. Even those who saw its wisdom faced the problem of how and when to start. It boiled down to what they would do when they got up in the morning in order to survive. But the old men prevailed: if nothing changed, they kept repeating, the world as they knew it would end.

Eventually Ron got permission to organize a symposium that included economists, tropical agronomists, and conservation biologists. At its end, the town would draw up a plan for a complete shift to organic farming and direct marketing within five years.

The meeting broke up after more than an hour. We walked back to our tents in the dark. Nearby, the mercury lights at the army base at San Quintín, the old Bulnes montería, polluted the sky.

That night, in the ejidos of the Jatate valley, the intimidation campaign against rebel communities would resume. Indian women would
sell themselves and their daughters to Indian and Latino soldiers.
Houses would be sacked, shots fired over the heads of innocent
people. Loudspeakers would blast the Mexican equivalent of the
Carpenters through the night and Dobermans would parade on
leashes. But for now, all was quiet. In the houses we passed, even
those serviced by electrical wires, candles burned.

In the morning Nicandro showed up, along with the usual crowd
of gawkers, as we crawled out of our tents. Nicandro wore a T-shirt,
polyester pants, black rubber boots, and a careworn expression. He
was about thirty. His father-in-law, a wiry old codger, and one of his
young sons accompanied him. They watched with folded arms while
we brushed our teeth.

Nicandro gestured to the old man and the boy. The men had left for
the fields, he said. Impatiently the old-timer fashioned a tumpline out
of cheap plastic rope and made a show of hefting two huge coolers
onto his back. Then he headed out, alone, down the four-mile trail to
Miramar. After some dickering, two more able-bodied men appeared.

I swung the Freedom onto my shoulders to start the carry while
Nicandro looked on, crestfallen. Fernando told me the men expected to
be paid to carry our equipment. I remembered the painful images of
Indians bent under gringos' burdens, and Stephens in his silla, but I
relented. I jammed the paddles between the center thwart and bow seat
and showed Nicandro and the other man how to carry double, with the
canoe inverted and the seats fore and aft resting on their shoulders.

The trail led through the village to a swinging plank bridge over
the Perlas. I crossed the bridge, stopping midway to look at the river.
Underneath, the current tumbled at a good rate and kicked up a riffle
of six-inch waves. A few thatched houses stood on both sides of the
river, cayucos hauled onto the banks behind them.

I was about to head up the trail toward Miramar, away from the
river, when Nicandro and the other guy carried the Freedom down the

bank behind me. They cast a quick look in each direction and launched, Nicandro astern. At first they looked wobbly and close to capsizing, and they held my lightweight bent-shaft paddles with the blades facing in the wrong direction. Then Nicandro snapped the boat into a perfect angle for an upstream ferry, the bow pointing forty-five degrees up and across the river. They paddled just hard enough to maintain their place in the current, and the boat leapfrogged across the waves.

The trail climbed slowly toward the lake. After a mile or so it crested on a height of land surrounded by overgrazed scrub. Milpa climbed the lower slopes of the mostly forested hills to the north and west. We hiked through groves of spindly cecropia trees, like wide-leaved aspens, the avant-garde of rain forest succession. The productivity of a plot using slash-and-burn methods declines 50 percent within three years, so we walked through an approximately twenty-four-year time line of one-shot farming. You didn't encounter working milpa until right before the cooperative area surrounding Miramar. In other words, in this direction at least, the community had nowhere left to expand.

Flycatchers and unwieldy keel-billed toucans flew overhead. It was hot and, despite the aura of destruction, beautiful. Trails led off through the undergrowth to milpas and coffee plantations. Families approached and passed us headed toward Zapata, barefoot men and women in traje carrying sixty-kilo loads of coffee beans and corn from communities beyond the lake.

After an hour the trail entered a wall of forest. We continued under the canopy for half an hour until we came out at a narrow beach curving gently for three hundred yards. Ranks of green palms bowed over the sand. Inland, enormous palo de agua trees fronted the forest, encrusted with epyphitic cacti, bromelias, and orchids.

The lake filled a wide, round bowl—a huge blue lens in the forest. The water was calm and clear, the sandy bottom rippled in the shallows. The encircling mountains rose dramatically. Puffy white clouds scrolled in from Peten, spawned over the Caribbean, casting shadows on the steep slopes, and the rounded green domes of the Lacandon archipelago hovered in the distance. I scanned for signs of houses or development and saw nothing but untrammeled shoreline, the irregular bays and peninsulas of the eastern lakeshore, three miles away, and a single cayuco in midlake. The ubiquitous drone of howler monkeys drifted over the water like a pedal tone.

It was the largest unspoiled lake in Mexico, completely within the Montes Azules Biosphere Reserve and filling a volcanic caldera approximately seven miles square and a thousand feet deep. The water, blue and clear, maintained a year-round seventy-four degrees. The mountains climbed 1500 feet above the surface.

Crocodiles, turtles, and a variety of fish endemic to the watershed inhabited its waters: mojarra, bobo, bagre, macabil, among others. Tilapia were introduced in the sixties in a misguided attempt at economic development, overpopulating and remaining too small to reward fishing for them. Rainbow trout, which could conceivably survive in the cold, oxygen-rich depths, may also have been introduced during the same period. It seems impossible—trout in the jungle?—but one old-timer I met at Miramar described a fish resembling a rainbow that ran into the cold feeder creeks during rainy season.

Miramar's forests supported dozens of neotropical birds and North American migrants, as well as monkeys, jaguars, tapirs, white-lipped peccary, and brocket and whitetail deer. Fernando, a former horticulturist from the state of Colima, had identified more than fifty species of orchid and bromelia growing around its shores.

I waded in up to my ankles. The communal motor launch, a big ponga with a 150-horse Yamaha, rocked in the shallows, awaiting the families we passed on the trail. A small group of men stood around the ponga. A couple of beached cayucos tottered in the swell.

The men came out of the woods behind me and carried the coolers and packs to the campsite, where two thatch-roofed palapas stood near the trailhead, one for sleeping, the other with a raised hearth for cooking. Fernando and his friend Alban Pfisterer, "Snoopy," pitched the tents and organized the kitchen. Ron Nigh slung a hammock between two palms.

A minute later Nicandro and his partner grounded the Freedom beside me. The men and children stripped to their shorts, waded in, and swam. By some wordless agreement Nicandro and I unwedged the paddles from the seats, floated the Freedom, and placed his eight-year-old son amidships. Then, while Fernando and Snoopy made camp, we shoved off.

We worked our way slowly offshore. The beach's curve widened in perspective and a break in the caldera rim opened a view of distant mountains looking back up the Jatate toward Ocosingo. The waters darkened steadily from pale aqua to deep indigo, the clarity thirty feet or greater.

The Freedom delighted Nicandro. He told me to follow the left-hand shore, where the beach gave way to travertine extrusions and the mountain sloped steeply to the water. Mature timber bristling with orchids and cacti hung over the shallows, and fish waited to eat their falling fruit. We paddled over pale shoals where calcium had coated the rocks and drowned limbs with petrified crust. We paddled into a narrow cave and out again, and rounded a point where Nicandro said jaguars came to drink.

We drifted wordlessly, examining the scene in silence. From the water, one cleared area could be seen on the flank of a northern range, and a recovering burn on the eastern shore. Otherwise, the view was pristine. I wanted to ask him about the uprising, what part he had played, if any (Fernando told me he had fought), but etiquette forbade it. Instead I told him his lake was lovely. Sí, he agreed, está sagrado, it is sacred.

•

THE DOMINICAN CHRONICLER Villagutiere Soto-Mayor drew a confused but compelling picture of the region in the century after the conquest, in which a subdued and pastoral highland area—a geographical perimeter—surrounded a lowland core of intractable tribes of hunter-gatherers and milpa keepers. In Villagutiere's writings the contrast of darkness and light, heathen and Christian, pastoral and wilderness, damned and redeemed, is every bit as sharp and unforgiving as you will find in the annals of the New England Puritans. In his chronicle, he leaves the cause of Lacandon resistance unaddressed.

Jan de Vos attributes Lacandon ferocity to offenses perpetrated by the first entrada led by Francisco D'Avila, in 1530. When the invaders appeared on the lakeshore, the Indians fled to the forest and down the Río Azul. The Spaniards and their highland allies then burned shoreline crops and destroyed the abandoned temples on the island ceremonial center. As soon as the Spaniards left, the Indians returned. From then on the Lacandons vowed vengeance on the invader.

Within a decade, religious and civil authorities had relocated many of the forest-dwelling Mayas, like those of Topiltepec and Pochutla. The Lacandons remained obdurate. Given a chance to convert them by peaceful means, even Bartolomé de las Casas, the author of *The History of the Indies* and the Indians' defender before the court of Spain, failed.

In 1552 Lacandons raided Bachajon, a Christian Tzeltal town near the highland source of the Jatate. (Bachajon still commemorates the raid in its annual carnival.) In the following years black-and-red-painted Lacandons turned up in villages all around the highland perimeter and as far away as Cobán, in Verapaz, killing and kidnapping their Christian cousins and Indian and European clergy. Parties sent in pursuit reported finding the captives' corpses bound and mutilated, in some cases with their hearts torn out, and sooty incense burners still smoking nearby.

Both sides committed atrocities. In 1559 the bishop in Ciudad Real, today's San Cristóbal, persuaded the government in Guatemala to send a force against Lacam-Tun/Miramar. Leaving Comitán, at the southwest corner of the selva, the army and its ax-wielding forerunners carried the parts for a landing craft eastward across four dangerous rivers, including the Jatate, and assembled it at the lake. Thus equipped, the Spaniards defeated the Indians, sacked the lake islands, and deported and enslaved many Lacandons. Enough escaped into the woods, however, to filter back and rebuild. Hostilities recommenced.

In 1563 Fray Pedro Lorenzo, Palenque's founder, moved to Lacam-Tun, living onshore like an Indian while preaching peaceful conversion. The Lacandons recognized the priest as a different breed of Spaniard and left him alone. Still they rejected his entreaties, choosing to remain in the selva, loyal to their gods.

In 1586 the colonial government sent a force to subdue the rebel Lacandons once and for all. The troops destroyed their island redoubt and all the fields and houses within a wide radius. The Indians, however, had already migrated from Miramar to the southeast and established Sac-Balam, "White Jaguar," their new town near the eponymous Río Lacantun. The Lacandons remained there, invisible to the Spaniards, for nearly a century, continuing their intermittent raids against outlying Christian villages.

We paddled around Miramar for three days, exploring caves and pictographs. On the main island we found the Lacandon ruins overgrown with mature timber. A single beheaded idol stood on the plaza. Every couple of hours we grounded the Freedom on one of the many low travertine shoals and swam in the clear, lukewarm water.

Cayucos passed slowly back and forth. Mornings they landed on the beach in front of the campsite carrying produce from the outlying villages. The men and women backpacked the coffee and corn to the airstrip at San Quintín, and from there it was flown at high cost to buyers in San Cristóbal, Ocosingo, and Comitán.

The men stood in the low-slung dugouts, making deft J-strokes with their cañaletes. All admired the Freedom. Superficially the two craft were unalike, the dugout a minimally shaped tree trunk, heavy and slow, though beautiful, unchanged over the centuries; the

Freedom a highly evolved product of design and technology, less pleasing aesthetically but better performing. They had in common their general purpose and use, and their irreducible, universal form—cognate to the waterlily, the vulva, the jewel in the lotus.

One evening Ron and I took a starlight cruise after dinner. We had both read Freidel and Schele's *Maya Cosmos,* with its exposition of the multilayered myth complex undergirding the Maya creation story and the metaphysic of canoes, its documentation of the continuity of belief and practice connecting ancient and contemporary Mayas. The Milky Way streamed across the sky like frog spawn: heavenly canoe, Watery Path, and world tree combined.

We felt suspended in a continuum of past and present and imagined dozens of cayucos drifting aimlessly, boys and girls from Lacam-Tun coupling under the stars and farmers and fisherfolk all the way back to the Olmec standing on calm lake surfaces or agricultural canals, the heavens reflected in crystal clarity and the ongoing story of creation unfolding above and below. The paddler would have had no trouble visualizing the explained cosmos and seeing himself poised between two worlds—both of them visible simultaneously—as a participant in the historical narrative.

One day Fernando, Snoopy, and I were paddling near the landing for the village of Tierra y Libertad when we heard music drifting over the water. Low clouds muted the light. The music blended strangely with the howler monkeys' figured bass and the trills of trogons along shore. We rounded a point and saw thirty men clustered about the trailhead at the top of a steep bank. Three of them played guitars, one a small drum, and another a guitarrón, the mariachis' potbellied six-string bass. We drifted to a halt at the foot of the bank. The music stopped and we asked permission to come ashore. The men hesitated at first, but they crowded around the top of the bank to inspect the Freedom, responding as if to some universal language encoded in its double-ended form and complex vectors, and they let us up.

They told Fernando they were from Nuevo Galilea, across the

lake, but had been visiting Tierra y Libertad for an "agricultural meeting." They were all in their teens and twenties, except for a few mid-
dle-agers. One viejo with white hair, gold teeth, and a big smile
seemed to be in charge. I didn't see any agricultural implements.
Most of them wore good military boots, however, and carried the
regulation nylon rucksacks of the EZLN. With rifles and masks they
would have fit the popular image of Zapatista fighters to a tee, and we
had no doubt that's what they were, probably training in the event
that tensions exploded and the army made its move.

While we chatted I picked up one of the small cheap guitars that
lay against a tree, strummed a few chords and tuned it. At Snoopy's
prodding I played an inept bluegrass version of "Greensleeves," which
they applauded with a chorus of laughter. Sing something, they said,
and I responded with "Freight Train." More laughter. When I asked
them to reciprocate they shyly declined.

While they waited for the launch to take them home, the men filed
down the steep bank for a closer look at the Freedom. I was sitting in
the stern, fielding the usual questions, when a gaunt teenager with a
sharp face and wispy mustache pushed me off and hopped into the bow
without invitation or comment. He took up the paddle and we backed
and turned without speaking into the bay. He wore a western hat, jeans,
and military boots, and displayed perfect canoeing form: shoulders
square, arms straight, head steady. He paddled me fiercely toward mid-
lake while I struggled to keep up in the stern, alternately ruddering and
paddling hard to compensate for his power. Off to our right the islands
of Lacam-Tun, where his forebears had resisted Spain, hovered over the
surface like disembodied green hills. It was slightly alarming, as if I were
being forced into a contest of strength and canoemanship, my canoe and
canoeing itself—a practice sanctified by history and necessity, its gestures ritualized and formalized—being reclaimed for all time.

We matched each other stroke for stroke far into the lake, the
shoreline falling away on either side, until we merged into the nacreous zone where water and sky came together and you couldn't tell

them apart. The universe expanded in both directions, history flowed both ways.

With the calls of monkeys carrying over the water, we stopped paddling and glided to a halt. He slapped the hull and shook the seat. I told him the boat was very strong, designed for running rapidos. Turning in the bow, he said he had run rapids on the Río Azul, but they were easy. At this level—as canoeists for whom canoeing meant more than recreation—we made an accommodation and understood each other. Slowly we turned the boat and paddled easily and smoothly back to the landing, under the overcast sky. Within minutes the ponga arrived and carried him and his compadres back to New Galilee and his people's dream of frontier independence.

Eight

CAÑÓN COLORADO

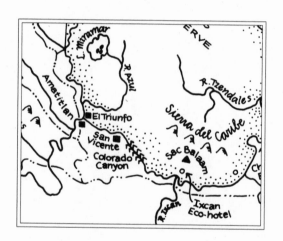

IN THE MORNING WE REACHED THE MOUTH OF THE Río Azul two
hours below camp. The tributary rose in the central Montes Azules
reserve thirty miles north and followed a looping course, draining
Miramar and pouring slowly but forcefully into the Jatate through a
channel about fifty feet wide, deep, blue, and clear as sapphire gin. It
contrasted starkly with the sullied Jatate. We paddled upstream a hundred yards to a place where the river roiled in a slow eddy, then
drifted, turning, over the clean sand bottom fifteen feet below.

On the south bank stood a tropical homestead par excellence, the only one we had seen on the river's shores: a neat thatched cabaña and outbuildings set amid ceibas and the romantic fronds of corozo palms, a couple of acres of open "pasture," ample milpa, and fruit orchard. The fishing would be good, the hunting iffy but adequate, at least for small game. The house's cayucos were gone, probably fishing or snailing upriver, but their landing was carved out of the bank on the Azul side. In the near background rose the forested Sierra del Caribe, unblemished by saw or fire.

The confluence lay at the geographical heart of the southern Lacandon forest and as removed from the outside world as we would get. Within a few miles a ganglion of rivers—the Perlas, the Azul, the Santo Domingo—added their volumes to the Jatate. Like many central places, it was beautiful but unassuming: an anonymous convergence in a wilderness. It perfectly symbolized the locus of Zapatismo. Within a thirty-mile radius the movement had coalesced and trained. Tierra y Libertad, not far up the Azul near Miramar, had maintained a clandestine hospital and refuge for Guatemalan rebels. The ríos Dolores (on whose banks the Zapatista headquarters at La Realidád were located) and Eusaba ran parallel to the Jatate a few kilometers over the Sierra de la Colmena to the west, feeding the Santo Domingo. With the peace agreement repudiated, the leadership had withdrawn, keeping on the move in and out of the remote villages, off in the caves and canyons it sprang from. Like the movement, the confluence was somewhere but nowhere.

All morning the river pushed us easily through long flats and riffles. We took off the spray cover and our helmets for the first time since La Sultana. Deep, high old growth extended in both directions, with occasional cultivated breaks. Between the Río Azul and the mouth of the Santo Domingo we saw four ospreys, one carrying a fish, many flocks of parrots, and iridescent green kingfishers, called "water hummingbirds" by the Maya, for their tactic of hovering over a quarry. The Sierra del Caribe rose steadily closer and steeper before us.

Josh, David, and I had now been paddling for two weeks. We had settled into the mind-emptying rhythm of the days, an effect of extended river travel I had encountered while working as a guide in years past, when the present expanded to absorb any question of past or future. In those days abstractions dissolved: everything became concrete, immediate, a perpetual immersion in the physical world. I had rarely felt so secure as I did then, despite occasional minor brushes with danger, the hazards of nature seeming benign compared to those of the mind or economy.

That security derived from the continuous sensation of buoyancy and from submitting to the imperatives of moving water, a discipline that required you to relinquish illusions of control, but that also connected you to the past and the hemisphere's prehistoric colonists, ancestors of geography and craft if not of genes. It often seemed to me that the motion of paddling called forth the shades of primordial paddlers the way a musician's fingers remember patterns of a composition the mind has forgotten.

A different safety resided in the shape of the canoe itself, which surrounded and protected the paddler and made a dent the shape of a willow leaf in the planetary membrane. C. Randall Daniels—Sakim—the Muskogee Floridian who instructed Freidel and Schele in his people's canoe culture, called it a "portable personal portal" that kept you hooked up directly to otherness, transcendence, as you moved through the landscape. When you stayed on it long enough, I knew from experience, the path would carry you.

I couldn't expect Alonso to share this conceit, though I hoped he would.

Around noon we reached the Santo Domingo, as beautiful as the Azul, and beached on a travertine shoal extending into the tributary. Alonso stripped and waded into the affluent, which, like all the tributaries except the Tzaconejá, ran high but clear, greener even than the Perlas. While Alonso swam, Josh reassured me privately that we could run the canyon. I asked him if he also thought I could run it solo should Alonso back out and carry around. He declined to answer. A minute later Alonso got out, dried off, and we began to eat lunch.

After a while I spoke to Alonso in everyone's hearing. I said Josh had been very careful, as he should be, not to make categorical statements about rapids or abilities. But based on what he had seen us do, and what the Freedom could do, he had assured me that the canyon was runnable. I told Alonso that if he still didn't want to run the canyon, that was fine. I understood and thought I could make it solo. We just needed to find the portage trail and ask somebody who knew the area how long it took to walk around—a daunting prospect in this place where concepts of time and distance bore little resemblance to ours. Alonso could carry a pack and whatever else he could in his hands to lighten my load in the Freedom.

I hoped in any case he'd decide to come along, I said. I was certain we worked well enough together to make it, but I couldn't guarantee anything.

No thanks, he said. He had a family to think about.

A few hundred yards downstream the Zapatista village of Triunfo sat on a high bank, a number of cayucos and a ponga resting on the beach at river level. We decided to pay it a visit to ask about the carry and possible porters in case Alonso needed help.

We drifted down the Jatate to the beach and walked up the bank to the village. On the opposite shore soldiers in the progovernment village of Amatitlán watched us through binoculars. There some of the early Jatate trips under Cully Erdman had taken out and hired mules to carry their equipment to the nearest road.

We followed a trail through high grass. It passed behind a building with separate rooms opening on the zócalo, a grassy area about fifty yards square with a ball court, pylons, and power lines. Beyond, the Sierra del Caribe glistened. Outside, some boys worked under the supervision of a man in his thirties dressed in jeans, T-shirt, and ball cap. All appeared listless in the heat.

The trail around the canyon started on the right, the man told us, not the left, as Cordan had claimed, at a village called San Vicente unmarked on Blom's map. It didn't take long to walk around and he thought we could hire a guide or porter there.

He said the power had been turned off since the protest began a month ago, though it was still on in Amatitlán, and in the army base. He shrugged. The other village also controlled access to the road. It was hard.

As we descended the bank to the river, the soldiers kept watching us from the opposite shore and we could see the shapes of Humvees, and tanks or Bradleys, hulking behind the trees. It was the most dramatic standoff we had witnessed so far—two worlds in opposition across a wild river, one poor and native, the other the vanguard of an aloof kleptocracy—and anger rose in my chest. Pushing off, we discussed checking for more information over there but decided against it.

Instead I burst out impulsively in a loud stage whisper, "Viva Zapata!" and immediately regretted it. Could they have heard me that far away? Alonso spun in the bow. Not everybody agreed with Marcos and the way the Indians had conducted their uprising, he reminded me, even Chiapas intellectuals. I was entitled to my romantic gringo fantasies, but I had no right to put him in jeopardy in such a remote place. If they decided to, man, the army could make things very hard for us.

I apologized immediately, and suggested that, technically, I had merely quoted a slogan of the revolution that belonged to all Mexicans. And in any case, I doubted they could hear us. It didn't matter, he said. Of all the places we needed to be cool, it was in sight of the army.

I observed chastened silence for half an hour, before David and Josh started razzing me. It dissolved the tension, though Alonso remained adamant.

Not far below Triunfo the river picked up speed, winding through separate channels and riffles, sometimes quickening into a class 1.5

rapid. The sierra drew closer to the river, looming to the northeast about a thousand feet above the river. Cayucos began appearing, tethered to shore, showing pronounced rocker for maneuvering in rapids, deep bodies, and flared prows. At one point we rounded a bend to see a paddler ferrying a cayuco across the river, a cow standing serenely amidships.

The mountains pressed close on either side, anticipating the canyon and increasing the sense of wildness and impending derangement. Cordan had referred to reports of Lacandons still evading contact in the area, implying he knew of some in the immediate vicinity of Cham Huitz, the highest summit in the Sierra del Caribe and sacred to both Lacandons and highland Mayas.

Such speculation harked back to the Chol Lacandons' 150-year resistance, when they were the "wild" Indians, heathen cannibals practicing unspeakable rites and surviving in elusive remnant bands after their official defeat.

Their persistence, or the belief in the persistence of some primal aborginal remnant, has fueled legends of various wild humanoids ever since. Nonbellicose modern Lacandons believed in cannibalistic people called lokin, "wooden men," subhuman castoffs from a previous, unsuccessful creation cycle (or possible Chol remnants) who lived deep in the forest and carried off children. Old Chan K'in's father had "seen" one of the last ones in the nineteenth century. Mexicans and Indians together believed in the duende, a sasquatch-like being with backward-facing feet which appeared to travelers lost in the jungle, usually with malign intent. (To Lorca and the Gypsies of southern Spain, duende was the death principle that enters a work of art at its sharpest, most piercing moment.)

To the highland Maya of Chamula and Zinacantán the modern Lacandon were themselves subhuman remnants, creatures of wood or mud instead of corn, no better than monkeys. They scourged effigies of tunic-clad Lacandons in their village festivals. Moises claimed to know of traditional Chol throwbacks hiding in the forest. No matter where you looked on the scale of cultural hierarchy, belief in a prior, inferior form of humanity persisted somewhere in the selva, waiting to supplant those among the "true men," the hach winik, who failed to honor the gods and the sacred contract.

Tales of lost cities, inhabited and uninhabited, reflected similar contorted memories and desires. Stephens encountered a friar in Guatemala who told of looking out over the selva from the Sierra Cuchumatan and seeing far off the pyramids and temples of a storied White City protruding above the canopy. Traven, Cordan, and Blom flirted with the idea. Even the unflappable scientists Maudslay, Maler, and Morley were not immune to it. Lacandons visited ruins and burned incense, fueling rumors. Discoveries like Bonampak in 1947, the three new cities on the Pasión in the sixties, and Site Q in just 1997 fed the flames. No matter how many ruins you could find on the map, another always awaited discovery.

Near the foot of Cham Huitz, on the biosphere reserve side of the river, we came upon four men resting on the bank in the shade, two of them mounted. The mounted pair slumped and smoked in their worn hulls, one on muleback, the other astride a handsome white horse. Buenas tardes, señores, we called, pulling to shore, cómo estás. Bien, they mumbled in unison, nodding. They all wore black rubber boots and jeans. Sí, they told us, smiling, the trail began at San Vicente, on the right, but we would never survive the canyon. The idea of running it in a canoe delighted them. You will die, they said, laughing. Some men—Mexicans, they called them—had tried to line a ponga loaded with arms upstream through the canyon a couple of years earlier, but the line had snapped and the boat had gotten away in the swift water. They had lost the boat, the arms. Men had died.

We talked some more, told them thank you, assured them our boats and skills were up to the task, and continued on. It was hard to know who had tried to bring arms upstream or why, but we assumed they were being carried to the Zapatistas from Guatemala up the Lacantún, a major route of contraband.

Soon the mountains drew close together up ahead. In the gloaming between them we spotted a narrow, muddy gravel bar on the right, at the head of a swift run. It was the only visible place to stop before the canyon. In the event that we found nothing better below, we would have been unable to paddle the canoe back up the swift run. We had seen no sign of San Vicente, and feared we had missed it.

Directly downstream, below the swift run, we saw a small beach with a single cayuco resting on it. Josh paddled down the riffles to check it out, landed on the beach, and disappeared up the trail. When he didn't reappear right away, we assumed he had found the village and began unpacking.

My solo whitewater skills were moderate in boats outfitted for the purpose with flotation bags, center seats, and thigh straps. In class 2-plus waters I could get down a rapid solo in a standard tandem canoe like the Freedom. With the Jatate running so high, however, and needing to carry some cargo, I faced a lot of unknowns. Without Alonso—and with a single-bladed rather than a double-bladed kayak paddle—I would lose considerable power, control, and maneuverability, and make up little in reduced weight.

Before dinner I placed one of the dry-packs loaded with clothes and sleeping bags under the center thwart and lashed it to the D rings on the floor. With the spray cover mounted, I would be unable to kneel in the normal solo position slightly astern of the center thwart—the position of stability and control for a solo paddler, where the weight balance would allow the maximum area of the bottom to touch the water and the bow would be elevated slightly to ride over waves. There, your power lay at the craft's pivot point rather than at the ends, and you braced and angled your way down a rapid.

The only solution I saw would be to face backwards on the bow seat, which was set closer amidships than the stern seat, and paddle the Freedom stern first. That would achieve the same weight-distribution effect.

I replaced the spray cover and sat in the bow cockpit facing stern first, approximating the normal solo position. The off-center spray skirt fit fairly well, though I couldn't tell how badly it would leak.

I practiced some solo turns, ferrying across a braid of current at the top of the swift run, leaned the canoe sharply, and eddied out into a bay in a small midriver island. Then I reversed the process, peeling out and bracing into the swift run. The Freedom pirouetted like a dancer. With the pack's low weight amidships, it remained steady no matter how far I leaned it over to one side.

I worked my way upstream, keeping to the eddies and surfing the small waves. The light paled in the cerulean sky. At the head of the island I rested behind a midstream rock, suspended in all the dimensions of space and fluid. Parrots flocked across the river, a flight of mealies followed by a smaller species, possibly green parakeets. The sun flashed in their feathers and nicked the summit of the forested sierra a thousand feet above.

Downstream Josh paddled up the swift run, working the eddies. I peeled out and negotiated the miniature rapid I had just paddled up, backing, bracing, crossing, and ferried back to camp. By then I had no fear of running solo through the canyon. Even if I swam we would avoid the time, possible expense, and labor of carrying the boat. At best, it would amount to my finest hour in canoeing.

Josh reported that the beach belonged to San Vicente—hardly a village, he said, more like a cluster of shacks in a cornfield. He had spoken to an elder who assured him we could hire a porter to help Alonso in the morning. The carry took an hour.

After dinner I sat with Josh on the inverted Freedom. The high water and our laborious lining and scouting had caused to us to run late, and he was concerned about our distance from Pico de Oro. He had to be in Palenque for his video shoot no later than the day after tomorrow, he said. We might have to pull a long haul.

While we talked, an old man and a boy launched the cayuco on the beach downstream. They started off ferrying together across the slack current opposite the beach, both standing, the taller man in the stern.

When we looked again, they had found an eddy along the opposite shore under the steep bank and high riparian trees. The man stood astern, the boy appeared to be fishing with a handline or a net.

The next time we looked, the man and the boy had worked their way up the river on the far side of the island. The moon had risen above the sierra and hovered there. They floated on the sun's low rays beaming down the river from the west. The light slammed against the forest wall behind them, magnifying the details of liana and mato palo on each tree—you could almost see the leaf-cutter ants parading up and down their trunks—and brought out their faces and the details of their boat. It was about sixteen feet long, short by cayuco standards, slightly hogged amidships like the ones we had seen earlier. Clearly it was designed for swift water and small rapids.

While the boy sat in the bow and fished, the man kept working the boat slowly upstream. Sometimes he used his cañalete as a pole, pushing against the bottom from the stern, or as a paddle to ferry from one eddy to another. Other times he leaned on the pole and let the boat pivot to the opposite eddy, where he would lean, plant the pole again, and let the boat swing across the current behind him. That way they moved steadily upstream and out of sight while the moon rose in the sky, the man in constant, fluid motion while the boy fished with his handline. I couldn't take my eyes off them. It was a virtuoso demonstration, a pas de deux between paddler and river, neither dominating, neither yielding. It had the effect of something we were meant to witness.

I was about to climb into my tent an hour later when the cayuco passed down the swift run near our shore on a stream of moonlight, the old man standing and paddling in the stern, solo. The boat, the man, the river, and the moon formed something iconic, just outside my conscious grasp. I wanted to own it, arrest it, and emblazon it in my mind, but I was tired. I took the picture mentally and crept inside to a moon-drenched sleep.

BY THE TIME I crawled out at first light Alonso had the water boiling and the air filled with incense from the last copal shavings. Mist obscured the river and the canyon. I stumbled to the water to consult the stick I had thrust into the riverbed at water level: overnight, after five days in spate, the river had receded three or four inches. It remained silty and opaque.

We were standing around waiting for the coffee to brew when a man and two boys walked out of the woods. We exchanged greetings and introduced ourselves. The man declined coffee and said they were from San Vicente. He examined our boats and asked where we were from and where we were going.

We told him I was headed for the gulf and that we were preparing to run the canyon. He paused politely and said, If you can. We asked if the village could supply a guide and bearer for Alonso. Sí, we can do that, he said.

Parrots flew across the river and we remarked on them together. I asked him if there were guacamayas (macaws) in the area. No, he said. There were tigres (jaguars) and monos (howler monkeys), however. The hunting was good.

He said the canyon was muy peligroso, very dangerous. Josh answered, Nosotros gustan lugares peligrosos, We like dangerous places. Ah, sí, he said. He reiterated the story of the lost ponga and arms shipment and we told him we had heard about it.

I asked how he felt about the biosphere reserve. It didn't bother him, he said—he paid it no mind. He wanted to know about employment in the States. There is much work there, yes? Construction or farm labor, I said, but it was far away and hard to get in. Claro, he said. It's very tranquilo, peaceful, here.

Bueno, pues. We told him we'd pack up and paddle down to San Vicente within the hour. All shook hands and told each other mucho gusto. He rounded up his boys from where they played on the Freedom and they disappeared back into the woods.

Immediately Josh paddled to San Vicente to line up Alonso's porter.

We packed and within half an hour drifted down the swift run to the beach. When we got there, Josh was sitting on the sand, waiting.

All the men were gone, he said. Nobody in the whole village but a few women who didn't speak Spanish.

Well, we had to try again, I said, hoping we could work it out. The men couldn't be far, could they?

David would wait with the boats, we decided, while the rest of us walked to San Vicente.

The sun had already steamed the mist off the river. I smeared sun-block on my face and took my fifteen-dollar polarized fly-fishing shades out of my life-jacket pocket. One of the lenses had come loose and delaminated. In my hand were two plastic lenses and a tinted, filmy cellophane layer that went between them, probably the "polar-izing" layer. I discarded the cellophane and fitted the two other lenses back in place. It seemed to work.

We climbed the bank and followed the trail into a wall of cornstalks eight to ten feet tall. After ten minutes we reached an elevated clearing of about two acres where a chorus of small spotted dogs with longish legs and flat faces greeted us. A quadrangle of eight to ten jacales—small, rustic houses with outbuildings and yards fenced with poles lashed together—surrounded the clearing. They in turn stood inside a forty- or fifty-acre maizal (corn plantation), recently cleared, with blackened trunks still protruding above the stalks. The dark walls of the forest rose at least three hundred yards off. In its present embodiment, at least, San Vicente could not have been standing there for long.

We elected Alonso as spokesman. Asking permission from an ancient abuela, we let ourselves through the gate into one of the rough courtyard enclosures. Alonso took the lead; Josh and I hung back. For some reason we had all left our life jackets on. Alonso wore his big-hat, shorts, and sneakers. I had on a green ball cap, black shorts, nylon sandals. There were big red sores on my knees and elbows. My vision was slightly skewed by the altered and smudged lenses of my shades.

The family confronted us with enormous bravery, it appeared, though their faces were rigid with fear. The tiny abuela couldn't have been taller than four ten. Like her daughters and granddaughters, she wore the black wool skirt and embroidered blue huipil of Tzotzil-speaking Mayas from San Juan Chamula. Her feet were wide and bare, and her toes gripped the dry dust of the courtyard. She stood defensively at the head of her brood, which included two or three daughters and daughters-in-law ranging from fifteen to about twenty-two, numerous naked infants and toddlers, and two boys of ten or twelve who regarded us with fascination as if we were really Michael Jordan, Pancho Villa, and Subcomandante Marcos.

Alonso removed his hat and commenced the required small talk, shifting back and forth between Spanish and Tzeltal, which the old woman spoke about as well as he did. (Tzotzil and Tzeltal are linguistic neighbors.) It took forever. While they chatted, the dogs kept barking at us and the boys cavorted, trying to attract our attention. The daughters stood in the rear, one nursing an infant, another going about her chores. The sun bore down. A pig lay in the dust, some chickens scratched. An enormous gobbler strutted and displayed for our benefit.

The abuela shook her head back and forth, locked in negativity. To a question from Alonso, she waved toward the distant forest. En el monte, she said. Muy lejos, she said. No sé.

We understood that. The men were all gone to the forest clearing land. She didn't know where they were, but it was a long way off. She didn't know when they'd be back.

She stood her ground before Alonso's importunings. Could anyone show us the trail? She waved toward the woods in a downstream direction. (Down there!) I told Alonso to ask if we could hire one of the boys, the older one, to carry some light equipment. I crudely showed my wallet and mentioned pesos, something in the range of five to ten dollars. I thought that would seem like a fortune to them. The boy perked up, eager to take on a man's job with these apparitions and pocket some cash. But she kept shaking her head no. It was too dangerous. We got the picture. The men of San Vicente had answered yes to all our questions, decided we were trouble, and cleared out, leaving grandma in charge. She was clearly no slouch.

We apologized for troubling them and began to leave when the older daughter, the one who had kept about her chores, said there was a man working on his roof at one of the other houses. She left it at that, but implied we might try talking to him. We thanked her, thanked the abuela, and backed out of the enclosure.

The man's house lay a few yards away through the corn. We came out in the yard where a tiny mother of no more than sixteen met us. She wore the traje of Chamula and bore at her breast an infant who watched us sidelong while nursing. Behind them stood a house of split hardwood planks with a caved-in roof of thatch. Her husband sat astride the ridgepole beside a gaping hole, dolefully pondering his fate. He looked hungover.

Alonso repeated his performance. He asked if we could speak to her husband. He's busy, she answered, though she retreated a few steps toward the house. Once again, even more crassly than before, I waved pesos at her. Dinero, I said. She shrunk back.

The woman turned and stepped into the shadow of the crumbling house. She spoke to her husband, standing on her toes and calling toward him in a loud stage whisper. He looked up from his work, at which he made small progress, and appeared ready to consider our request. He was in his early twenties, not the community's brightest bulb, I suspected, but the village's sole adult male at the moment. He seemed surprised to hear Tzeltal emanating from Alonso. He listened, a fog of bewilderment clouding his features.

At this point I opened my wallet even wider. Tell him fifteen dollars, twenty, I told Alonso. I didn't care if I was being vulgar. Cash, I was sure, would smooth our way. I removed some gaudy peso notes and waved them while Alonso transmitted my request. I thought the man twitched just perceptibly at the cash offer. Mom, however, stood fast.

She whispered upward toward him emphatically. You didn't have to be a linguist to understand what she was saying: They'd been living without a roof since the rain quit. It was time for him to fix it, no excuses, before the rain returned. These gringos would never pay him what they offered, and might leave him bloody and beaten at the end of the trail.

When she finished, the clearing throbbed with a painful, embarrassing silence. The air darkened with the accumulated gloom of four centuries of cultural miscues and solitudes. We were goblins, spacemen, Vikings—duendes and lokin combined. We were Cortés, Tonatiuh (Alvarado), Mazariejos (Chamula's conqueror), banditos gringos, devils who seduced with offers of money before murdering the parents, enslaving the children, and devouring the corn.

The man wore an expression of long suffering. Ceding defeat, we apologized, bid them adios, and turned down the trail. Vaya con Dios, said the man, graciously. Gracias, we replied, looking back and waving.

All it meant, I decided, walking down the trail, was that I would carry a slightly larger load in the Freedom, Alonso a smaller one. The man on the roof had said the trail was easy to follow. The villagers didn't object to Alonso passing through to reach it.

At the beach I repacked the Freedom and had already set aside a single pack for Alonso when I looked up and saw Alonso and Josh off to the side, talking privately. After a moment, Alonso came over to the Freedom.

Put that stuff back, he said. Josh says we can do it, so let's do it.

For a split second I was crestfallen—there went my chance for whitewater immortality. Relief followed just as quickly, but I moderated my reaction. None of us wanted to make too big a deal out of it, but we were all happy, Josh and David as much as Alonso and I. The right choice had been made by the person who had to make it, without ridicule or pressure. Nobody felt bad. In my experience of such situations, this one was exceptional.

My hero, I said.

We refitted carefully and launched on the brown and roiled though falling river. The head of Cañon Colorado lay a hundred yards down-stream. Unmatched, my lenses impaired my binocular vision, so I dropped the shades to my chest on their neck cord. We made ourselves comfortable, tightened the drawstrings on our spray covers. I went over some basic principles with Alonso: get your right and left straight, keep your head pointed at the sky, lean downstream no matter what.

Then we were in it—Josh leading the way, David behind as sweep. The current piled up against a wall on the right, bounced off into a long, narrow sluice to the left. Josh disappeared into the left-hand sluice. The current accelerated and wanted to slam us against the wall. I angled the boat slightly away from it, we leaned just a few degrees *toward* it and dug in with our paddles. The wall slid by.

Ahead of us the morning light shone through a long, narrow chute of five-foot waves. The channel had shrunk from about two hundred feet to thirty feet across. The gradient increased, the current speed went from three miles an hour to close to twelve. It felt like being shot through a hose nozzle. We plowed through some of the waves; others we rode up and over and into the trough on the opposite side, alternately paddling and bracing.

The close-set walls sped past, scalloped and scoured like the canyon of the Santa Cruz, tree limbs nearly joining overhead. After fifty yards, water sloshed in the boat and in the skirt, elevating our center of gravity. We braced continually. To keep the boat straight I undermaneuvered, so we just clipped the eddy lines of two hydraulics.

After five to ten minutes I saw Josh waving his paddle from an eddy downstream. We were getting heavy and needed to bail. The eddy lay on the inside of a long flat between rapids. We avoided a last hydraulic, made the turn, and paddled hard to pull ourselves up the eddy's long skirt. After a moment of struggle we reached the calm water and floated beside Josh. David turned in sharply behind us.

We bailed in silence, breathing heavily. Josh said we were about halfway through. It had been somewhat easier than we had expected, yet all we could handle, a continuous class 3-plus, pushing the limit for canoeing but intermediate for skilled kayakers. I told Alonso he was bracing like a champ.

As I looked around, the canyon seemed narrower and not as deep as I had thought it would be, more like a tube or culvert a hundred feet in diameter with a thirty-foot slot cut out of the top. The 1980 hydro survey had located one of the proposed dams precisely at its mouth.

Blom had marked minor ruins just below the canyon, and around the mouth of the Río Ixcan, which flowed in from Guatemala just to the south, one of which Cordan roughly mapped. Little or no work had been done in the area since then. The proximity of the canyon's mouth—the terminus of a carrying place, and the head of upstream navigation on the Lacantun—and the mouth of the Ixcan, one of the main upstream routes to the highland resources, would have given the vicinity strategic and commercial importance predating the classical era. A dam, it goes without saying, would cancel the possibility of more extensive archaeology in the area.

The second half of the canyon reprised the first. We couldn't avoid one hydraulic and pounded our way through, emerging full of water in the skirt and belowdecks, wallowing dangerously. The hole had pushed us out of the main current into an indistinct, nebulous swirl. We bounced along, half in, half out of the current, until the remolino pulled us off-line toward the left-hand wall. I pried on the right and called to Alonso to lean and draw right, which he did to no avail.

Water sloshed in the boat. I saw us approaching a ledge and reversed our direction, calling for Alonso to switch sides and draw left. While I ruddered in the stern we swiveled slowly 180 degrees to the left until we faced upstream. The current swept us stern first at top speed down the canyon.

I kept reminding Alonso to lean downstream and brace. We inched our way left until we had turned 360 degrees and climbed back atop the waves. Just in time we straightened out and shot the eddy line around the hole on the right.

Still the waves came, and we braced, braced to stay upright just a lit-tle longer. It got harder; we were tired. Below us the placid surface of the Lacantun came in view, flanked by high forest, but two rapids remained to go. Down there Josh again waved his paddle from an eddy.

We ran the two rapids without incident and plowed through the last hole, the boat foundering sickeningly one way, then the other. But it was over. The walls spread open like the mouth of a bell. We slid off the right hand edge of the waves, gingerly crossed the eddy line, and paddled hard to reach the calm water tucked just underneath the final ledge. If we had swamped at that point, I wouldn't have cared.

Before we even stopped paddling we were laughing and hooting hysterically, venting an enormous amount of pent-up anxiety. From here on everything got easier. The river ahead bore a different name than the one that had just ended, even though the second proceeded from the first. The next significant whitewater, the Roudales de Anaite, lay a hundred miles downstream, below Yaxchilan.

By the time David pulled in behind us, we had removed the spray cover and toasted each other from our water bottles. We drifted in the eddy, loafing, and went over the run yard by yard: the odd light, the unending wave trains, the near misses, the incredible speed of the current, the three-sixty.

We heaped praise on Alonso, who had undergone an ordeal by water, swum in class 4 rapids, opted out and then, by inexorable logic, back in, and performed flawlessly and without whining.

Now he took his place beside Blom, Traven, Maler, and all the selva's self-appointed explorers and interpreters. Not one of them, including Cordan, had run Cañón Colorado at any water level. Josh and a handful of kayakers had done it, but nobody as far as we knew had made it in a tandem open canoe with or without a cover. Among living Chiapanecos, that distinction belonged to him.

He turned around in the Freedom and faced the stern, leaning back against the bow decks and stretching his feet out on the dry-packs, smiling. Josh and David floated beside us, holding on to the Freedom.

The sun had risen higher and grown in strength. I lifted my shades on their neck cord and absentmindedly put them on. They seemed to work, though with the same binocular distortion as before.

Man, what happened to your lens? Alonso said.

I told him the polarizing layer had come out, but they were better than nothing.

Man, your whole lens is out, he said. You look like a cyclops or something.

I took them off and held them before me. The lens I had replaced that morning had disappeared. I mentally followed my tracks from the moment I had discarded the cellophane and repaired the lens. In fact, the glasses had never really worked any better than they did now. I must have lost the lens right after fixing it and not noticed. My brain had compensated for the exposed eye, making it seem like I had 50 percent protection, only on both sides.

Which means the lens must have been missing the whole time we were in San Vicente, I said.

It sure was gone when you got back from the village, David said. I didn't want to say anything because I thought you knew.

Jesus, no wonder everybody seemed so afraid of me.

Alonso laughed. We were like aliens to them, he said. By now they think you're either dead or a god. They're talking about the one-eyed god who came to kidnap their babies and sacrifice them to the canyon. They'll talk about that for years: the Time When El Ojo Came.

We disintegrated in laughter. We laughed arrogantly. We laughed for making it. We laughed for the spectacle we had made, bullying around in bizarre get-ups, beyond civilized witness, like trees falling in a forest observed by other trees. We laughed at the expense of the Chamulan pioneers whose lives we had disrupted, who may have kept custody of the ancient caves of Cham Huitz across the river, who may have grown a little pot on the side for cash (Alonso suspected), whose men probably fought as Zapatistas and viewed us suspiciously, concerned for their anonymity. Why had we asked about the wildlife, what was our concern about the biosphere reserve? What was our angle? We must have had an angle. Why else would we be there, in the current climate of fear and repression, dressed as clowns, as demons?

We laughed as cosmopolitan, self-important, imperious canoe merchants—sexually ambiguous enema-takers and toad-lickers—may have laughed at the rubes who peopled the outposts, the settlers, the pious farmers.

Nine

THE LACANTUN

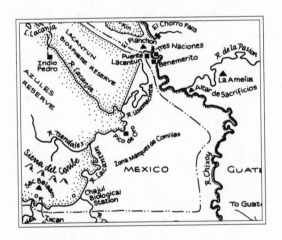

ANCIENT TRADERS COULD NEVER HAVE RUN THE CANYON AT ITS
present volume. At normal dry-season levels, however, you
couldn't say categorically one way or the other. In the shorter rock-
ered cayucos like the ones we had seen yesterday, young hotshots
might have tried anything.

The flood had impaired my appraisal of the trade route's ancient
viability below La Sultana, but only slightly. Geography still supported the idea, as did the Olmec carving at Xoc, the deployment of

ruins, the named rapids, the little clues of the carry trails and appropriately designed cayucos. Once long-range traders were headed
downstream from Toniná, I was sure, little would have thwarted
them—not the prospect of waiting out a flood, of running, lining, or
poling down a rapid at normal water levels, nor even of launching
empty boats through the canyon, à la Cordan, and walking around.

The descent thus far, including the vehicular approach to the put-in,
had begun to show me the arc of the land, the relationships of scale
and distance at the watershed's upper reaches—its "form." Already I
had put a large measure of the journey's anticipated uncertainties
behind me. The visible habitat losses were no worse than I had
expected, in some cases not as bad, and the people, while immobilized
by politics and habit, showed an awareness of their limits and the need
for change. Beauty still governed in the cañadas and Montes Azules.

Miramar's villagers especially remained canoe-centered, while
straddling the transition from one world to the next—on our last day
they had even requested a Freedom of their own as formal economic
aid. Their attachment to place and their effort to protect it encouraged me. Now I wanted to reach the forest-dwelling CPRs near El
Desempeño, whom Tammy Ridenour had visited, 150 miles downstream, and hear from them.

Only one big uncertainty remained (that I knew of), though a couple of weeks of clear sailing lay ahead before I needed to confront it.

The head of the Lacantun told its own story. The Jatate poured out
of the canyon as out of a tunnel. Here, travelers moving upstream
would have reached the head of navigation and been forced to turn
around unless they lined up or carried around the canyon. From
below, you could see how the Jatate and the interior it drained
would have appeared an impenetrable refuge, the Jatate an entirely
separate river.

Immediately below the canyon the channel widened by hundreds
of feet. Macaws flew across the river over our heads; three together,
their colors muted against the sun and their long tails trailing behind.

The river was still cloudy and high from the Tzaconejá, but unruffled. The Guatemalan border lay four or five miles south, and we would approach within a mile of it a little farther downstream.

I watched unsuccessfully for crocodiles and endangered white turtles, a species endemic to the upper Usumacinta whose eggs and meat were a local delicacy. Ignacio March, a wildlife biologist in San Cristóbal, had told me the turtles were staging comebacks in the area, after being nearly wiped out by market and subsistence hunting in the sixties and seventies. But floodwater drowned the gravel bars and mudbanks where the species would have congregated and made themselves visible.

The name Lacantun derives from the original name of Lake Miramar, Lacam-Tun—"Standing Stone" in Maya. Its commoner form, "Lacandon," applies to the lowland forest on the Chiapas side of the Usumacinta, a mountain range flanking the river in Guatemala, and to both groups of unconverted, furtive Mayas who held out in its fastnesses at separate though overlapping historical periods.

Not far inland and downstream the Chol Lacandons of Miramar made their last stand in Sac-Balam, a remote village located on a level savanna just over the Cerro Los Gemelos to our left, where they had moved to escape the Spanish marauders. Jan de Vos confidently placed it about halfway between the mouths of the ríos Ixcan and Chajul. Modern Lacandons, such as Chan Bor, lived along the Lacantún as recently as the 1950s.

A Franciscan missionary, Antonio Margil de Jesús, found the Lacandons at Sac-Balam in 1694, decades after they abandoned Miramar. The Indians sent him packing and he appealed to the authorities in Guatemala to retaliate, bringing on the three-pronged entrada of 1695, in which forces left simultaneously from Chiapas, Huehuetenango, and Verapaz. The troops from "Hue-hue" got there first, following the Río Ixcan downstream to the Lacantun from the Cuchumatan Mountains, capturing Sac-Balam on Good Friday, 1695, without resistance. They changed the town's name to Nuestra Señora de Dolores, "Our Lady of Sorrows." The Lacandons were "converted," and Dolores made into a Mercedarian mission with an armed force of thirty soldiers. Soon the Indians started dying from disease. Many of the survivors slipped away.

IN 1714 DOLORES was decommissioned and the Lacandons removed over the Cuchumatans to the town of Retalhuleu. In 1769 a census there found only three left alive.

The Lacandons of Sac-Balam had been considerably reduced even before their defeat. Unlike Lacam-Tun/Miramar, their new village had no stone temples or palaces and no regular priesthood. They performed ceremonies in a house restricted to men, called the "god house," like modern Lacandons. Their clan leaders or chieftans acted as shamans, also like modern Lacandons. Spanish records preserved these leaders' names—Cali, Canan, Cuat, Chan, Batz, Itzquin, Quetzal, Zelu—some extant in the region.

They lived in pole-and-thatch houses and were great milperos, growing maize, beans, chiles, plantains, sweet potatoes, jicamas, plums, cultivated zapotes, cacao, and pineapples, among numerous other plants. By the time of their subjugation they had apparently given up human sacrifice, instead sprinkling turkey blood and copal incense on pine sticks, then burning the stick. They kept howler and spider monkeys, macaws, and probably curassows. Pet coatimundis would have been useful for controlling snakes, scorpions, and other vermin.

We don't know to what extent the Chol Lacandons interacted with long-range canoe traders from the gulf, if at all. We do know their lives revolved around navigating lakes and rivers by cayuco, and that they frequented the Jatate and Lacantun and their tributaries on raids against their traditional enemies, the Itzas of Tayasal, and the Christian towns of the highlands. In the postclassic period, they are the ones most likely to have run Cañón Colorado on a regular basis.

Depending on whether you believe accounts of a 1537 expedition, the 1695 entrada also mounted a European first descent of the Lacantun and beyond. After installing the garrison at Dolores, commander Jacobo de Alcayága ordered fifteen "pirogues" to be built from logs. He wanted to learn the route by which Lacandons traveled by cayuco to attack the villages of Peten-Itza, and explore the "Great River of the Lacandons"—the Lacantun—in the process.

The party launched on March 4. According to the Dominican chronicler Villagutiere Soto-Mayor, the party traveled downstream thirty-two leagues, landing frequently. At the river's mouth, a notoriously murky zone geographically and historically, Villagutiere says they turned right, *up*stream into a larger river, the Usumacinta. They then navigated a further 140 leagues, stopping often and finding a huge city with stone foundations.

No one has ever been entirely certain, however, which direction Alcayága traveled from the mouth of the Lacantun. Villagutiere's distances are notoriously unreliable. Morley asserts the city they found may have been Seibal, but doubts it. Maler says it was most certainly Yaxchilan, though Yaxchilan is only fifteen leagues below the mouth of the Lacantun. Peter Mathews discredits both theories.

All that is known is that Alcayága paddled from the Lacantun into a larger river—the Usumacinta, Pasión, or Chixoy—and found some ruins. The expedition consumed fifty-seven days.

Soon the mouth of the Río Ixcan, the route of the 1695 entrada, appeared on our right, sweeping across the Lacantun like a big mountain river, pushing the currents of both rivers to the left and piling them against the bank. High water had deposited enormous sweepers (floating logs) on the gravel beds that flanked its mouth and against the opposite bank of the Lacantun. The current speeded up and swept around a wide bend to the right.

In the last decade, racial and ethnic bloodshed had again followed the Ixcan and Chajul rivers down from the highlands. In the sixties and seventies, highland Mayas from Guatemala's Cuchumatan Mountains had settled in the forests along the lower Ixcan and Chajul, seeking land and a measure of distance from the strife going on at home. Many came from the notorious Ixil Triangle, a region suspected of high guerrilla concentrations surrounding three mountain villages at the Chajul headwaters. In fact, like the region along the Usumacinta near Piedras Negras, the remote rain forests of the lower Ixcan and Chajul did attract significant numbers of rebels, and CPRs, their social base.

In the early eighties, the Guatemalan government, frustrated at failing to eradicate rebels from the mountains and jungles, started terrorizing CPRs located on the lower reaches of both rivers, and farther west along the border, near the Santo Domingo headwaters, in an effort to cut off their support system. Contemporary reports said the communities suffered bombing raids, torture, and mass executions.

At the same time Mayas at home in the Cuchumatans suffered forced relocations. Villages in the Ixil Triangle were razed and their people moved to new state population centers—basically concentration camps. Refugees streamed over the border, establishing improvised camps all along the Lacantun. The river, always a route of contraband, became a conduit for rebel movements and arms shipments.

In all, at least fifty thousand Maya fled Guatemala. During the resettlement campaign, so many refugees poured in along the Lacantun that the Mexican army and immigration department closed the river to any but local boat traffic. The Guatemalan army attacked refugee camps, and cross-border skirmishes became common.

In 1985 Mexican immigration officers held Cully Erdman and one of his crews in a Lacantun refugee camp for three days, while confirming their disinterest in the conflict. While they waited, Erdman watched Guatemalan artillery shell Mexican camps from emplacements across the border, as well as aerial flyovers and bombings by the Guatemalan air force. In 1985, officers detained a National Geographic Society expedition near the mouth of the river for twenty-four hours. An article on that expedition, written by archaeologist Jefferey Wilkerson, later made the public aware of the Usumacinta and its political, environmental, and economic currents.

The border, always porous, turned to cheesecloth. Some of the refugees earned immigrant status and settled along the Lacantun. The more restless or fugitive of them filtered up the Jatate, deeper toward the heart of Montes Azules and its solitudes, reprising age-old retreats to the Lacandon wilderness. In turn, lowland settlers in Chiapas absorbed the liberation politics that had been thrust upon their Guatemalan cousins by history (and the left), and inclined toward the indigenous movement then attracting adherents in the caves and mountains—the Zapatistas. Previously, the idea of a pan-Maya identity had not caught on because of geography, self-interest, and local rivalries. The cross-border exchanges of the eighties fostered a new ethnic solidarity.

Early in the peace process, most of the refugees reentered Guatemala under UN protection and began rebuilding, but the true horror of those years is just becoming known. One of the last Guatemalan military campaigns before the cease-fire attacked an innocent village on the lower Ixcan. Many of the army massacre sites investigated by forensic anthropologists have been located in the Ixcan-Chajul lowlands. One of those farthest west, near the Santo Domingo, consisted of half a dozen mass graves in the shadows of some minor pyramids, each containing dozens of bludgeoned and gunshot bodies, primarily of women and children.

We stopped at a Conservation International ecotourist hostel going up on the left just below the Ixcan, and spoke with the architect and project coordinator, a Japanese-Mexican named Toshiro Culebro. Builders from an ejido across the river worked on a geodesic-dome-like structure of concrete and beams Culebro had designed, and other workers dug terraces in the steep bank for tent sites. Below, sweeping panoramas stretched up and down the Lacantun, and up the Ixcan toward the Cuchumatan Mountains, rising blue in the distance.

The hostel would be managed by members of the nearby ejido, he said, and the proceeds would benefit the community school and health center. Visitors would fly or take a bus to Pico de Oro and ride a lancha upstream from there, sleeping in beds or hammocks in the main building or pitching tents. Local Indians would cook and guide birding and hiking expeditions. As yet, no trails had been cut into the biosphere reserve, Culebro said, but the lodge would be ready for guests within a month.

Soon after we left Ixcan, the Lacantun reached its southernmost extent, almost in sight of the Guatemalan border, turned ninety degrees to the northeast, and began winding its way back toward the Usumacinta.

We had decided to get as close to Pico de Oro as possible that day, to ensure my rendezvous with Todd Kelsey and Josh's timely return to Palenque. We drifted along at two or three miles an hour, headed for the ecological research station opposite the mouth of the Chajul. The left bank was an undifferentiated continuum of high, gleaming forest; the right bank a scrubby mass of milpas, orchards, patches of forest, and small ranches. Macaws kept flying over at regular intervals, trading sides of the river like smugglers, or agents of undetermined affiliation.

We paddled through late afternoon, the light softening, the adrenaline of the canyon long since worn off, losing track of where we were. By three o'clock, when we had not arrived at Chajul, we began to doubt we could make Pico, though the river continued pushing us along at a good rate. Time and distance expanded and contracted. We were getting tired, but not so tired we couldn't keep going, if necessary.

The Chajul appeared suddenly, sneaking in on the right through the high bank and mature timber. Opposite the mouth and slightly downstream appeared the landing for the ecological station at the foot of a high bank. We grounded our boats on a narrow beach beside a big lancha and an aluminum motorboat and climbed the stairs.

On top stood a small palapa with bunks and hammocks overlooking the river, and a limestone obelisk marking the biosphere reserve, all shaded by tall trees. A large wooden sign announced the aid and spon-sorship of Grupo Pulsar, the Japanese conglomerate and one of numerous multinationals, like Corona, vying for resource access to the selva. A wooden walkway led a hundred yards across a low, wet area to the station proper: a collection of palapas, metal laboratory buildings, and an outdoor kitchen arrayed around a clearing in the forest.

From here, wildlife biologist Ignacio March had led a 1990 trek north across the biosphere reserve to the settlement of Indio Pedro to take a rapid visual assessment, in biological terms, of the reserve's interior, its wildlife, and the impact of illegal hunting and logging. The party included the writer Peter Canby, Archibald "Chuck" Carr III of the Wildlife Conservation Society, and local guides.

The crossing took nine days, and they were more or less "lost" from the moment they stopped walking upstream along the Río Tzendales and struck out overland. They carried minimum equipment and food, forgoing tents and sleeping bags in favor of hammocks and tarps, and followed a compass heading north, reasoning that by keeping one of the northwest-to-southeast–running ridge spines on their right they would emerge near their destination. From ground level, however, the landforms and stream courses grew progressively more confusing, the ridgelines on the map got mixed up with the ones missing from the map. Small rivers blocked their progress where none were expected. Entire untenanted valleys and ranges had to be crossed where the group had thought Indio Pedro would be.

Yet along the way they saw spectacular morpho butterflies. A jaguar visited their camp at night, coming so close Canby could feel its breath on his face. A stampeding herd of endangered white-lipped peccaries forced them into the trees. They found signs of tapirs, and encountered many of the commoner insects, primates, and reptiles associated with Montes Azules, including an obligatory close call with a fer-de-lance. And by keeping to their compass heading they eventu-ally emerged at Indio Pedro as they had planned, where numerous families had just settled, encroaching on the reserve's wild core.

The Chajul station's manager, Ricardo Hernandes, said that while our visit pleased him, he was too busy to meet us. A Mexico City rock band, Los Jaguares, had just helicoptered in to make a video at a small ruin in the nearby selva, and he had to oversee the shoot.

He invited us to a party that evening and gave us a guide, a young Lacandon from Lacanjá named Enrico Chan K'in, who would show us around and take us for a walk in the woods. Enrico Chan K'in wore his hair short and was dressed in a T-shirt, jeans, and sneakers. He told us he wanted to study wildlife biology in college so he could come to understand his home place from both the traditional and western scientific points of view.

Twenty feet down the trail we entered the filtered, purified twilight of the deep selva. The temperature plummeted and the acoustics at once clarified and dampened, yet in the background you could discern the low throb of the universal, unmediated organpipe of evolved life echoing back to the Cretaceous, barely audible, impossible to dismiss.

We followed Enrico Chan K'in over the bare, black-dirt trails through the shade, stepping over ranks of leaf-cutter ants. Mato palo and liana vines depended like beaded veils from the canopy, dispersing the thin light. Somewhere, far off, howler monkeys roared.

WE ATE A leisurely dinner and drank two pots of coffee on the high bank overlooking the Lacantun and the mouth of the Chajul, resting for the long haul while the moon peeked above the ceibas across the river. An old staffer at the station came over and shared gossip about the Jaguars' visit and the excellence of Pico's Guatemalan whores. He said Ricardo Hernandes had seen an ocelot a few feet from where we sat, in broad daylight, that very afternoon.

We waited for the sun to disappear, then set off. The air cooled. The river ran in a strange twilight, part milky lunescence and part sunset afterglow. Gradually the moon rose higher, displacing the sun and reflecting off the river before us. We formed a rank with the canoe in the middle and the kayaks aflank. Occasionally one of the boats strayed to the side a hundred feet or so, fading to a shadow, then to nothing, inducing castaway feelings in the rest of us. For the most part we stayed together, speaking only when necessary to keep track of each other or to consider questions of river navigation.

Venus and Jupiter materialized in the darkening indigo vault over-head, amid pale outlying stars. We paddled easily, the river moving swiftly through the dark galleries. At twenty-minute or half-hour intervals we converged, held each other's boats as we rested and let the river carry us. The current flowed mostly flat and soundless, at least two hundred yards wide, wider in places. We watched carefully for sweepers, snags, and the odd riffle or class 1 or 1-plus rapid, dis-covering them chiefly by sound, but also by peering into the thin moonlight. A dull liquid roar revealed their approach, and we all looked toward the sound until one of us spotted the offending tangle of branches or tree trunk and directed the others away from it.

The rapids came up silently, most of them simple waves or riffles that we ran without incident, though in a state of heightened, ecstatic awareness.

My mind wandered as the moon rose higher and sharpened in focus. A Lacandon might have said my soul left my body and wan-dered abroad.

Mile after mile we paddled, every so often lying back against the decks, gazing skyward, talking softly. Darkness swathed both banks, the canopy silhouetted against the sky. On the right we passed occa-sional ranchos, former monterías, the moon gleaming on their metal or tile roofs, yet no lights within and no one outside. Ceibas stood ghostlike against the sky. A dog barked.

Evening turned to midnight. The moon shrank, became sharp and clear, its light eclipsing the stars except for the Milky Way. Somewhere we passed the mouth of the Tzendales, flowing in through the forest on the left. Sounds started coming from that direction, far away at first, muffled and low: roars, screeches, whistles. Then the canopy grew higher, the river slowed and narrowed, and the sounds grew louder and more intense. The howler monkeys' calls stood out, sounding savage, however benign their purpose. Separate voices, harder to identify, wove in and out of the howlers' chorus, some lower in pitch and timbre, others higher, louder; more muted, melodic, horrific. The grand finale reached a crescendo that lasted for an hour. We identified—or imagined we did—the calls of crocodiles, macaws, and coyotes; the cries of lokin and duendes, dying Spaniards, rebelling monteneros, and, we thought more than once, the low cough of the jaguar. Depending on your point of view, it was either a hellish or an angelic concert. To us, its captive audience, it was both; loud enough to be not just heard but felt, simultaneously unnerving and mesmerizing. After an hour of it we were as thoroughly unhinged as if we had eaten every psychotropic mushroom in the Zona Marqués de Comillas, or ingested them through other, more fundamental orifices.

All night we followed the moon across the heavens. Six, eight hours passed. If one of us had suggested, risking ridicule, that we had uncoupled from earthly gravity and paddled among the galaxies, he might have found agreement from the others. Every sense stimulus supported the notion. Everything told us the strata of creation had been upended, we had "entered the road" and commerced among Otherworldly manifestations, accompanied by the gods and their terrible voices.

It was the kind of episode you could find recounted from Point Barrow to Tierra del Fuego, and that you could probably find prefigured among tribal people in Siberia and Southeast Asia, a primal exercise of Stone Age pedigree, predating and erasing any notion of recreation. You could easily imagine African or Asian tribes, compelled by necessity or a perverse appetite to devour geography, conveying dugout technology with them from west to east, forgetting and remembering it, improving it over millennia, until they used it to people Australia and Polynesia fifty thousand years ago; and following seals, whales, salmon, and waterfowl along the southern rim of the land bridge, down the coast of the new world, twenty, forty thousand years ago, as some were now suggesting, traveling on calm waters under the moon when the opportunity arose. By all means these were creators, these progenitors who carried human consciousness to the western hemisphere in canoes.

Around 1 A.M. a veil drifted out of the east (the direction of prevailing weather) and softened the edges of the moon and the planets. The return to "normal" awareness jarred us. We drifted off in our boats, and despaired of reaching Pico de Oro. No campsites appeared. We drifted back and forth across the permeable veil of consciousness, between waking and sleep, the rational and the suprarational, like macaws crossing a river from one nation to the other.

Around two Alonso spotted a fan of bulldozed cobbles extending into the river. We dozed there until dawn, our tents pitched precariously in the softball-sized stones, neither quite asleep nor exactly awake.

Alonso roused us with the coffee already made. I stood beside him and drank it in the overcast dawn while macaws and parrots crossed the river in flocks. Josh and David stumbled over, took away their coffee, and went back to strike their tents.

Within half an hour we launched again, sloppily packed, aching and sore. We filtered water into our bottles straight from the river and drank deeply to restore our fluids. On the right-hand bank pastoral scrubland mixed with constuction debris. We heard machinery roaring and figured Pico must be close by.

Ranch buildings began appearing more frequently along the right shore. Then the town came in sight, a few buildings atop a high bank to the right. We landed on a muddy, slimy verge at the base of the steep bank.

At the top of the bank lay a grassy parklike area, some overturned boats, and a street leading to a small commercial center a couple of hundred yards away. I wandered around, dazed with exhaustion, looking for Todd.

By the time I slid back down the bank, a marine patrol boat had pulled up to the Freedom, the officer talking to Josh. Six or eight typical Indian recruits, kids holding M-16s and other U.S. government issue, sat in the motorized inflatable wearing passive expressions and life jackets. They looked at us and our boats with shy but undisguised fascination while Josh and the officer chatted. It was the matter of a body, a drowning reported the night before, according to the officer. No, Josh said, we haven't seen it. Ah, bueno, the officer replied, glancing upward in my direction. They exchanged small talk and the officer thanked us, gave an order to the soldier at the outboard, and they putted away upstream.

The encounter disoriented us even more than we already were. Josh walked to the centro to ask after a bus or a camioneta to Palenque. The others joined him while I stayed with the boats and began hauling equipment to the top of the bank.

The Freedom rested near a rill that drained gray and bilious-looking into the river. I sat on the stern peak and washed and dressed my sores. I hurt everywhere and couldn't decide if I was feeling spent or built up by the week's exertions. A little of both, probably, with a large dose of overload thrown in.

I lay across the packs amidships and closed my eyes, returning for a short time to a hypnagogic state. When I opened my eyes, the men were standing around me organizing their gear. Todd Kelsey was with them.

He had rolled into Pico the previous evening on the back of a camioneta from Benemerito, a few miles down the road, which he had first reached by a five-hour bus ride from Palenque. He spent the night in a closet-sized room in one of the brothels the old-timer at Chajul had recommended to us. The other patrons' exertions, painfully audible through the paper-thin walls, had kept him awake. Josh had found him by inquiring around the bus stop after a recently arrived gringo backpacker.

Josh had also discovered a camioneta preparing to leave within minutes for Palenque. I had barely greeted Todd and lacked the energy or emotion necessary to face the others leaving so abruptly. But they insisted, so I embraced Alonso, thanked him as effusively as I could, shook hands with Josh and David, and promised to see them in Palenque. They turned and hauled their kayaks and equipment up the bank and into the village.

Todd and I sat in the boat and started catching up. I had left him only sketchy instructions on how to reach our rendezvous, and he had been unable to locate my York pack, a hard-plastic canoe pannier that I had stored for him under Moises's care, packed with food, books, and other items for the run to the gulf. Its absence left us short on food.

The only thing to do was shop in Pico to round out what I had left over from the past week. As we made our way down the short main drag, I refreshed him on the political situation.

I avoided mentioning the bandits, though I figured Todd would be game for most anything. In the sixties he had hitchhiked from Norway to South Africa and spent a year on a farm learning pottery. In Stony Creek, in the Adirondacks, he had transformed an abandoned, over-grown hill farm into a productive, thriving, and idiosyncratic homestead. One year, when his gardens had favored flowers over produce, he had justified the indulgence as "more visual than victual."

Everything he touched bore his wry signature. For years he had designed and invented ingenious and sophisticated devices of stage magic for a scenic-design company in Glens Falls, New York. As a problem solver he had no equal. On numerous projects, usually involving some kind of rough outdoor labor—roofing, slaughtering, milling logs—his resourcefulness astonished me. After I left Stony Creek and faced problems caretaking sporting clubs or guiding trips on lakes and rivers, I often asked myself what Todd would do, and arrived at a solution. I wished I could apply the technique to the question of the bandits.

Beneath the overcast, Pico de Oro made an unappetizing impression. The main drag, which flanked a grassy, deserted square, was about a hundred yards long, with a garage, a couple of tiendas, a small café, a smokeshop. Todd's "hotel" was a little farther out, beyond the single crossing street. A cinder-block Catholic church faced the side of the square at right angles to the row of shops.

We saw Alonso, Josh, and David sitting at a table in a café. The camioneta, not surprisingly, was running late, so they had decided on a quick breakfast despite the place's questionable appearance.

We joined them while the Guatemalan owner fussed over us and took our orders for coffee and a meal: the choices were scrambled eggs or chicken, with fresh tortillas. The chicken was a spicy red mole of chiles and pumpkin seeds, called pepian, that exploded in our mouths. The coffee was delicious. We ate so fast we got sauce all over ourselves, then we ordered more coffee. But it ended quickly. Alonso, David, and Josh rushed to catch the camioneta; Todd and I had to get out on the river and away from Pico de Oro. David was the last person I spoke to as the others hurried away.

He said he'd get my missing York pack from Moises and send it to Benemerito by combi. Then he looked at me sternly and said, Don't try to sneak past the bandits. It's not worth getting killed over.

I told him thanks and waved goodbye.

WE BOUGHT FRUIT, pasta, chiles, and tortillas, and left. The Lacantun slackened, making us paddle laboriously to make headway. The overcast burned off and the sun bore down. After more than two weeks afloat, after yesterday's marathon, and with Todd's arrival, everything pointed to a layover day.

The river widened and separated into braided channels. The landscape opened out, the sky extending eastward over the Pasión watershed and Peten, the right bank distant, settled, imponderable.

The mouth of the Lacanjá snuck up on us within the first hour. A campo militar stood on the southern point of the confluence, the site of Chan Bor's original caribal. A sign announcing biosphere reserve access faced the river, mounted on a fence post. The base would have repelled most nature lovers. It covered the space of a football field, surrounded by a pole-and-razor-wire fence with log blockhouses at the corners. A heavily bunkered gate guarded the entrance, atop a stairway that zigzagged up the bank from a boat landing. I ignored the armed guards who waved, calling us over for questioning.

Just below camp the Lacanjá entered on the left. Across it high canopy shaded the bank, now part of the Lacanjá Biosphere Reserve, one of two smaller reserves established to round out the Montes Azules grant. We decided to paddle a short way up the tributary, swinging around a point where soldiers bathed and swam in a deep, clear pool. One of them, possibly an officer, frowned and asked if we had been questioned as we passed the checkpoint. Sí, I told him, too exhausted to be bothered.

We proceeded up the Lacanjá between high forest walls. The current pushed against us blue and clear, coming down from the tierra templada around Bonampak and Lacanjá village. Loaded with gear, we made little headway against it. The trees hung with moss, mato palo, and epiphytes, the shaded water the clearest I had seen since the Río Azul.

The Lacanjá rose in the limestone breaks of the tierra templada not far east of lakes Naha and Metzabok, homeland of Chan K'in Viejo. A dozen ruins clustered around the river's headwaters, many discovered as recently as the 1940s and 1950s, including Bonampak, with its extraordinary murals.

From there the river dropped more than two hundred feet over numerous falls and rapids, to the Lacantun. I swam in one of its upper pools in 1989, a pellucid jade-colored lagoon below a travertine ledge. The river was marginally navigable, though a Cordan protégé, Dimitar Krustev, had run it in the sixties, in a folding kayak with a wooden framework and a canvas hull.

Krustev thought himself a great adventurer and artist. He spent weeks hanging around Lacanjá seducing women and photographing nursing mothers under Chan Bor's approving eye. His trip became a nightmare when his Tzeltal guides, after successfully navigating dozens of rapids, wrecked their dugout. They ran out of food until they reached the flats before the Lacantun, where they caught numerous mojarras, one of the Usumacinta's many endemic cichlids, and tortugas blancas, or white turtles.

Moving upstream, we found the current prohibitively strong and the banks high, with no obvious campsites. In the shade and silence of the tall timber you could hear the thunk of zapote fruit hitting the ground. Reluctantly we swung the bow downcurrent and let the river carry us back toward the Lacantun. The soldiers waved again and wished us a good voyage, and we passed out into the Lacantun, then into a shady side channel that skirted the open river, hugging the left shore behind a long island.

We entered a bewildering maze of more islands and shallow channels. Two large iguanas skittered up the bank and into the undergrowth. One island rose gradually from the river level, a long reef rising to a low height covered with tamarind, cecropia, and mimosa scrub. A narrow channel separated it from the left mainland, where the timber grew tall and generous, and it looked far enough from the agricultural right bank to discourage ranchers from grazing cattle there, so garrapatas were unlikely to be present.

We landed and carried the equipment up through the soft mud and sand. A marginal campsite stood on the crown of gravelly alluvium that formed the island, far from the water's edge, devoid of shade. There we flipped over the Freedom and pitched our first camp together.

In late afternoon I set up my folding camp seat along the shadow line that had started to advance over the island from the high forest across the channel. Todd joined me and we watched through binoculars as a half dozen scarlet macaws ate fruit in the riparian canopy.

The last Todd had heard, when I had phoned him from Palenque, was that Tammy Ridenour's trip had ended safely. Now I told him the story I had heard about Mauricio's ambush by AK-47s, the equipment's theft, the abuse of his cook, and Machete Jim's escape and survival. To Todd, who had flown in just three days earlier from the cold but nonviolent southern Adirondacks, it all must have sounded bizarre and inconceivable. Understandably, he pleaded his eight-year-old daughter and declared that unless we could establish that the situation had improved, he'd be unwilling to risk the passage.

I suggested that we could inquire after conditions when we reached Bethel, a village on the Guatemalan side just upriver from Corozal. People there would certainly know of the situation. Once past Yaxchilan, however, that was it; we were committed. The current was too fast to paddle back up from Piedras Negras. If things looked bad we might catch a motorboat ride from Bethel down to Piedras Negras and back, but it would be expensive.

I asked him to keep an open mind, to keep talking as we went along, and left it at that. Todd looked up and glassed a pair of howler monkeys in the canopy. Shortly afterward their guttural calls began echoing over the water and continued through the night.

All the next day we paddled on slack water, passing a couple of Guatemalan Indian settlements. The river wound through sweeping oxbows that took hours to navigate. The biosphere reserves fell behind, and with them the tall timber. Now both banks were cultivated, though some of the grandest ceibas I had seen stood sentinel on the right. We had entered the great zone of ambiguity near the confluence of the Usumacinta's three main affluents: the Chixoy, the Pasión, and the Lacantun. Landscape referents were hard to come by. Without consulting the compass, we lost track of which direction the river was flowing.

We camped on a muddy gravel bar across from some cabañas and the road to Pico. The next day we reached the highway bridge at Puente Lacantun around two. Across the bridge passed the periferico de la frontera sur, the ring road of the selva, begun in the early 1980s when Guatemalan refugees streamed across the river, to serve as a buffer against the incursions and as an emblem of sovereignty against possible invasion. At the same time, the road was meant to "open the frontier" and prevent exactly the kind of contraband activity in arms, drugs, refugees, endangered species, and artifacts it now fostered.

The road began at Palenque, ran due east to within a few miles of the Usumacinta, and paralleled the river a few miles inland, cutting a swath of devastation extending half a mile on either side, and circumscribing the selva as far as the dusty frontier hamlet of Benemerito, near the mouth of the Lacantun. Soon it would be paved completely as far as Comitán, closing the circle and tightening the noose on the republic's securest refuge of wilderness and rebellion.

Todd rested in the bridge's shadow with the Freedom and read a book while I left to see if the York pack had made it to Benemerito. I hoped to flag a bus or a combi, but knew I might have to walk.

We had packed some superfluous equipment for shipping back to Palenque. I shouldered the hundred-pound pack and started walking up a stock trail through scrubby pasture, passing through a gate and waving to a family resting on the patio behind their run-down jacal. In a minute I came out on a new section of the periferico, on the eastern end of the bridge. Some women, and a Lacandon boy dressed in the traditional tunic and long hair, stood in the sun awaiting a bus. The boy carried bows and arrows for sale. I couldn't see a village or settlement of any kind, though an army checkpoint stood a few yards east of the bus stop, and a closed tienda across the road.

The checkpoint made me nervous since my two-week Chiapas visa had expired while I was on the river. Almost immediately a bus pulled up bound for Palenque. The women and the Lacandon boy boarded. I crossed the highway to wait for the Benemerito bus in the shade of a solitary tree. Then I recrossed the road toward the checkpoint, figuring the best approach was to present myself and my papers for inspection voluntarily. Nobody noticed my approach on foot. I stood before the soldiers' canvas and nylon shelter and said buenas tardes.

Inside, the soldiers were opening a round of Coronas. A young Indian in combat gear and a beer in his hand stepped forward and requested my passport, which I handed over, reserving my expired

visa in my pocket. He glanced at the passport and called for an officer. A squat but jovial Ladino emerged from the shade and greeted
me cordially. He flipped through my passport, put his beer down, and
copied down the number.

He asked if I was a writer, un escritor. Sí, I answered, shocked. My
mind reviewed an assortment of possible catastrophes, including my
arrest—the power structure didn't take kindly to gringo writers nosing around the conflict zone. The officer disappeared in the shade of the
ramada. After a minute he came back and handed me a piece of paper.

This is for you, he said in English.

The paper read, in Spanish: To the Comandante, Ejército Mexicano,
Puente Lacantun: Estimado Comandante, This letter is in reference to
the American writer Christopher Shaw, who will be passing Boca
Lacantun in his canoe on his way to the Gulf of Mexico between
February 23 and March 1. Please extend him every courtesy and con-
vey him this message with all goodwill. Many thanks. Respectfully,
David Kashinski, Guide, Ceiba Adventures, Palenque, Chis.

Below, it went on, in English: Chris, Your yellow box will be wait-
ing at the combi stand in Benemerito. Return anything you want to
Palenque by the same carrier and I will pick it up for you. Good luck,
El Ojo! Adios, Dave.

I gazed at the letter, astonished to be reading a personal hand-
delivered message in that blasted landscape. I thought its confident
temerity an especially fine touch.

Está bien? Everything is all right? asked the comandante.

Uh, sí, comandante. Muy bien. Muchas gracias.

You are having a good asperience? You like our cowntry?

I love Mexico. I love Chiapas, the selva, the rivers, the people.

Bueno, bueno. You write about us nice things, okay? He drank from
his Corona.

Okay. I promise.

I started walking. The road traversed a rolling scrubland, a gleaming black straightedge superimposed upon a chaos of low monte and

hilly karst. The heat reflected brutally from the tarmac. A lone tree stood at the roadside a good half mile ahead, like something left over from a stage set of *Godot*.

A bus soon cleared the checkpoint and stopped when I flagged it down. We sped down the rigidly straight, newly paved highway between scrublands extending to the horizon where twenty years ago high-canopy rain forest had stood.

After ten minutes Benemerito rose abruptly from the karstland like a wart, halfway across a spit of land a few miles wide separating the Lacantún from the parallel-running upper Usumacinta. The tarmac turned to rutted and hardened clay laterite down the village's single main street.

I got off and walked down the quarter mile of zapaterías, comedors, bodegas, bars, and brothels, all catering to Pemex workers. A decade ago oil exploration had followed the bulldozers and opened the floodgates for laborers, ranchers, lumberers. The Guatemalan exodus filled out the population. Benemerito had become a port of entry, a center of "commerce," but it still had an unfinished, provisional look.

The street was strewn with shredded light blue plastic, the kind used for shopping bags everywhere in Mexico. Trucks and combis roared past. Nasty characters lay about drunk—or dead—in the shade. My yellow plastic York pack lay incongruously just inside the door of the combi station, a small café run by Salvadorans.

I waited around town half an hour, then clambered aboard the combi back to the bridge with two Indian women, one of whom nursed an infant. The driver, a young Ladino, sped out of the village. Just outside town young boys rode double on a wobbly bicycle far down the road, one on the handlebars. As the driver approached, the boys, oblivious to traffic like all kids, veered in front us on a direct line to get hit. The driver waited until he was right on top of them, then hit the brake, sending the combi squealing across the tarmac. The momentum threw me onto the women in front of me. The driver yelled at the boys. The infant screamed. Its mother looked toward me, frightened, and I growled at the driver to slow down.

The soldiers waved me through the checkpoint. I scrambled down the trail under the heavy pack-box, relieved I had made the exchange so easily (thanks to David) and spent so little time in Benemerito. I had been gone little more than an hour and a half. We wasted no time repacking the Freedom and setting off toward the Usumacinta.

Ten

THE AMBIGUOUS ZONE

IN FEBRUARY 1992, I WAS SITTING IN A CAFÉ IN THE OLD COLONIAL
city of Antigua, Guatemala, the day Mexican president Carlos
Salinas de Gortari came to town to sell the latest version of a massive
Usumacinta dam project to his Guatemalan counterpart, Marco
Vinicio Cerezo Arévalo.

The newspapers and the relatively independent magazine *Crónica*
had been deconstructing the project for days, their commentaries
reflecting Guatemala's resentment of Mexico's economic success and

its harboring of Guatemalan rebel leaders while Guatemala was still mired in warfare.

On the day of the Salinas visit I took my Spanish homework to the peaceful, shady square. The cathedral's earthquake-scarred facade flanked the square on one side. Maya women and children from the outlying villages, working in squads of three or four, sold traje aggressively to the corporate and governmental language students who, like me, constituted, along with tourists, the town's chief source of revenue.

The morning started quietly, like any other. Around ten, advance men wearing plastic IDs around their necks began showing up along with television vans and reporters from the capital. When it got too hot I moved to the café, drinking coffee on the colonnade, then agua mineral. Some gringos awaited the festivities at a table nearby, one of them a florid gentleman in a white linen suit. They discussed the presidential visitation in refined accents while eating pepian and getting hammered on successive rounds of Gallo beer.

For hours nothing happened. Then rifle barrels bristled on the rooftops, silhouetted against the twin volcanoes Agua and Fuego. Plainclothes security thugs materialized on the square as the crowd assembled. I ate a simple, delicious pepian and waited. After a final coffee I took a walk. Tanks had been drawn up a block or two down the streets feeding the square, forming barricades. Army and security personnel turned away sullen Indians from the checkpoints.

I returned to a bench on the square and concentrated on my work. Every so often I looked up while workers converted the wide, ample porch of the cathedral into a stage, with risers and huge speaker cabinets. Little by little, men dressed in satin guayabera shirts and palm-leaf hats began setting up marimbas in front of the cathedral doors, dozens of them, all caparisoned in satin and brocade. Embroidered drop cloths on the fronts of the instruments told the names of the villages, neighborhoods, and civil patrols they represented. Some of the men began tuning up and practicing, filling the square with disorganized tintinnabulations.

To this accompaniment now entered hundreds of schoolchildren between the ages of eight and twelve, both Indian and Ladino, proceeding single-file out of one of the barrios off the square, led by nuns. Each wore a T-shirt reading I AM A STUDENT FOR PEACE. The girls were dressed in smart blue skirts and pumps and had their hair tied in ribbons or cut across their foreheads in bangs; the boys, pressed blue slacks and polished shoes, their hair slicked down. A drum and a four-string guitar called a quattro broke into a typical hybrid tune of the highlands: part Caribbean, part Spanish, part Maya. The marimbas joined in. The students climbed the steps of the cathedral and mounted the risers beneath the guns of the rooftop snipers and by now numerous soldiers cradling Uzis and Galils. It took forever. Finally they made an array of exquisite faces on the risers, hundreds of innocents dragooned as a first line of defense against rebel attack.

Soon a brass band sounded in the distance, its music echoing in one of the narrow streets. Ornately decorated Harley-Davidsons swerved into the square, followed immediately by security agents on foot, running, the band playing something martial while the marimbas blared. The two musics were utterly irreconcilable to the ear. The effect was chaotic and stirring. Behind them came more motorcycles, then, on foot and waving to the multitudes, the two presidents, Cerezo tall and aristocratic, with wavy gray hair, Salinas short and bald—"the Atomic Ant," as the Mexican press had dubbed him. Both wore blue suits and purple sashes across their chests.

The bands fell silent as the presidents mounted the stage, still waving to the cheering crowds. After a pause, a conductor raised his baton and two or three dozen amplified marimbas launched into a grand orchestral cacophony. It sounded like a cross between the Mummers' Parade and Mahler's Tenth, a jangling uproar of nationalism. When they stopped, the children sang a hymn and the national anthem in their thin, sweet voices, conducted by a nun.

The spectacle ended quickly. The presidents made short prepared statements and repaired with their entourages to the halls of a ruined convent off the square. In the evening they emerged with an agreement to further improve relations and economic cooperation between the two countries. The chief emblem of this new partnership, the papers related, would be the long-delayed monument to regional cooperation and modern Latino-Americano technology, a massive hydroelectric project on the Río Usumacinta, a "purely binational" effort involving three Mexican ministries and their Guatemalan counterparts.

It was an extravagant display of amistad, a quality that had seldom characterized relations between the two countries. The original, failed dam proposal and the cross-border skirmishing of the eighties had fanned latent bad feelings. Grand gestures were in order if the latest proposal were to succeed.

That earlier, larger project had fallen to poor planning and inherent economic disincentives. Archaeologists and environmentalists had protested vehemently as well. Archaeologist Jefferey Wilkerson's 1985 National Geographic article exposed the project to international criticism. The reading public responded vigorously, protesting the losses of habitat and the drowning of the obvious archaeological sites like Piedras Negras, Yaxchilan, Altar de Sacrificios, and the cities of the Pasión. So did Mexicans and Guatemalans, for whom the concept of "patrimony"—the fund of art treasures of its ancient civilizations—rose to the level of a secular religion. Many feared the environmental and archaeological damage new access roads would cause. By 1987 Mexican officials were denying the plan existed, or claiming it had been shelved, citing environmental problems and the public outcry.

In fact, engineering and financial drawbacks were more to blame. Mexico City, the project's largest single market, lay a thousand miles to the west. Guatemala would supposedly sell kilowatts to other Central American countries, though no transmission infrastructure existed. Even after it did, enormous amounts of energy would be lost or stolen in transit. Leakage through the porous limestone, rapid siltation due to highland erosion, and the rebels, who had sworn to sabotage the effort, added major impediments to the project. Funding fell through.

When Salinas resurrected the plan in '92, it was as a scaled-down project with only one damsite, at Boca de Cerro, located entirely on Mexican soil near Tenosique. It left most of Piedras Negras and Yaxchilan above water, but would still flood dozens of smaller archaeological sites and an unknown quantity of undiscovered ones.

The engineering and marketing difficulties remained the same, despite Mexican assurances to the contrary. This time Mexico would *sell* electricity to Guatemala, though a second, joint project might be mounted upstream later on. Oddly, in the face of predictable protests, no environmental impact studies were undertaken. To this day no water-quality monitoring goes on along the lowland rivers of the watershed, and the system's aquatic life is only little understood.

The new proposal went unremarked. In the United States four years had passed since the environmental "wake-up" summer of 1988, with its record heat waves, brownouts, and polluted beaches. Chico Mendes, the Brazilian rubber tapper and labor leader assassinated by ranchers for protecting rain forests, had been dead for three years. Even archaeologists shrugged: the new dam, some implied, would make it *easier* to reach Piedras Negras by boat.

In the new post-Communist era, indigenous concerns counted less than ever. Editorials portrayed little Indians carrying beat-up rifles, covering their faces with bandannas, living in the jungles and ruins, as anachronisms of failed leftist ideologies, pawns of power-hungry Latinos. Free trade, NAFTA, were the new rallying cries. Foreign investment could be had for the asking. Salinas's stock as a financial wizard was so high he was up for the World Bank job when his term ended. And the legwork on the dams had already been done.

On his way to Antigua in February 1992, just before announcing the new project, Salinas stopped at Yaxchilan, offering lip service to the ideas of patrimony, indigenous rights, and environmental protection by expanding the selva's existing ecological reserve by some 136,000 acres, fooling nobody on either side of the Usumacinta.

Within a month, Homero Aridjis, the Mexican poet and founder of the Group of 100, an informal colloquium of international environmentalists, went on the offensive, complaining in press releases and op-eds that Mexico had performed none of the archaeological surveys required by international aid agencies for such projects. He further asserted that government sources had told him no plans existed to "remove, protect, or safeguard the valuable historical and archeological artifacts" along the river. No funding agency would touch it after that. The project died again.

Yet it would be safer to think of it as dormant. Rural electrification remains a hot button in the selva. In 1994 some U.S. newspapers reported that Zapatistas were calling for the hydro project's renewal to provide jobs in the conflict zone. In 1996 Mexican papers said a group of private businessmen were trying to attract World Bank funding for an independent project on the river. The electrical-rate protests in the cañadas would surely ratchet up the pressure.

ONE OF THE first archaeological treasures to be flooded by dams would be El Planchón de Las Figuras—roughly translated, "the Flatiron of Figures"—a flat travertine slab carved with extraordinary pictographs that extends into the river just inside the mouth of the Lacantun. Maler had spent twelve days transcribing its carvings in 1899. Jefferey Wilkerson, echoing Maler, had termed the planchón "an ancient stopping place for canoe travelers on the vast Usumacinta network."

Photographs showed the planchón to be an enormous limestone slab sloping toward the current, the kind of place any paddler would seek out on a canoe journey. In a region of high riverbanks, wetlands, and marginal campsites, it would have stood out dramatically. Around such a prominent and inviting irregularity fish would gather. On cool evenings its stored warmth would attract iguanas and other edible cold-bloodeds.

It occupied the hub of Mesoamerica's network of waterways, where the great trade routes of the Usumacinta, the highlands, the Pasión, Jatate, and Lacantun came together. Voyagers from the gulf would pass it en route from the Tulijá-Jatate up the Pasión or the Chixoy. Olmec travelers could not have missed it. For those on their way down the Usumacinta, venturing to the gulf from one of the Pasión's cities or returning there, it was a short paddle up the easy-flowing Lacantun. It would have been well known to the postclasssic Chol Lacandons and classical putun.

El Planchón's location had been known for a century, but it baffled the few Mayanists who had paid it much attention, its iconography was so distinct from the mainstream art of the nearby ruins. Its carvings consisted of odd whorls, geometric designs, animals, and stick figures—proletarian, nonelite images, unlike the highly stylized and refined paintings, inscriptions, and bas-reliefs of the nearby cities, which were almost entirely concerned with the doings of royalty. Erosion had effaced some of the planchón's carvings, faded others.

To record the inscriptions Wilkerson had beamed floodlights over the slab, casting the sixty-eight figures into high relief. The lights revealed cartoonish crocodiles and birds, huge spirals, and something Wilkerson called a "strange, striding, monkey-like creature." Some showed maplike representations of pyramid temples. The largest of these, some ten feet by fifteen, resembled the main plaza at Tikal.

The site lacked structures, so no other scholar had expended much effort there. Nobody had searched for buried remains such as trade articles or pottery from formative, pre-, or postclassic canoe travelers, or attempted to date the carvings separately or together. Such information could show the extent of the planchón's significance and use, its continuity over time.

We left the shadow of the bridge and floated between high,

scrubby banks down a full-flowing river still sullied by runoff from the Tzaconejá. Clouds drifted out of the east, obscuring the sun and flattening the light. I expected to see rock formations as we approached El Planchón and I soon did, a narrow rim and flat shelf reaching a few feet into the left-hand side of the river.

It looked too small to be the planchón. No other formations showed themselves downstream.

We examined it just in case. The bench disappeared underwater, showing little above the surface, maybe an eight-by-ten-foot flat area, hardly enough room for one of the larger carvings Wilkerson had mentioned. Todd stood to scan the rock, but couldn't see any incisions. Evening approached. I felt like we had a ways to go before reaching the planchón and, shortly beyond it, the Usumacinta. We needed to find a campsite. My map showed the planchón's position but not the highway bridge, so I was unsure of our exact location. I quickly decided the planchón lay around the next bend and that we should be on our way.

We paddled a long straightaway to the bend. Turning the corner, we saw no rock formations on the left shore, just another bend. I felt disoriented, uncomfortable. The sky spit slivers of rain. As we passed around the second bend, the river suddenly opened up, widened, and the sense of disorientation resolved itself. An osprey, one of dozens I had seen along the rivers, pitched forward out of a ceiba on the right and whistled low over the water. We had left the Lacantun behind and entered the Usumacinta, hardly realizing it, and now rode down a much stronger and more voluminous current.

This, I said, is the Usumacinta. That was the planchón where we stopped. We missed it. (I did not remember until later, going over my notes, that Cordan too had missed the planchón at high water.)

Shit, I said, shit, oblivious to our arrival upon the "big" river, the river of sacred monkeys. The volumes of the Pasión and the Chixoy came together a few short miles upstream. We considered paddling back upstream but the current kept pushing us on past the old trading station of Tres Naciónes which occupied the point, and where in Maler's day milperos brought their corn to sell and built huge fires of the dried husks at night.

A large island split the current just downstream and we landed on its steeply slanting shore, an alluvial agglomeration higher and longer than the one we had camped on below the Lacanjá. I had no idea which country it belonged to, Mexico or Guatemala, though Guatemala was visible across the narrow channel on the other side, its shore denuded like the roadside around Benemerito and covered with low scrub. High water had coated the gravel with scum from the Tzaconejá, 150 miles upstream.

Exhausted, we hauled our equipment two hundred yards to high ground. The sky rained tiny shards. The wind blew, racing the clouds and ripping out my tent pegs, but I managed to start a fire with driftwood and put on water to boil. The occasional aluminum boat or lancha moved upstream loaded with produce, their kickers laboring against the strong current toward Puente Lacantun, or Sayaxché, a small Guatemalan river port on the Pasión. Two boys fished along the island shore facing Guatemala.

Todd fiddled with the tarp while I grew morose and scrutinized the landscape expanding to the east. Clouds flew out of Peten. Monkeys roared within earshot, where I couldn't tell. Not even the smallest stand of forest could be seen, all of it cut in the last decade by settlers or high-tech madereros who airlifted logs with helicopters.

While I cooked, the boys ambled shyly toward our camp, rods in hand. They pointed vaguely toward Guatemala when asked where they lived. They had caught nothing and their expressions evinced no pleasure. Their main interest was the Freedom, now inverted with dinner laid out on its hull. While we talked, a marine patrol motoring upstream on the Mexican side looked our way but kept on going. One of the boys said, American soldiers are working with the Mexican army.

Claro, I said—I know. The river and the border were fluid in many ways. In Guatemala, thirty years of burnings and killings had ended, but the conflict had jumped the river. Now American "advisers" had joined in, if the kids' gossip had any merit. I had already heard of a Mexican doctor on one of the raft trips who told David Kashinski he had treated American soldiers wounded in the Zapatista uprising. Such intelligence rarely surfaced in the mainstream American press.

While we talked, macaws and parrots, remnants of populations once as numerous as gulls, kept crossing back and forth, feathered ensigns of change.

The area of the Chixoy-Pasión-Lacantun confluence had always been geographically and politically murky. On his descent, Alcayága had become confused at the confluence and confused succeeding generations of scholars. For a hundred miles upstream the tributaries were navigable year-round, their courses sinuous and indeterminate. Numerous lakes and secondary tributaries created aquatic labyrinths and seasonally navigable wetlands. The rivers paralleled each other in places, separated by short distances and connected by intervening ponds and creeks. Water levels, while not as mercurial as in the mountain or canyon regions, flooded low-lying and shoreline areas in the rainy season.

Marginal types took advantage of the region's ambiguous character. Cordan had met a fugitive from Ocosingo at Tres Naciónes, a murderer, whose descendants made a "regular clan." Maler had endured troubles here, witnessed the Pasión's paradoxical upstream current at high water, and encountered an old Swiss hermit, almost a countryman of his, who had numerous Lacandon wives and cared not a whit for the concerns of the world. That these aimless channels delineated national borders accented the region's obscurity. Neither Mexico nor Guatemala really controlled it. Instead, it was a liminal, nongovernable zone of transition and passage.

Yet the Pasión, just upstream from where we had camped, had sustained as many as seven major classical cities, including Altar de Sacrificios and Seibal, Aguateca and La Amelia, all benefiting from their proximity to the canoe-trade crossroads. Maler found ruins "at any suitable high ground, the rest being low and swampy and ready to flood." By the mid-eighth century the ceremonial centers, outbuildings, suburbs, raised-bed growing systems in the wetlands, terraces, and milpas around the confluence must have covered thousands of square miles. Dos Pilas alone covered an estimated 3,700 square kilometers.

At its height this concentration of wealth and humanity would have made a scene of richness, beauty, and variety rivaling the grandeur of the Aztec capital, Tenochtitlán. At Altar and Seibal, and smaller centers along the shore, ranks of idle cayucos would have lined the shore beneath pyramids and palaces painted red and blue, yellow and black, the temples at their summits painted and thatched. Markets filled the plazas, selling every trade article in Mesoamerica, surrounded by decorative plantings, caged or tethered songbirds and parrots, wild cats and monkeys. Lowland and highland languages and cultures mixed with those of Costa Rica and Teotihuacán.

Along the river, channels would have led through the banks to aquatic raised beds and their interlocking canals. And always, upstream and down, cayucos passed: the small local boats of individual milperos; larger trade vessels carrying salt, jade, obsidian, and feathers down from the highlands for the delta and beyond, or orange slip pottery, cacao, and stingray spines up from the coast; deep, highly-rockered boats from the swifter and steeper highland streams; and larger boats, ornately carved and caparisoned for the royal tours and visits that cemented alliances.

If a golden age existed, it included—along with art and writing, highly developed religious and political systems, artificers and scribes, ritual torture and human sacrifice—cayucos floating in waterlily beds, canals thick with protein-rich fish, and the finite cosmos reflected in the waters. If it "fell," as many scenarios insist it did, the region became crowded and degraded at the denouement of the classical era. Drought came and apocalyptic wars ensued. In their aftermath, people forgot the old ways that connected them to the past. With the cities reeling, merchant nobles from the coast—putun—imposed themselves and took power. Some of them, in their bourgeois, sentimental fashion, tried to maintain the trappings of grandeur. But the thread had been cut. In the great pyramid temples of the centralized state, the gods fell silent, though not in the houses of the campesinos.

The putun—simultaneously "barbarian" intruders and "merchant warriors," to Linda Schele and David Freidel—apparently tried to keep alive the connections to tradition, dynasty, and place that lay at the root of the classic people's success. But the collective consciousness had moved on. The people "turned their backs on the kings to pursue a less complicated way of living," as Schele and Freidel put it. They turned to the forest. In the words of the *Popol Vuh,* they retreated "under the vines under the trees."

Factions of nobility may subsequently have migrated to the highlands and evolved into the tribes that live there now. But a hollow existed in the Usumacinta lowlands, the Maya region's core. The land returned to wilderness. Isolated pockets of old-fashioned Indians—with temple pyramids, priesthoods, and human sacrifice—persisted. Some, like the Lacandons of Miramar, lasted until the end of the seventeenth century. For the most part the people reverted to an aboriginal life of hunting and gathering, family-based milpa management, and religious observance. And they remained close to the religious centers, visiting them for seasonal ceremonies.

Many explorers and scholars, Maler among them, viewed this apparent regression as a tragic irony. The forest dazzled and appalled him with its beauty, impenetrability, and dangers. That a complex civilization had risen and fallen there, the land reverted to wilderness, its people devolved to a tribal level, had disturbing implications. Lawlessness seemed a natural consequence of such a history. It didn't surprise Maler that smuggling prospered at the turn of the century, and that desperadoes routinely jumped borders after every easy murder or hijacking.

The boys left, poling their father's cayuco home. We sat under the tarp by firelight eating fresh guacamole and tortillas from Benemerito. It was a blustery, forbidding, and ominous camp. Something about it turned us inward, made us focus on our pasts. We revisited old friends and characters from the Adirondacks, the forgotten and the dead, the beloved, the betrayed, the abandoned, the wasted, the lost. We had "wandered" of old, both of us, had known it, and had found our ways back by different paths. It seemed weird to recount personal histories and errors of thirty years ago in such a place, so far from anywhere, yet no wilderness. The "wilderness" as we thought of it—the museum of biological evolution, intact primary habitats, and a birthplace of human consciousness (we evolved there as a species)—was somewhere else, nearby perhaps, but out of sight. We, however, were as godforsaken, castaway, as in any haunted and haunting landscape where old spooks rise from the depths of time and assert their lasting, unforgiving presence.

The tent leaked all night. I heard the roars of monkeys and of distant trucks on the periferico and the voices of fishermen or smugglers singing in the dark. Toward dawn I had a recurring dream of high bluffs overlooking the Mohawk River near Schenectady, where I grew up. Nearby, the Iroquois culture hero, known as the Peacemaker, had performed a miracle and revealed his powers to the skeptical, disbelieving Mohawks, persuading them to join the Six Nations Confederacy under the Great Peace. In my dream the river was no longer ponded behind the dams and locks of the Barge Canal but wound freely from bank to bank over riffles and easy rapids. I had seen it like that only once, when the dams were under repair. In the dream I viewed it from atop the bluffs, from a distance, on high. The dream brimmed with wish-fulfilling sunlight and a sense of restoration.

In the morning the marine patrol passed upstream while we ate and packed and the macaws flew predictably from Mexico to Guatemala under lugubrious skies. The boys returned and watched. When everything was ready, we paused for thirds on coffee. The patrol drifted downcurrent on the Guatemalan side and landed their boat near the boys' cayuco. A pair of officers and an enlisted man sauntered up from the water, bid us buenos días, asked for our passports but not our visas (not their concern). The usual palaver ensued: point of departure, destination, purpose. The formalities complete, the officers seemed genuinely intrigued by our journey.

I asked them which country the island belonged to. Nada, the officer replied, es la mitad. It's the middle. Unclaimed territory. The assonance of "la mitad," with the word for friendship, l'amistad, rang in my head.

FOR A CENTURY visitors regarded the few miles below the Lacantun as among the most spectacular on the Usumacinta. Maler found the area wild and beautiful, with huge crocodiles sliding noisily off the sandbars at his approach. Thirty-some years later Alfred Tozzer's Harvard student, Louis Halle, found it unchanged. In the sixties Cordan described it ecstatically. "As soon as the rainy season is over bromeliads, orchids, and lianas bloom profusely on the walls of greenery enclosing the river, and on the Guatemala side crystal clear streams tumble over white-terraced cliffs into the deep-blue Usumacinta. There is nothing to compare with it, unless in Yellowstone Park, in the United States." Monkeys followed his boats along shore. A few years earlier the archaeologist Ian Graham, on his first trip by cayuco from Sayaxché to Yaxchilan, termed it a paradise.

After the marine patrol departed we set out from La Mitad Island. In the first mile we saw no "walls of greenery enclosing the shore." At least on the Guatemalan side, all the timber of any size had been skinned, leaving the usual mixture of ragged recovery species. A few downtrodden homesteads stood along the bank.

We pushed the loaded Freedom through the eddies and swirls made by the deep channel, limestone bed, and high water. We reached the fabled El Chorro Falls, pouring in on the right, by 10 A.M. The clouds had burned off, leaving a hazy, muted light. The falls themselves were as spectacular as Maler, Halle, and Cordan had advertised, and of old must have attracted flotillas of cayucos. A great travertine fan spread along the Guatemalan shore for two hundred yards, forming watery cells, pools and side channels, a miniature version of the staircase of drops and pools I had run below La Sultana on the Jatate. The water fell over a final drop of five or six feet that continued for a hundred yards along the length of the falls, broken only by irregularities in the rock, grass, and shrubbery that had rooted there, including a frail white blossom that rimmed the ledge. At its base the clear water purled and oxygenated the discolored Usumacinta like spun crystal.

It was a natural gathering place, and a portal of rare distinction. Now a poor shack stood on the top of the bank where the falls roared out of the scrub, shaded by an enormous fig. (Who wouldn't build there if left to themselves?) The yard was worn to the muddy rock by livestock and human feet. It made me long for the neat, well-kept homestead at the mouth of the Azul.

The region had seen intense rebel and military activity. Now women washed laundry in the shallows, just downstream from the falls. Yellowish detergent foam rotated in the eddy, with white bleach bottles and the ubiquitous light blue shredded plastic of discarded shopping bags.

Fears of road construction and its negative impact had proved justified, only they were fulfilled even without the dams. On the Pasión, not far upstream, the recently improved road from Flores to Sayaxché, in Guatemala, had increased the traffic of highland campesinos seeking land in the forest. The demand for land was growing, but the balance between the concerns of campesinos and those of big land interests— large landowners, resource extraction industries, and conservation organizations—had never been addressed. The country's lack of a fair and equal land-tenure system amplified the problem.

Along the Pasión, what land the army generals hadn't claimed had likely been placed in some kind of archaeological zone or "extractive

reserve," for harvesting forest produce like xate, where it was managed corruptly and ineffectively. Campesino invasions of unoccupied
land occurred frequently. Shortly before my trip, members of a native
land cooperative had burned a nature station at El Peru and set up a
community amid the ruins and in the surrounding forest.

Immigration had increased artifact looting in the ambiguous zone,
where polychrome ceramics—among the most coveted pieces of classical art for collectors—were common, and easy to smuggle. Mostly
clayware plates, bowls, and vases for both ceremonial and household
use, typical polychrome pieces are inscribed and painted in characteristic color combinations of black, orange, yellow, and red, with scenes
taken from myth or the history of the local dynasty. At a glance the
lowliest campesino knew a marketable piece. Anything with visible
"Indian" imagery, even fragments, brought the highest prices.

More ambitious, higher-end looters employed helicopters normally used for airlifting logs from remote timber stands to remove
whole stelas from ruins such as Aguateca. The looters severed stelas—carved stones erected at intervals in the plazas—from their
bases using chainsaws with chiseled-diamond chains: ironically so,
since the stelas symbolized trees. A technique learned from early
archaeologists was to skin a few inches off the face of a carving on a
stela or a temple, thus reducing weight. Both countries had strong
laws restricting the practice, but the market remained, and the river
made an easy corridor to the gulf.

After El Chorro the channel narrowed and the banks steepened.
The sky cleared. We ran some easy class 1 riffles and practiced brac-
ing in the low waves and eddy lines to prepare for the rapids below
Yaxchilan.

Squatters' cabins appeared at regular intervals now, clinging to
slopes at the feet of hills, surrounded by milpa planted up to the windows and doors. Chemical defoliants used to clear land left swaths of
jungle dead brown but as yet uncut against the surrounding green.

We stopped for lunch in the shade, at the head of a canyon and across the river from one of the homesteads. Children swam and fished at the foot of the bank, beside two tethered cayucos. Above them the house clung to the base of a sheer cliff that rose six or eight hundred feet above the river, catching the sun. It had a small corral and a lean-to for livestock. The milpa ran upstream for two or three hundred yards on the narrow strip between the bank and the base of the cliff.

We ate on a rough outcrop where water seeped from the base of the cliff and across the steep mudbank. The trickle had precipitated a brown reef that spread along shore in frozen whorls and globs, reminding me of Thoreau's "brains or lungs or bowels, and excrements of all kinds." It was not a comfortable landing. The children watched us from across the river. For a moment I admired their situation and the rough simplicity of their lives, however hard, dangerous, and poor they might have been. Most of the western hemisphere still revered the frontier impulse that drove their parents. At home, back-to-the-landers of my generation, second-home owners, and various factions of the libertarian right revered it. I harbored some of its more simplistic fantasies myself.

Unlike them, however, these settlers degraded the global biosphere hardly at all. There were no SUVs in the driveway, no ATVs, no snowmobiles, no satellite dishes, no riding lawn mowers, no leaf blowers—not that they wouldn't have had those things had they been available. They probably had a chainsaw. To let them live there for however many years they lasted—before flood, politics, low crop prices, or corrupt deed holders drove them off—seemed a small indulgence, and a healthy way of life for humans generally. When they left for bad jobs in Guatemala City and lived in a cinderblock hut beside an open sewer, their homestead would return to earth, leaving no Celotex wallboard to scar the bank, no fiberglass Sana tubes, no vinyl siding. A few rusty appliances, maybe, and an unfortunate chemical legacy in the soil, from the fertilizers, pesticides, and herbicides they were addicted to. With some education however (and a better homesite), they might actually figure out a way of life that merged with the principle of living harmoniously in nature, which was the driving concept behind the UN's biosphere reserve program.

THE NEXT FIVE miles passed through a shady narrows flanked by high walls. On the Mexican side the river paralleled the Reserva de Chan K'in, one of the smaller, more recent additions to the selva's biosphere reserves, the name suggested by Ignacio March in honor of the Lacandon headman. The Guatemalan side fell within the vaguely delineated Zona de Amortaguimento, the "buffer zone" of the new national park and Guatemala's Maya Biosphere Reserve. The current speeded up.

Settlement disappeared from the river on both sides. Trees and rough terrain shaded the narrows, another potential wildlife corridor between the Chan K'in reserve (which inexplicably didn't extend to the river) and the opposite buffer zone. Guanacaste trees growing on the steep banks shed yellow blossoms into the current. The water level had receded somewhat. You could catch a glimpse of its natural jade color through the silt, persisting there like a memory, or a shadow on a canyon wall, when you looked straight down into the water. I had begun to think I had imagined it.

The narrows widened into a giant rotating eddy, beaches and rock outcrops lining both sides of the river. We pulled in on the Mexican side and filtered some water, then dropped down to a crescent beach where the old montería Agua Azul, later known as Filadelphia, had stood.

Agua Azul had been a largish river station with numerous buildings, an airstrip, and a trading post. Lacandons had occupied the site before pulling back from the river in the nineteenth century, and continued to trade there while the montería lasted. When it was abandoned after the war, the site became the haunt of chicleros, looters, crocodile hunters, and other unsavory types. When Cordan ended his trip there, the bloodstains from a recent murder still streaked the boards of one of the run-down buildings.

Two dozen cattle now occupied the beach at Agua Azul, one a big old Brahma bull who eyed us biliously when not attending his ménage. We decided Bethel could not be much farther and we should try to get as close to it as possible. There, I thought, we could assess the news from downstream and I could have my passport stamped.

An hour later we landed on an island, Isla la Puleta, opposite the landing for Bethel. A squad of boys ferried over from the village as a greeting party, landing and hovering at a discreet distance while we pitched our tents in the dunes. While I cooked, Todd put up an elaborate awning. A low, ground-hugging mimosa covered the island, its floral aroma filling the air. Flycatchers, nighthawks, and mangrove swallows swarmed over the flats.

While we ate I started lobbying Todd in favor of continuing past Yaxchilan and completing my seamless descent. Moises was old friends with Yaxchilan's caretaker, Manuel ("Manuelito") Perez, I said. Moises had sent him word we were coming. I thought we could stay there for a few days. There would be an opportunity to plan a strategy for the miles below.

Leaving Yaxchilan, I told him, we could camp on the big playa at El Desempeño, upstream and across from El Cayo, where I had seen the mysterious aquatic creature in '89. In the morning we would follow the trail to the gray tarn in the forest. From there we would continue another couple of miles inland to the CPR community left over from the war, whose people wanted to remain in the forest to work for the park and the dig at Piedras Negras.

I praised Piedras Negras and the magnificent uncut forest that mantled it, its beautiful setting on the river. I told Todd about the new dig going on, and my appointment with Nature Conservancy staff. After Piedras Negras we could leave just before dawn and sneak past Budsilhá at first light, before the bandits shook off their hangovers. They would be looking for big groups of rafts who started late and moved slow, not a dark green canoe zipping past at sunrise. This I felt had become the best idea. We agreed to keep talking.

Again it rained all night. The zipper on my tent broke. Everything got soaked. The roars of monkeys blended with Mexican corridos playing on a radio in Bethel.

In the morning I ferried across the swift current, hitting shore just below the landing and working the eddies slowly upstream. A dozen children greeted me at a rocky beach. They examined the Freedom and declared it a canoa, in the local idiom. I left them to watch it for me and climbed the steep trail to Bethel.

Modest houses clustered around unplanned lanes shaded by ceibas and corozos. I made my way through yards planted with plantains and bananas, hibiscus and ginger, out to a rutted clay street. A PA blasted corridos and salsa all over the village.

The street led to a grassy square with a concrete government block on one side and a tienda, immigration office, meeting hall, and a row of rugged wooden shops on the other. In the meeting hall, four timber cruisers for the Guatemalan forestry agency, FORESTAL, told me they supported the biosphere reserve, the national park, the peace. The army base in town was inactive now, they said. The killing had stopped. Life was good.

I asked if they knew of anybody running boats to Piedras Negras. No, they said. They knew nothing of bandits downstream, but the news concerned them.

They directed me to the office of CONAP, the national conservation agency, a few streets away. I navigated the shady dollhouse lanes past a dinky army base where soldiers played Frisbee to a small courtyard with two frame buildings, an office, and a barracks. The office was empty except for a calendar, a desk, and some nature posters hanging on the walls.

From the barracks some men saw me nosing around. They were rougher-looking, and older than the FORESTAL workers, probably patronage employees. They called themselves "natural resource guardians" and liked their work, saying they were excited about the national park. Banditos? Never heard of 'em.

At migración it cost fifty pesos to get my passport stamped. The officer expressed concern that rafters were being ripped off on the Guatemalan and Mexican sides below Piedras Negras, though he had heard nothing about it. In the tienda I used Mexican pesos to buy fruit, avocados, and batteries.

Back on the island the river urchins had returned, with reinforcements. They played war among the dunes, expertly imitating high-tech weapons fire, dying in dramatic falls to the sand. When I landed they ran down to the shore to greet me as if we were old compadres, their bare soles throwing up puffs of sand behind them, and helped me haul the Freedom out on the gravel.

They hung around shooting each other while we broke camp for Yaxchilan. Then they helped us carry the equipment to the water and Todd took our picture with the whole gang crowding around me, aiming their sticks at each other and striking muscle poses. Wasn't it better now that the war was over? I asked them, disturbed by their expert mimicry of war and death (no worse than my own at their age). Sí, they answered. No more killing. Then they erupted in another outburst of oral gunfire.

I gave them pasta, spools of thread, soaps for their mothers, and antacids for their fathers. We told them mucho gusto and pushed off, letting the Freedom glide down the clear slicks. Looking back, we saw them solemnly boarding their cayucos to return to the village.

Eleven

SPLIT SKY

WITHIN HALF AN HOUR WE COASTED PAST FRONTERA COROZAL, a former landing for mahogany on its way to the sawmill at Chancala. During the Guatemalan insurgency it had been made into a Mexican point of entry and army base. Now it was a sizable though makeshift Chol Maya town, with numerous bad streets and fairly well-built cement-block houses.

With my passport stamped in Bethel, I no longer worried about my expired Mexican visa. Nevertheless, the closer we got to Budsilhá the more I wanted to avoid Corozal and anybody in the Mexican army or immigration. I couldn't ignore the possibility that members of those institutions were passing intelligence to the hijackers downstream.

I angled the Freedom toward a midriver island, planning to pass behind it out of sight of the village. Just as we moved offshore we heard somebody blowing a loud whistle and turned back to see an armed guard, at least two or three hundred yards off, waving us emphatically back toward Corozal. Reluctantly we switched direction. A rapid pushed us far below the army camp, and we landed on some limestone outcrops amid the currents. Houses and storage buildings stood on the bank. Dozens of children just out of school swam in the eddies in their dresses and underwear.

No soldiers came to meet us. After waiting a few minutes, I climbed a trail and looked over toward the military stockade. Still nobody appeared. I jogged down the bank and back to the Freedom, and we slipped quickly downriver.

On this stretch I had gotten my first glimpse of the Usumacinta and met my first cayuco paddlers. The forest on either side had made a wall, however lacking in mature mahogany. Less than ten years later the wall was gone, leaving only scrub. The river pushed and boiled, high and brown, the clarity I had enjoyed while gliding over the gravel shallows off Bethel besmirched by a roiling current and soft clay bottom. We passed the landing for Nueva Jerusalem on the Guatemalan side. At the top of the bank, thatched houses stood in the sun amid banana fronds and hibiscus blossoms.

We stopped for lunch in a bay on the Mexican side, where two iguanas rested on the bank, one pale green, the other a gray-brown five-footer. There was logging slash everywhere, drift timber tangled along shore. Scum and plastic circled in the eddy. We ate in the boat, drank from water I was happy we had filtered upstream, and continued on.

I grew progressively calmer the farther we dropped downstream. From here on everything—the river, the ruins, the forest, the people—existed on a grander, richer, less altered scale than above. On the approach to Yaxchilan the mountains rose higher on either side, the homesteads sparser. One new homestead stood on a prominent Guatemalan headland, formerly untenanted, at the head of a bend near the mouth of the Arroyo *Yal*chilan. An enormous ceiba overshadowed the point.

The light left the water, casting a reflective sheen over the surface. A pure white hawk spiraled overhead. We entered the ninety-degree bend to the east that signaled the edge of Yaxchilan's protected area, and the approximate extent of the ancient city's ceremonial precinct. For the next three miles the river described an enormous omega, a nearly circular bend narrowly pinched at the neck. The peninsula's narrow neck and its prominent heights made it one of ancient Mesoamerica's most formidable defensive positions.

The temples and palaces of Yaxchilan's ceremonial center climbed the east slopes of the mountain that dominated the peninsula. We watched for temples, but the forest was thick, and the approach took longer than I remembered, stretching out over two or three miles. In the eighth century you would have seen the raw terra-cotta reds, ochers, and greenish-blues of the pyramids through the trees, especially those of structure 33, and structures 40 and 41 on their solitary summit, the enormous braziers billowing black clouds of copal, sacrifice victims hanging from the roof combs. Ranks of stelas carved with warriors in battle gear lined the bank. On ceremonial occasions you would have heard drums, conch trumpets, ocarinas.

Maudslay, after learning of the ruin from a German academic named Rockstroh who had visited the area while doing research into the ongoing border dispute, reached the ruin from Sayaxché, in March 1882, with a crew hired from the nearby monterías. The water was low. Drifting between unbroken forests on both sides, he had no idea where he was until he sighted "El Pilar," a rubble cairn jutting out of the river near the left-hand shore, which he assumed was an ancient bridge pier. He estimated its height at fourteen feet above the river surface.

Maudslay believed the ruin marked the limit of downstream navigation, raising the stakes for drifting by accidentally. Below, "the river is totally unexplored, but is vaguely reported to consist of a series of impassible rapids running between high cliffs," he wrote. To support the assertion he pointed out that a recent attempt by "drunken wood-cutters" to reach Tenosique by canoe had failed. Though their cayuco had made it, the woodcutters hadn't.

On landing, Maudslay climbed the grand stairway and took lodg-ings in structure 33, the Temple of Bird Jaguar, amid the copal streaks and broken shards of abandoned Lacandon incense burners.

His privacy was short-lived. Desirée Charnay, a French writer of popular travelogues, had also heard of the city and followed rumors of its existence upstream from the gulf. At Jonuta on the lower Usumacinta, Charnay's boat ran aground in the low water, forcing him to continue overland to Tenosique. From there he sent men ahead to build a cayuco, then hired guides and mules and followed the north shore of the river upstream over the ravines and ledges of the Sierra Lacandon for six days. The appointed rendezvous was on a trib-utary named the "Chontal," after the lower river's eponymous ethnic majority—surely, in fact, the arroyo better known as Yalchilan.

The dugout builders were drunk when he arrived and the boat unfinished. Dejected, Charnay cast his eyes over the water. Just then a Lacandon poled by on his way upstream and Charnay hailed him over. The Indian told Charnay that Maudslay had reached the ruin only hours earlier. At Maudslay's request the Indian had been returning to a band of his fellows camped upstream to buy food. Instead, Charnay ordered the man back to the ruin to inform Maudslay of his arrival. The next morning Maudslay arranged for his vogas to fetch the French gentleman's expedition.

Their meeting was a model of noblesse oblige, each pledging to share credit for the "discovery," as quaint an "after you, Alphonse" narra-tive as the literature affords. Later, both admitted their disappointment.

Charnay wrote lyrically about the Usumacinta throughout his vividly detailed *Ancient Cities of the New World,* and illustrated it with accurate engravings as compelling as any photographs taken by Maler or Maudslay. Of his camp on the arroyo, he wrote: "The forest around is teeming with life; parrots and avas fill the air with their shrill cries, yellow-crested hoccos [curassows] move silently among the higher branches, while howling monkeys peer inquisitively at us. . . . Here and there traces of cultivation are still visible, and huts which have been abandoned on the approach of timber merchants plainly show that they were inhabited not long ago."

The engravings included "a kind of votive pillar" set on limestone outcroppings exposed by low water—the cairn. It had been described to him at Tenosique as a bridge piling, a supposition he found impossible in the absence of evidence of an additional piling across the river, or knowledge of Maya engineering capabilities.

A few years later Maler also rejected the bridge pier theory, estimating that the river had cut into and carried away as much as one hundred meters of riverbank since the classical era. The city's masonry embankments, which now reached almost to the water's edge, Maler thought, would then have extended *into* the river, and the "little circular structure—which was perhaps once surmounted by a small temple—[would have] stood close to the foreshore even in the rainy season." Elsewhere he called the cairn "the substructure of a small temple consecrated to the water deities."

Part of the cairn's function, from that point of view, might have been to mark a landing. A jetty of rubble such as ran underwater from shore to the cairn would have softened the eddy line, making it safer for cayucos to cross. The deadwater behind it would have acted as a staging area for ceremonial occasions, as well as a trade dock. In fact, given the shore's continuing westward curve, a jetty might have extended the reach of its calming effect far downstream and into midriver. The presence of a temple there would be consistent with the ceremonial practices of other river-oriented societies, especially those on swift, mercurial rivers like the Usumacinta, and may even have housed a torch for night landings.

Recently, however, the bridge theory had been plausibly resurrected by an urban-planning engineer from Atlanta named James Okon. Using diving gear, Okon found remains of a piling off the Guatemalan shore, and possible anchor points for suspension cables carved in limestone outcroppings on the Mexican shore. He examined records of ancient and contemporary bridge-building techniques in the Andes, where the technology has existed for centuries, and fed them through a computer. Like the Andean bridges, the cables at Yaxchilan would have been six inches thick, and woven from sisal fibers. The bridge would have been wide enough for four people to pass abreast, and 600 feet long—with one of its three spans extending 230 feet—making it the longest suspension bridge in the world at the time. Archaeologists remain unconvinced of the theory, despite its strengths.

The river changed course to the west, rounding the top of the omega. We followed the leftward curve back toward the waning sunlight, watching for the cairn. But high water had submerged it entirely, and I saw only the doors and windows of structure 11 peering from the forest shadows. Next came the landing, with half a dozen lanchas tied to the bank, each forty feet long, awninged, and colorfully painted.

We hopped across the lanchas' rocking hulls, tied the boat by a long line to a root, and climbed the steep, horribly eroded bank to the airstrip. The palapa we had used in '89 had been expanded tenfold, and was hung with the hammocks of fifty or sixty visiting workers. The workday had ended and the men lounged and smoked or bathed in their underwear, radios blaring salsa. A couple of boys kicked a ball around on the airstrip.

Tents belonging to European tourists and their guides were pitched under trees at the top of the bank, beside the airstrip. We found a reasonable site between two tent clusters and began relaying equipment up the steep, slippery bank. Across the strip stood cinderblock housing for INAH scholars and students. The ruin proper lay behind a barrier of forest and limestone ledges at the upstream end of the strip. You reached it by following a path that led through the woods for a hundred yards.

While we carried the equipment, a German couple, both fit and in their thirties, came down to the water to bathe. Not to be denied their Club Med moment, they stripped, swam in the easy current along the bank, then stood knee deep soaping themselves under the undisguised stares of fifty or sixty lonely workers.

We started the camp stove, donned our headlamps in the gathering dusk, and prepared to explore the grounds for two or three days and plot our next move. The waning light flashed green and gold through the trees. The last tourists returned from the ruin and descended the bank. Gradually the landing emptied of lanchas as they carried the tourists back upstream to Corozal and the long ride to Palenque.

While I cooked, a young man of no more than twenty wandered over and introduced himself shyly as Sebastien Virginia, one of the ruin's official guides. Manuelito, the caretaker, had been drunk for a week, he said. (Sebastien had had a nip or two himself, I judged.) He asked if we were balseros, rafters. I told him we had come by canoe from Ocosingo, and that we were friends of Moises Morales and Alonso Mendes. Ah! he exclaimed, Don Moises!

He said he would guide us in the ruin, adding that free access was no longer allowed while the restorations were under way. People sometimes took things of value.

While we talked, the German woman, now dressed, ambled past on her way to the rustic comedor-café that stood atop the bank a few yards away. Sebastien looked at me with dark, bloodshot, utterly earnest eyes, and cupped his hands in front of his chest. Hay muchas chicas, he said, smiling.

WE ROSE AT dawn. The workers crossed the airstrip to a mess hall for breakfast, then headed out up the trail to the ruin in groups of two or three, smoking cigarettes. The forest filtered the gray light. Monkeys and toucans called. Todd had left his pants hanging on a tree overnight and found them full of fire ants, fortunately before he put them on.

Sebastien joined us for coffee. He was fresher than last night, though slightly bleary and mesmerized by the roar of my lightweight gas stove. To my question he said he was Chol Maya, from Corozal. The workers were all visiting Yucatecs, from Yucatán, where they had been restoring ruins all their lives.

He told us Mauricio's second trip had just left Yaxchilan two or three days ago. The chastened outfitter had transported his customers by lancha back to Corozal, rather than run the river and expose more people to robbery and death. The last ambush had done him in—Fue lleno, as Sebastien put it—he was full. Mauricio was a little loco, anyway, I said.

The bandits had been there, at Yaxchilan, some months earlier, he said, appearing at the downstream end of the airstrip, where the trail to El Cayo began. There were more than a dozen of them and they carried AK-47s. They lined up all the tourists and demanded money, credit cards, and jewelry before disappearing.

He finished his coffee. We could go ahead in the ruin on our own, he said, as long as we didn't touch any stelas or inscriptions and stayed out of temple 20, which held the best of the ruin's remaining door lintels.

The wide trail to the ruin began at the end of the airstrip. As soon as we entered the forest the trees arched overhead and signs of construction appeared. To one side a sizable visitors' center had been staked out and studded with reinforcing rods, ready for a foundation to be poured. Then the trail passed over one of the limestone reefs and into leafy twilight.

A shapeless mound rose before us, camouflaged by thick moss and leaf mold, out of which the forms of hand-worked stones gradually resolved. Trees grew from its spine. The trail led into a single narrow passage, like a trench, about fifteen yards long and open at the top, which disappeared into the mound through a tunnel opening. On the right side of the passage a row of shallow niches opened, housing short masonry benches (beds?) under peaked, "corbel-vaulted," ceilings. (In corbeling, a series of stones, each projecting a little farther than the last, rises to a peak, spanning an opening in a primitive kind of arch.) Then you entered a dark shaft. Inside, you groped along until thin daylight led you up a flight of stairs and around a corner, and you stepped out onto an earthwork platform overlooking the sunken main plaza.

Maler had camped in the structure (number 19) and named it the Labyrinth. The walk through the dark and ingeniously twisted interior replicated the soul's descent to the Otherworld at death, or in the throes of sensory derangement (to which Yaxchilan stood as a singular monument), and its resurrection. It recalled the Hero Twins' descent to Xibalba in the *Popol Vuh,* their triumph by guile and imagination over the Lords of Death, and their subsequent rebirth.

As you emerged into the light, your eyes fell on the plaza—the model of the world, a cosmogram, with symbolic mountains, caves, forests, and waters arranged intentionally to strike awe in the observer and open his senses to the gods.

It worked.

Todd and I blinked our eyes on the platform as the scene slowly came into focus. The silence was complete. We were early, and alone. The lanchas had not yet returned with the day's new visitors.

I followed a low earth-and-stone rampart toward the river and climbed an unexcavated structure numbered 76 on Ian Graham's 1977 site map. There I looked out over the plaza and, through a window in the trees, the river.

The plaza lay under a soft mat of grass kept trimmed by maintenance workers using machetes. A canopy of scattered ceibas, crusted with epiphytes, filtered the light into flickering bars and motes. The trees' spacing among the empty plinths where stelas had been hauled off to museums was as aesthetically pleasing as the spacing of the existing stelas themselves. You could very easily imagine them linking the realms of the visible and the invisible, the upper and the lower, and holding up the sky.

At spatially harmonious intervals, intact stelas blended their verticality with the ceibas they symbolized, low altars interspersed among them. Surrounding the plaza, the temples, in various states of restoration or decrepitude, enclosed the open space and distinguished it from the profane exterior surroundings. The scale was at once human and monumental, and thirteen hundred years after its construction instilled in us a profound tranquillity.

A pair of collared aracaris—medium-sized black and yellow toucans—nibbled fruit in the understory screening the river. Flycatchers and motmots evanesced in the foliage. Monkeys roared.

Descending to the plaza floor and heading toward the grand stairway of structure 33, I came to an indistinct complex of buildings facing the river and undergoing restoration. Workers mixed mortar and carried stones up from shore in baskets on their shoulders. According to the archaeologist Carolyn Tate, you would have stood here after beaching or tying your canoe (or stepping off the bridge, according to Okon) and climbing the stairs up one of the shoreline structures. The entry maximized the visual impact of the soaring main pyramids.

The grand stairway, facing the river and moldering under moss and grass, climbed the steep natural slope of the mountain. Above, on one of the mountain's false summits, rose Bird Jaguar's temple and its "roof comb"—a wall of masonry gridwork, typical of classical architecture, extending above the roof and acting as counterweight for the interior arches.

I pictured, as others had, a busy riverfront, with trade, recreation, household, and ceremonial activities going on simultaneously, and canoes hauled on shore, some resembling the low-profile boats common today, and others the cosmic cayuco carved on the bones from Tikal—deep amidships rising to high bow and stern peaks.

At that spot all the divine and mundane significances of rivers and water converged. Mesoamerican plazas, designed to hold water, to flood, created living tokens of the Watery Path. Moises remembered Yaxchilan's plaza flooding in heavy rains. On the plaza floor the prostrate sculpture of a crocodile stretched at my feet, as if to emphasize the point. Emblem of creation, of earth, and transformation; of rivers, canoes, and perhaps of Yaxchilan itself, it lay at the exact foot of structure 33, miraculously unlooted, beside a low altar. There it anchored the cosmos, and the entire Maya cultural sphere by extension, high and low conjoined in a masterwork of public art, a shared vision of creation that Tate termed "a cognitive map of reality."

ON THE USUMACINTA you apprehend the futility of classification. Everything corresponds: crocodile, cayuco, ceiba; canoe, origination, civilization. Form is fluid, contingent, metaphorical. In classical art quetzal plumes and maize leaves stand for each other, evoking transformational motifs embedded in the region's consciousness. The muan bird—the cosmic soul, perched atop the world tree and ready to take wing—is at once quetzal, macaw, and crested guan.

At Yaxchilan this shape-shifting achieved an apotheosis, producing a body of art vast enough to identify distinct styles, or "schools," and to perfect a handful of genres endemic to the watershed. These included inscribed stair risers, bas-reliefs, and the carved undersides of door lintels—a site-specific form that required the viewer to squat in doorways and crane his neck backward to view the work.

The flowering took place over a five-hundred-year period of stability and continuity between 320 and 808, dominated by a family of rulers we may refer to as the "Jaguar" Clan: Shield Jaguar, Bird Jaguar, and their forebear, the redoubtable Penis Jaguar, Yat Balam. The artists and scribes came from the elite and priest classes. In return for support, they glorified the royals in stone, justifying their wars and usurpations, commemorating their sacrifices, and rendering into dogma the visions they had achieved through bloodletting and psychotropic drugs.

For generations western eyes found the imagery, its patterns and motifs, an indecipherable grammar of form and image. It took Mayanists a century of collecting, photographing, cataloguing, and concentrated *looking* before the shapes meant anything to them.

Maudslay had recognized the city's remarkable vision, carting off numerous lintels and stelas to the British Museum and instituting the archaeology of theft in Mesoamerica. Among his prizes were two sequences of door lintels numbering 15 through 17 and 24 through 26, masterpieces that depict, in successive narrative panels as in a comic strip, a historical occurrence of ritual bloodletting, the vision it produced, and the subsequent captive sacrifice the vision justified. The work is among the most striking in the art of the western hemisphere. Maudslay, however, was so careless in removing the pieces that he neglected to mark the locations of each lintel in structure 23's respective doorways, leaving Maler and Morley to piece the sequence together forensically years later, like detectives, analyzing the dust left behind by Maudslay's workers.

Morely and Maler added their incremental early observations, but little organized archaeology went on at Yaxchilan until the early 1970s. Yet the collecting work of those three pioneers helped Tatiana Prouskouriakoff, squinting at photographs, arrive at her historical thesis and usher in the golden age of Maya glyph decipherment.

Using references from Piedras Negras and from monuments collected, drawn, or photographed at Yaxchilan, Prouskouriakoff identified three rulers whose reigns stretched across more than a hundred years. Shield Jaguar I, according to the inscriptions, born in 647, reigned from 681 to 742; Bird Jaguar, born in 709, from 752 to 772, and an unnamed descendant of Shield Jaguar, born in 752, from 772 to 800.

Prouskouriakoff also deduced the meanings of several "event glyphs" that record specific ceremonial occasions—bloodletting, birth, death, the capture of enemies, the accession of rulers—and demonstrated, according to Tate, that the sculpture record contained images of historical women. One of them, Lady Xoc, was featured in the famous bloodletting rituals of lintels 17 through 26, shown kneeling and drawing a string of thorns through her tongue.

Her name alluded to the river's eponymous monster, the xoc, root of the classical Usumacinta's appellation, Xocolha. The Mayanist Tom Jones, in a paper that amounts to a scholarly tour de force, argued that the xoc-fish of the Usumacinta was nothing other than the bull shark, the anadromous shark of Lake Nicaragua and tropical rivers worldwide. (One was caught far up the Mississippi.) In the seventeenth century, after an unsuccessful privateering cruise to the Bay of Campeche, Jones asserted, coldwater English mariners aboard the ship carried back the native name for the fearsome predator, and it entered the English lexicon as the word shark.

Following Prouskouriakoff, subsequent studies filled gaps in the glyph record and honed the historical details of the Jaguar Clan. The record contained accounts of state visits by and to surrounding cities, especially Piedras Negras and Bonampak, as well as Tikal and the Pasión cities. These visits, and the art and inscriptions that commemorated them, all served to maintain the intricate balance of divine right and popular consent that allowed the royal families to rule and their dynasties to flourish.

Yat Balam, "Penis of the Jaguar," established Yaxchilan in 320. His descendants ruled until 808, when the city was abandoned. His principal achievement, Tate says, was his selection of the site itself, giving the city, through its geographical location—on the mountain, in the river—its "spiritual identity." Its historical name, she says, was something like Tsah Kanak, or Itz'am Kanak—"Split Sky," after a prominent cleft in the Sierra Lacandon, visible across the river from the south acropolis on the city's summit.

Before Yat Balam's reign, Tate believes, the summit had served as an observatory for tribal Mayas. Later, Yaxchilan's astronomers, like their neighbors, not only kept track of planting and harvest times, they also used the stars to explain "the establishment of dynasties and the justifications of reign." Every civic occasion or royal act was meticulously timed by the movements of the heavens. Every accident of fate recorded in the glyph record happened on a specific date, under a specific configuration of sun and planet. By the time of Bird Jaguar, all the major temples had been aligned astronomically, the sunlight falling through their open doorways at the solstice dawns. Summer solstice temples celebrated births, plantings, accessions, captures; winter solstice temples commemorated deaths, defeats, harvests.

On the summer solstice, when the sun rises in the cleft across the river, the "split sky" provided a natural and dependable geographical fix from which to track the annual transits of the sun, the moon, Venus, the Milky Way, and the star cycles associated with creation narratives.

Yaxchilan's "emblem glyph," , which identified it on inscriptions all over the Maya area, portrays the split-sky cleft as a simple *V*. The Basal Monster, an ornate zoomorph, or imaginary beast, that supports stela 7 on the plaza, boasts a more imaginative rendering. Tate calls it a "sky caiman" (or crocodile), recalling the prone crocodile sculpture at the base of the grand stairway. The creature's profile is "saurian, with an upturned snout," the head cleft in the middle, like the range across the river, and also like the many almond-eyed supernatural figures of Olmec iconography, whose notched heads symbolized the volcanic craters of the Tuxtla Mountains in the Olmec heartland—an artistic homage or leitmotiv stretching across two thousand years.

The Sierra Lacandon resembled the ridged and cratered back of a crocodile, the foundation of the earth. The people of Yaxchilan considered the cleft in the sierra the very source of creation, the ultimate portal, analogous to the split turtle shell from which First Father emerged in the heart of the sky.

Thus the sky, the topography, and the specific geography of the city constituted the "world," the cleft its omphalos. The view contributed as much to the city's identity and greatness as the strategic location. Afterward, what self-awareness its people may have enjoyed as individuals or as a polity coincided with its specific geography, placing them at the center of the cosmos, a situation they shared with every other classical city and with a number of the chief municipal centers of their twentieth-century descendants.

WE DAWDLED ON the plaza for an hour. Structure 20 was closed, but restored, and we spent a few minutes examining the lintels in structure 23. Then Sebastien appeared and showed us around structure 33, Bird Jaguar's monument to himself. Inside, the decapitated idol that the Lacandons identified as "Our Lord Hachakyum," their principal deity, sat in state. (It actually represented Bird Jaguar.) The head lay a few feet away, lopped off a century ago, most likely by falling timber or masonry. When it was restored, Lacandons believed, the celestial jaguars would emerge from their ageless sleep and devour the hach winik and foreigners alike, ushering in a new creation cycle. This was prophesied to occur on or about December 21, 2012. (Whether the current restoration project planned to test the prophecy remained to be seen.)

I drifted away from Bird Jaguar's self-referential palacio, drawn upward into the forest. Todd caught up with me. We climbed steadily through the xate and heliconia understory until we broke out on the true summit, the south acropolis. Its two temples, numbered 40 and 41, loomed above us.

I mounted the ramparts and sat on the roof ledge of Shield Jaguar's solstitial observatory, the oldest surviving structure at Yaxchilan, temple 41. The sky was clear and blue, the sun high and sharply defined, the canopy below me green and shining. The air hadn't felt so dry in weeks, and I stripped and sprawled across the temple's old stones, letting the sun pound on my wounds. It was a dubious spectacle, yet not altogether inappropriate for a temple of the sun.

Birdcalls accented the silence. The view for 360 degrees contained nothing but forest and mountain: to the west the ridges of the Sierra Cojolite in the direction of Bonampak and the Lacanjá headwaters; to the east the serrated ranges of the Sierra Lacandon across the river. The impression from here was of unmediated biological and topological integrity, whatever the picture from shore may have been. No sign of logging or other human agency betrayed itself to the naked eye, nothing that admitted of the concepts "Mexico" or "Guatemala."

The jagged Sierra Lacandon, all of it within Guatemala's new park, paralleled the opposite shore for miles. The cleft in the range, which gave Yaxchilan its name and locative authority stood out against the blue sky, separating two summits, the higher one rising to 2,050 feet. Beyond it the land telescoped in range upon seemingly infinite range into the blue distance.

The river paralleled the range, at the bottom of the expanding, replicating topographical tableau that was at once the world itself and its own projection. I had asked Mayanists whether a glyph existed that referred specifically to the Usumacinta, as you might expect, or whether the river had been represented by some other logographic device in the artistic record. No other river figured so centrally and formatively in the classical era's evolution. But I drew a blank.

It seemed so odd. From up here, above the reach of the most ambitious hydro engineer, you couldn't avoid comparing the Usumacinta and the Nile, with its crocodile deity, or the Tigris-Euphrates. Perhaps the river had been so central to the classical Maya identity that they took it for granted. More likely Yaxchilan's numerous crocodile and zoomorphic xoc renderings, each signifying some aspect of foundation, stood simultaneously for the creature and its habitat, neither existing without the other.

A little after noon we climbed down off the temple and made our way back to camp. Just below the south acropolis we took a side trail to the left. The trail rose and fell through thick understory past unexcavated mounds and emerged on the wide-open expanse of the north acropolis, a vast and rambling residential complex well above the river. Instead of continuing down to camp we drank from our water bottles and peeled some mangoes I had bought in Bethel.

In the sharp, clear air we wandered around the terraces of the palace compound, a salubrious residence if not a profound religious statement like the plaza, overlooking the river and kissed by breezes. Then we sat on a low wall in the shade, mesmerized by sun and silence and the nearby drone of howler monkeys.

Gradually individual monkeys came into focus in the trees no more than twenty-five yards off. (This resolution of form out of chaos is the selva's most persistent perceptual attribute.) There were three of them, then a fourth apart from the others. They hung in the midlevel branches, torpidly stuffing leafy boughs into their mouths. The big male had a long beard, and a prominent goiter hanging from his throat where his eerie call resonated—not, frankly, an especially endearing visage. Occasionally one of the monkeys reached out a long arm and followed it with his body to the adjacent tree, where he resumed browsing. Through the glasses we could tell they were watching us, too, primates viewing each other from different points on the evolutionary spectrum.

To the classical and Lacandon Maya alike, monkeys were imperfectly designed humanoids from the previous creation, corresponding to the *Popol Vuh*'s "men of wood," who had failed to recognize their makers and render them just tribute. Along with crocodiles they were grandfathered-in to the present existential phase in somewhat modified form—consigned to the trees that formerly constituted their flesh. The monkey-human connection, it seemed, was more obvious to Native American shamans and scribes of the first millennium than to Christian clergy and scientists of the Victorian era, or to those of today's drive-in, multiplex god houses of the millenarian Bible Belt.

While the monkeys fed and shat, distributing fruit and seed and guaranteeing future generations of trees, I worried over the downstream miles ahead, ran over them in my memory, then projected them at the higher water volumes we now faced, questioned all over again the Freedom's seaworthiness and Todd's skill level. We hadn't agreed yet to go on, but I had sensed a crack in his resistance.

I knew he could no more resist the pull of wild beauty than I could, that he wanted more.

I imagined the whine of the bullets across our bow, the tense paddle to shore, the raised gun barrels and harsh voices. What could I say to them? That I was an amigo of the revolution, of the indigenas, that I sympathized with la lucha? Could we work out a deal for the passage of boaters? In the event of an ambush I could account for myself. But who would account for Todd?

In my dehydrated fugue state I visualized spider monkeys following us through the trees along the Guatemalan shore as they had in '89, edging to the ends of the flimsiest branches and vaulting to the next, cradling their young at their chests. I remembered their faces in the moss-covered walls at Piedras Negras, venerated not for preexisting the hach winik and failing to render proper sacrifice, but for surviving the last apocalypse and affirming the cycles of creation. They came before, and the failed experiment they represented made way for modern humans, the people of corn.

AT DUSK WE ate in the comedor run by Manuelito's wife, Margarita Perez. The building, which also housed the Perez home, was long and low, with a metal roof and rough-sawn mahogany siding. Gas lamps lit the spacious, dirt-floored sala. A tough-looking but friendly Indian woman brought us agua minerals and a piquant chicken in red chile sauce, with black beans and fresh tortillas, the only thing on the menu.

After we finished I approached a counter that stretched across the far end of the room. Behind it, Doña Margarita, a tiny ash-colored woman, flipped tortillas on a comal set over the fire. A Dutch door opened onto a yard where chickens scratched. I told her I was looking for Don Manuel and wondered if it would be possible to speak to him in the morning. I said I was friend of Don Moises Morales, who sent Don Manuel his best regards.

Margarita never stopped flipping tortillas, but erupted in a torrent of unintelligible, high-pitched invective. Then she looked at me and apologized. She said Manuel was ill and nobody knew when he would recover. I thanked her, and conveyed my deepest apologies.

In the morning we quickly reached the mutual decision to proceed to Piedras Negras. After discussing possible strategies in case of ambush—say yes to everything, let them have whatever they wanted, walk out via the Chocolha if they kept the Freedom—we began to pack. Certain valuables we could possibly leave in the care of Manuelito, should that august and elusive personage make an appearance before we left.

We would camp that night on the playa at El Desempeño and walk into the CPR village in the morning. At Piedras Negras we would spend at most three days, then slip through the dire straits below at dawn. If we made it past Budsilhá, we would decide then whether to continue through San José Canyon or take out at Francisco Madero.

We did our chores in an atmosphere of rising anticipation, convincing ourselves that all would be well.

While we packed, Sebastien appeared for coffee. I told him I wanted to consult with Don Manuel about conditions downstream. Don Manuel was still on a bender, he said. I told him our decision and plan. Ah, sí, he said. You should remember, he said, shrugging histrionically, that the bandits were operating almost all the way through San José Canyon, not just at Budsilhá. Last year they got Mauricio at Boca de Cerro, almost to Tenosique. (Todd spoke enough Italian to comprehend simple Spanish. I glanced at his expression to gauge his reaction to this news, but read nothing there.) I asked Sebastien about the possibility of catching a supply boat back upstream from Piedras Negras, but he had no idea when or how often they ran, and the dig wasn't scheduled to begin until next month.

Sensing our resolve, Sebastien pointed out that no other paddle trips had gone through since Mauricio's ill-fated revenge mission. That would be in our favor, he said, because the bandits would have no pattern of regular descents to keep watch by. He agreed the best thing to do was to go to Piedras Negras and play it by ear from there.

We kept packing, relieved to have made the decision and stuck to it. Todd projected useful scenarios and stratagems: we could tape valuables—passports, etc.—to the undersides of the decks, squeezed on top of the flotation bags. We could stash pesos, dollars, and traveler's checks (our diminishing supply) in assorted places where we could produce them in succession. What if we encountered tough-looking guys but didn't see guns? he wondered. Should I tell them I was interested in their grievance and they could communicate it to the world through me?

Sebastien thought the banditos would have little to tell the world. They weren't guerrilleros, we agreed, sólo pendejos—only assholes.

We jettisoned as much superfluous equipment and food as we could. The lighter the Freedom, the faster we could slip past Budsilhá. I put aside two cartons of tomato sauce, three pounds of pasta, a big bag of freeze-dried chili, a bottle of oil, and a roll of paper towels, and carried them to the back door of Margarita's kitchen.

The abuela stood behind the lower half of the Dutch door. She looked puzzled when I offered her the items, then accepted them gratefully when I explained we were heading downstream and no longer needed them.

I kept finding things to give her. On my fourth or fifth trip to the back door, she looked worried on our behalf and said it was very dangerous downstream. There were a lot of rapidos, and also men down there, ratos, who were robbing and killing people. I said we knew about the hijackers. I told her my boat was specially made for rapids, we were experts, and we intended to sneak very carefully and craftily past the banditos.

Well, all right, she said. She told me good luck, held up her hand, and *blessed* me.

Minutes later we had reduced our gear to its appointed dry-packs.

It was another perfect morning. I couldn't wait to get out on the river before anything changed.

Just then a man looking extremely disheveled emerged from the side of the comedor facing the river. He waddled directly toward us, barefoot, fly unzipped, shirt stretched open over his belly. I knew immediately it was Manuelito.

He confronted us and demanded our names, asked if we were the gringos balseros who were planning to run the river. He reeked of liquor and stale sweat. His speech slurred and halted so badly I could barely understand him. Rheum caked his bloodshot eyes, and he squinted through a mask of acute alcoholic withdrawal.

Amigos de Don Moises! he shouted, emitting a fog of halitosis when we answered affirmatively.

Sí, sí . . . Don Moises, I admitted, ready to make a run for the Freedom.

His breath came in choking gasps. He began to wheeze. In a dry rasp he said under no circumstances were we to continue beyond Yaxchilan! He would not bear the responsibility for harm befalling friends of Don Moises, one of his oldest, dearest, and most treasured compadres, etc., etc.

There were men downstream, he went on, many men, twenty-two or twenty-five of them, maybe thirty, who had ametrelladoras, armas automaticas—he made the sound of automatic weapons fire, like the boys at Bethel—who had robbed and wounded many balseros, and who had killed an archaeologist the previous November (news to me). No, it was not even safe between there and Piedras Negras, they were spread out along the river. Quien sabe? he said when I asked him who they were, though I wondered how he could not know.

They were involved in narcotraffic, arms traffic, refugees, smuggling of all kinds, he said. He described the raid on Yaxchilan in December. Every night their dark lanchas passed downstream carrying who knew what. The people up and down the river were terrorized, and still the government did nothing.

We formed a triangle amid the green and yellow packs, the old man wheezing and scratching, but adamant. We would leave, it seemed, over his dead body. I realized that Doña Margarita had roused him from his stupor on what she considered our behalf.

I thought about telling him we would turn back, then going on anyway. But I could see that Todd understood enough Spanish to follow the exchange, and his face told the story: End of the line, ol' hoss. That's all she wrote. Katy bar the door.

I resisted but could not ignore the force of the message, nor the circumstances of its delivery. I considered sending Todd to Palenque and continuing solo, but rejected the idea immediately.

I sat on a bench, trying to think. We would need to take a lancha to Corozal and a combi to Palenque, but there wasn't much cash left. I asked Manuel if I could leave the Freedom and some of the equipment there, at Yaxchilan, and return for it in two or three days. By that time, I thought, I could uncover extenuating intelligence and persuade somebody local—Moises's son Chato Morales, or Manuel Oca—to finish the leg with me. To carry everything back now would cost too much.

The old man equivocated. He shuffled, casting his eyes one way, then the other. Do you have anything to drink? he said. He made the universal drinking sign, spreading his thumb and little finger and tipping them up. I told him no, but I could bring it on my return. Did he prefer rum or tequila? Tequila, he said. Bueno. When I return, I said.

The deal struck, I followed him around the back of the comedor and he showed me a storage shed where we could stash the Freedom and other equipment. It was safe, he assured me, and rattled a big padlock on the door.

I thanked him, both for his warning and for letting me leave the Freedom in his bodega. He commended himself to Don Moises and I assured him I would deliver his greeting. We parted and I retreated to the bench to sulk.

The morning kept unfolding in dazzling increments of glory, the river noticeably lower and greener, less murky, the sun climbing rapidly in a cobalt sky. Todd wandered off, snooping in the workers' palapa and taking pictures along shore.

Sebastien returned and joined me on the bench.

Manuelito was right, he said, it was better we didn't go on. I liked Sebastien.

It's very mysterious, Sebastien, I said, ten or fifteen guys with armas robbing Mexicans and foreigners, and the government wouldn't lift a finger, even though the river corridor was such an important resource for tourism and archaeology.

Sí, es muy misterioso, he said softly, resigned.

He claimed not to know who the bad guys were, but reiterated they were not Zapatistas. They were mostly good people, he said, a phrase that instantly caught my ear and cast suspicion on the whole river community. How else could all of Bethel have claimed ignorance of the bandits? I left it alone, however. I did say it was very bad for me and very bad for Mexico, what was going on, and it made me very sad to stop.

Sí, es triste, he agreed, looking genuinely sympathetic.

Is it I have sadness, or I am sad? I asked him.

Estoy triste, he answered. I am sad.

ALL THE CANOEING equipment—the Freedom, paddles, life jackets, safety lines, helmets—stayed in Manuelito's bodega, along with my tents, tarp, and kitchen gear. We packed one dry-pack, the York pack, and a couple of day packs for Palenque.

Sebastien helped me carry the Freedom up the bank and deposit it in the bodega. Afterward he left to guide a tour and I was alone.

I walked over the trail, through the labyrinth to the plaza, and climbed the stairs of structure 30. On the plaza French and German tourists meandered in expedition gear, glassing the canopy for toucans, motmots, trogons, and North American migrants, accompanied by Sebastien and another guide. They carried themselves better, in their confident hauteur, and were better informed politically, than the few Americans I had encountered in the watershed—not counting paddlers. A little conflict didn't bother the Europeans—they were used to it. Except for rafters and mochileros, American tourists avoided the region.

They spread out over the plaza, the tan white women with their sleeveless pastel T-shirts, the men in their sandals, socks, hairy legs, and tropical shorts. The ceibas, the stelas, and the clothed erect primates made an attractive pattern of vertical and horizontal contrasts in the architectural surroundings. Orange heliconias, flowering red bromelias, the depending tendrils of spider plants and mato palo, the textured blackish-green layerings of xate and philodendron—all seemed to have found a nook that produced the effect most pleasing to subjective human observation. As usual in the selva, only concentrated looking rewarded the eye.

I sat on the pyramid steps and consoled myself. Our turning back was fated, I realized, inevitable since I had reached Palenque. But then whether I could begin at all had been in doubt. Every mile was a crapshoot. I only hoped I had conducted myself and my voyage with an acute eye, and had given my best attention to the world that presented itself.

And yet, I thought, we could have made it.

I returned to camp. The day droned on in torpor, indolence, and boredom, the river bleeding away to the gulf. After two weeks high and muddy, it had dropped a foot overnight. We ate lunch, read, lay in the hammock. About noon the first lancha arrived and we began negotiating a reasonable fee to Palenque with the boatman, an endeavor that consumed three hours and provided welcome comic relief.

Around three our lancha prepared to leave. I thanked Sebastien and said goodbye—Manuelito had disappeared again—and we unceremoniously boarded the brightly painted forty-foot craft, stashing our packs in the bow. The boat fought the current upstream, veering back and forth seeking any eddy or obstruction it could use to its gas-saving advantage. But the lambent surface betrayed nothing obvious—the water was still too high. You had to read the subtler aquatic stretchmarks and rufflings the underwater formations projected on the surface.

It reminded me of Traven's circular banality, that the Usumacinta was mysterious for being so little known. Nothing about it was clear. It was opaque, like Maya reality, discontinuous in history and in reality, a free-trade, free-fire zone of the purest kind. A new putun—disruptive, river-borne agents of an invisible economy—controlled its villages. For all intents and purposes the river ran into a hole, an ontological portal, beyond Yaxchilan. The Watery Path of Mesoamerica, the region's binding energy, its main artery of topological integrity and historical identity, was blocked.

I had dreamed an Usumacinta after my own designs, and up to a point I had found it consistent and continuous with my expectations. But it ran into a void of doubt and unreason, and shattered into glittering fragments.

Twelve

THE COSMOGRAM

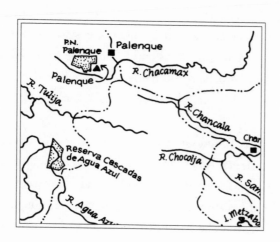

ALL THE CAMPSITES AND THE ROOMS AT PANCHAN WERE FULL, SO Alonso and Susan let us pitch our tents in the space behind their champa where the chickens scratched.

After two days, when I realized it would be harder than I thought to get back on the river, I took a cab to the village and bought Manuelito a fifth of gold Hornitos, leaving just about enough in my account to cover repairing my car, which had refused to start after sitting for a month in the rain.

Chato, Moises's son, who was building more cabañas at Panchan, said he'd think about accompanying me to Piedras Negras when he finished his work in two or three weeks. Manuelito, like everyone along the river, had been implicated in dubious affairs, Chato said. If he liked you and knew you were Moises's friend, however, he would do anything for you. I decided to waste no time dispatching to the old man the bottle I had promised, sending it and a note to Yaxchilan with some tourists who went over for the day.

On the roads you saw more and more military and state security forces than before, in higher numbers, and the checkpoints were harder to pass. Chato, never at a loss for an opinion, believed martial law was imminent. Mexico City had replaced (temporarily) its drastically corrupt law enforcement officers with military police. Chiapas, Guerrero, and Oaxaca would be next, he said. National elections loomed in July. Many Mexicans and Palencanos were fed up with the Zapatistas. The PRI, Chato and many others believed, would wait for the dry season and begin a massive entrada, a clean-up operation, in the cañadas.

I called Tammy Ridenour at Maya Expeditions, in Guatemala City, from a long-distance office on Main Street. I knew her next trip to Piedras Negras was scheduled for mid-March, two weeks away. If she hadn't canceled because of Mauricio's debacle, I thought I might be able to join her. But she had heard nothing and was furious none of the outfitters had informed her of the ambush. No, she said, under no circumstances would she run another commercial trip on the Usumacinta, not until the situation was resolved.

She thanked me for my call. It was too bad I couldn't finish, she added, but I had made the right decision.

When the car was fixed we drove to San Cristóbal so I could find Fernando Ochoa, whom I had asked to arrange a meeting for me with Subcomandante Marcos. Until recently, the rebel leader, who approved and supported Fernando's work, had been reasonably accessible to journalists and high-profile allies, his insomniac midnight interviews a charming peculiarity. But things had deteriorated in the backcountry, Fernando said.

He looked haggard and thin-lipped, suffering from a cold and just returned from Miramar. He couldn't believe we had made it down Cañón Colorado. We spent a couple of days tracking down code-named Zapatista operatives around the city, to no avail. Marcos had gone to ground. No more interviews.

We shook hands, parted on the street, and I left to reunite with Todd. The air was cold. My own joints ached, my energy level diminished by the city's seven-thousand-foot altitude, cold, fatigue.

The clouds broke up and thin, high-altitude winter light laved the paving stones and plaster walls of the city, where only three decades ago Indians still ceded the sidewalks to members of the white upper class. I wandered toward the zócalo and our cheap hotel. "Respect the agreement of San Andrés," declared a newly sprayed graffito. Another pronounced, "Chiapas needs a transitional government," from a pillar on the municipal building.

Crowds clustered around the EZLN booths beside the cathedral. In the streets, armed state police, soldiers, and Humvees patrolled. Repression was in the air, yet nobody, nobody, knew what was going on.

As I crossed the zócalo my path intersected that of a mature, distinguished gentleman, handsome, intellectual-looking, dressed informally in black. He looked up and our eyes met—his sad, mine tired. We nodded. Only later did I realize the man was Don Samuel Ruiz Garcia, the Catholic bishop of Chiapas.

THE NEXT DAY the newspapers reported increased troop movements in the cañadas, new encampments near Miramar, and complaints by human rights organizations of government harassment in the Zapatista-sympathizing villages along the Jatate. They mentioned

Betania, La Soledad, and San Quintín. The human rights office added that in February a group of Indians had been "violently detained" at the Agua Azul crossing, protesting the army presence.

In Palenque we heard that while we had been in San Cristóbal state security forces, justice department agents, and guardias blancas had moved against San Martín Chamizal, a long-established squatters' colonia on the periferico near Chancala, outside Palenque, on the way to Corozal. The squatters, members of a campesino union called Xi Nich and supposedly allied with the Zapatistas, had armed themselves with AK-47s. Two policemen and an undetermined number of campesinos had died. Nobody knew how poor Indian farmers had acquired such expensive weapons.

Sam Libby, a freelance reporter staying at Panchan, had watched hundreds of state police and their supporters gather on the zócalo and parade their dead compadres' coffins before the church, blaming its support of the squatters for the deaths and demanding government retaliation. The Indians had held the land for more than a year while their suit for ejido status moved through the courts. It didn't matter. Local businessmen told Libby that no matter how legal the campesinos' claim, Palenque's cattle boom took priority over the revolution. Even marginal land, like San Martín's, would be held at a premium.

It looked, in other words, like a garden-variety expulsion that had met with surprise resistance. Rumor had it that twenty to thirty campesinos had died, but nobody knew for sure. It could have been more. The periferico remained hazardous, and a high level of security prevailed.

Eventually the time came for Todd to fly home. In the morning after our return from San Cristóbal, I dropped him off at the bus station in Palenque on his way to the airport in Villahermosa.

Afterward I read the (bad) Villahermosa papers, which said Palenque's Spanish priest, Geronimo Hernández, the one whom I had heard deliver the New Year's homily, had been arrested with another priest for "presumed implication in the ambush" at San Martín, and with supplying the campesinos with weapons. A machine pistol had supposedly been found in his personal belongings. With his beard and long hair, the non-Indian Hernández had long been confused with Marcos. Both priests were being held in the state penitentiary in Tuxtla Guttiérrez.

Gonzalo Ituarte, the bishop's spokesman, decried the arrests and denied the accusations. A government spokesman, contradicting charges by a Jesuit university in Mexico City, denied that the arrests were premeditated to obstruct the path of peace.

I drove out of the village, through the colonia Pacal-Na, to the ranch of Raul Roca, the local DJ and martial arts instructor, and Scott Davis's right-hand man. His American wife, Rita, a baker, had just sent her loaves off to Palenque's hotels and restaurants. We sat around a table eating hot bread and butter and drinking tea in a yeast-charged atmosphere.

I had not seen Raul since he dropped us off at Tecojá. I told him everything that had happened. Regarding turning back I could not repress a note of disappointment, which infuriated him. You saved us the anxiety of worrying about you, he snarled, curling his brow.

He wasn't the least interested in canoeing troubled waters with me. A friend of his, an immigration officer in Tenosique, had told him that many illegals came down the Usumacinta—Salvadorans, Hondurans, Guatemalans. Some had drowned at high water the year before. Usually the man's office followed up leads and intercepted the immigrants, but frequently the office was told hands off—leave this one to the army.

Along with the illegals, Raul's friend claimed, came cocaine. The boats passed Tenosique and continued out through the mouth of the river at Frontera, or the Laguna de Términos, where they supposedly transferred the drugs to submarines. Traffickers didn't use planes anymore.

His friend thought the bandits might be connected to the drug trade, that they kept people away from Budsilhá for that reason, but

Raul said ultimately it didn't matter. They just didn't want anybody around.

The hijackers may also have been related to the (nearby) Xi Nich campesinos, he said, sharing their legitimate beefs and viewing all outsiders as threats. They had good reason. There were new forces in town, Raul said, who worked under the judiciales, semisecret agents of the justice department, something like a combination of the FBI and the KGB. The town had a permanent office, but the department moved the agents around a lot to reduce corruption. Nothing criminal happened without their approval, and they always took their cut. You never got to know one of them before he got transferred and some other thug, just as bad, took his place.

A year ago Raul had been walking down the street in Palenque when a Bronco pulled alongside and a tinted window rolled down. It happened a lot: he looked like a narco—long hair, a beard—or what a cop thought a narco looked like. Amigo, the guy inside said—he wore expensive reflector shades and a Rolex—you're not a narco, are you? No, Raul told him, giving him his best samurai face, I'm a campesino. He took Raul to the office, pulled out a big nickel-plated magnum, and grilled him for an hour. Said Raul was a tough guy, would he like to get tough with him? He waved the magnum in Raul's face. Raul calmly told him he was a black belt in tae kwon do and karate. If he didn't put the gun away, Raul said, he was going to shove it up his ass, blow his guts out, and leave his body in a ditch by the side of the road. The headline would read JUDICIAL FAGGOT SUICIDE.

You think he beat the shit out of me or something? Raul said. No way, man. Now he had his arm around Raul, a big smile on his face, and he invited his partner in from the other room. Hey, this is our new amigo, Raul, he said. He is muy macho. We can depend on him for help some time, maybe. Hey, Raul, you gonna come help us kick some Indian ass, or what? Raul just thought, What a fucking cabrón, and he didn't say anything else one way or the other.

They let him go. A month or two later Raul was walking down the street when the Bronco drifted around the corner on two wheels, like in the movies, and stopped diagonally in front of him, almost on the curb. The same guy threw open the back door. Raul, man, climb in, the guy said. Choose any gun.

It looked like somebody had just dumped two or three armloads of automatic weapons in the backseat—Uzis, AKs, Tech-9's, just clattering around together. Come on, man, the guy said. We're gonna go shoot up a village.

You're crazy, Raul told him.

What, are you a pussy? It's easy, the guy said. We just drive up, get out of the car, and start shooting. Nothing to it.

Get away from me, motherfucker, Raul told him.

I thought you were macho, man, the guy yelled. You're nothing but a faggot and a pussy. He slammed the door and peeled out. Raul didn't know about a specific village being shot up, but there were always reports. You never heard for sure because in most cases the campesinos didn't shoot back.

After two days the government dropped the charges against the priests.

MACHETE JIM LIVED in his motor home at Mayabell campsite, a mile down the road from Panchan. In the old days Mayabell had been a destination for mushroom pilgrims whose mind-bending quarry sprouted in the rich, humid cow pastures along the road. Today Mayabell had an in-ground swimming pool and you were as likely to encounter vagabond retirees from Phoenix or Orange County as mochileros, who had moved their headquarters to Panchan's more sylvan acres.

One day I walked to Mayabell from Panchan, past mushroom dealers haunting the ditches and whispering from the culverts, Psst, señor, quieres comprar champiñones? Machete Jim sat in a canvas director's chair under an awning outside his fancy thirty-foot caravan. He was fifty-five-ish, thickset, short-haired, somewhat less imposing than I had expected. He wore deck moccasins, striped T-shirt, bermudas. Before moving to Chiapas, he had been a developer in the Dallas suburbs, converting agricultural land to industrial parks and strip malls.

Along the way he and his ex-wife had stumbled upon Palenque and discovered rafting. He began renting rafting equipment to outfitters, and they soon depended on him to relieve some of the logistical and equipment headaches brought about by operating far from their summer bases in the United States or other Mexican states. In return for a consideration on the rental fee, they often let him row the equipment boat and go along for nothing.

He told me of the recent fiasco, when he had rented Mauricio all his equipment. The trip had included twenty-nine people in seven boats, including the five incognito federales and Jim's dog. Mauricio had hired Jim's girlfriend, a much younger Indian woman, to cook on the trip. Jim rowed his own boat to help out and keep tabs on her.

The morning after leaving Piedras Negras, a month ago now, they swam and camped at Budsilhá. They had just rounded a bend a mile below the falls when Jim heard machine-gun fire coming from the Mexican side. He had four hundred dollars on him, a marked decrease from the previous year's thousands. Nevertheless, he "knew he would be killed this time," so he rowed for Guatemala and climbed five hundred feet up the canyon wall.

He hid in the heavy timber while they made his girlfriend haul everything out of the boats, beating her and verbally abusing her while holding the others at gunpoint.

He passed the night in the rain. In the morning he lowered himself down the canyon wall and swam to his raft, but it was gone. He couldn't follow the steep shoreline on foot, so he inflated his dry-bag for flotation and continued drifting downstream, the dog swimming alongside. They fell into a hydraulic, and he had to let go of the dog to save himself. The dog drowned.

Entering San José Canyon, he climbed out on the right bank, removed everything but his shorts and sandals, and built a raft out of three narrow drift logs, lashing them together with his belt and rain suit. The raft was too small to sit on but it supported his weight in the water and he could guide himself by kicking. In the hydraulic he had lost his cigarettes, but he still had two joints in his waterproof match case. He smoked both of them.

He maneuvered through the class 3 rapids in San José Canyon and made his way to Tenosique. On reaching Palenque, he reunited with his girlfriend and appealed to the Mexican tourist bureau without success. He had faxed a letter to the DEA and copied the U.S. embassy in Mexico City, describing his ordeal, condemning the impunity of cocaine smuggling along the Usumacinta, and demanding action. He had received no reply and I doubted that he would.

Why had Jim carried so much cash with him the year before? He said he always traveled with a lot. Was he concerned the bandits may have bought their AK-47s with that money, and that those were the same arms used in the San Martín shoot-out? It genuinely seemed of no interest to him. He was more interested in telling me he was writing a book about his experience, and suggested we might collaborate.

THE WEATHER GREW hotter. My camp took on a lived-in appearance: hammock hung with stiffening hand-wash, packs dangling at either end, tent frayed and torn. Water bottles, first-aid stuff, and books lay scattered around. Everything looked weathered, reduced, going back to earth. The chickens, and the leaf-cutter ants, perhaps a generation or more of them by now, had folded me into their cosmos.

The scene attested to the derangements all voyages are subject to. It was my own "last camp"—the temporary station where expeditions or civilizations founder and come to ground, or move on to accept or resume membership in the "real" world, the "present." It also symbolized a fact that surrounds us so utterly that most of the time we don't see it—that we live atop others' ruins, programmed for extinction. The imprint of former eras shows through the threadbare fabric of the present, coloring its assumptions and convictions, though we exert enormous energies to avoid its influence.

A picture taken of Robert Bruce in the far-off fifties, after some months at Naha, showed him in Lacandon tunic and long hair, straddling his hammock in a rough palapa. There was a typewriter between his knees, his bare feet grazed the dust. A bottle stood nearby, and a cigar hung from his lip. A pistol in a holster and a hurricane lamp hung from a post.

The earth was littered with notebooks, clay ollas, bones. A net bag and a scabbarded machete hung from the rafters.

Here, the picture said, the vestiges of faded time caught up with and overtook the voyager. Worlds flowed together, as they did during the early stages of contact, when the lines were not so clearly drawn. The frontier relied on marginal individuals of either and mixed race who mediated between worlds: missionaries, traders, guides. Later some anthropologists and ethnologists participated in their subjects' lives and communities while observing them, identifying with them (that is, acknowledging their humanity), and thus shading, somehow, their conclusions—though not necessarily for the worse.

Like others, Bruce's was an undertaking begun in deep study, with long, concentrated hours in libraries, the acquisition of essential and frivolous supplies. There was a goal, a scholarly design, a conclusion vaguely anticipated. The goal set priorities through the planning process and the initial stages in-country.

Like so many expeditions (and scholarly lives), the picture said, his took an unexpected turn. The plan and the circumstances changed; the student himself changed. Perhaps he stumbled on a gap in his learning, a hole where everything became clear and clouded over again, and it seemed as if everything had been that way forever— glimpsed once, then obscured. At that point any expedition would cross a line and become permanent. From such an exile there could be no homecoming. Indeed, Don Roberto was still considered, by many standards, out there.

The glimpse through a cloud would have been the student's true destination, and it would have revealed something essential about the nature of our presence here.

For we remain, five hundred years after our arrival on this side of the world, strangely unaccommodated to our geography, and disconnected from our human predecessors.

While paddling the Usumacinta and its tributaries, then researching and writing the first versions of this book, I kept hearing the words "the shape of the world" over and over in my mind. The phrase hounded me. I tried to ignore it, but it kept rising to the surface.

It came from my reading of the poems and essays of William Bronk, which I had devoured twenty-five years ago as I came to terms—historically, perceptually, cognitively—with the geography I inhabited, the Adirondacks. The idea ran throughout Bronk's work, i.e.: "To live in a hogan under a hovering sky / is to live in a universe hogan-shaped." Bronk himself lived just outside the Adirondacks and had traveled throughout the Southwest, Mesoamerica, the Andes. His words made me look at how the structure of creation and our identities, our beliefs, and our habitats—our specific residences on the planet—cannot be separated: "To live in a hogan under a hovering sky . . . "

The Maya preoccupation with shaping space out of amorphousness, replicating the perceived cosmic structure, inspired some of his most luminous pieces. The "world" (the universe), including the invisible parts, he viewed as finite, tangible, rather than distant and abstract. We are here, he wrote again and again (while nowhere). History is short. The past isn't past.

His poems and essays on Tikal, Palenque, Copán turned my attention to Mesoamerica. One evening under his influence I canoed around the fifty-acre pond where my wife and I were caretakers, as I did most evenings. The pond lay on the edge of a public wilderness area at 2,300 feet.

t was September, the air cool. I followed the shoreline, rounding each headland in hopes of sighting a bear or coyote coming to the water. The faces on Gore Mountain held the sun's last rays. Eventually I stopped and drifted, bracing my knees against the hull's curving inner walls. Venus appeared in the west, the sky turned violet. The air and water were perfectly still.

The mountain, the water's surface, and the ring of forest formed a diametrical middle plane separating two identical, equally spacious and complementary concavities—one above, the other below. I floated, my canoe making a soft indentation in the sky, a portable personal portal connecting me to both hemispheres simultaneously. It was the clearest picture of the universe as we experience it I had ever known. Thoreau's observation, previously obscure to me, that the "universe is insular, not continent," sprang into focus. We live inside a sphere, as much as on the surface of one.

After that I could never countenance the proposition that such an apparently elegant structure would ever express itself in meaningless forms. The very shapes and details of the land and sky, I saw, expressed themselves through us, our perceptions, our identities.

Soon I began a decade of guiding whitewater rafting and flat-water canoeing trips, living for months every year according to the whims of the upper Hudson, Moose, and Black rivers, in northern New York, and making constant critical decisions based on shadings of weather, safety, and the illusions of simultaneity induced by rapid downstream movement.

Over time the practice changes (mostly for the good) the people who do the work, notwithstanding the dubious reputations of raft guides generally. While the proliferation of the paddling and rafting "industries" raises valid questions of nature consumerism—that running rivers is somehow akin to shopping for exercise videos on-line—the discipline of following rivers affects the way you live, think, view the world. When business was steady you entered a rhythm like the one we entered on the Jatate when things went well, but which lasted for weeks. You were married to the immediate, the physical. You kept a sharp eye downstream, but not too far, or else you lost sight of what went on in front of your nose. After a while, time fell away and you existed in a continuously unfolding present. Sailors and nomads report a similar experience. Ancient canoe travelers, from the peopling of the Americas to the rise of the pyramid cultures, chiseled their reactions to the experience in lakeside cliffs and limestone reefs, and carved them into miniature canoes that carried the mind afar.

It makes the business of thoughtfully traversing the earth on foot or by water look like something more than recreation—a puritanically inferior activity. Rather, it is the very work of being human.

When I came across the principle of the Watery Path, fifteen years after my guiding days, I felt like it had floated up from beneath the layers of time, where I had already intuited it, and surrounded me. Later still, it formed the framework of my perception of the Usumacinta River and its cohesive basin.

Contemporary American scholars invented the term, but it expresses a basic cosmological principle endemic to the western hemisphere. West of Greenland and east of the Bering Strait, water is the universal metaphor for everything ambiguous, purifying, mercurial, uncertain, forgiving, transformative; death into life, being and nonbeing. It symbolizes the route from one phase of existence to another.

The more I read—and the more I paddled—the more the reality of a water-oriented metaphysic for the western hemisphere, grounded in early human experience, took shape. In Maya studies the idea's primary exponent was the late Linda Schele, who consolidated a century of far-flung researches into a cohesive vision, left sadly incomplete at her death in 1999. Yet she realized, unlike Thompson, that the Maya saw rivers as only a single aspect of the metaphysical path. Iconographically, it required the addition of the canoe and canoeist, the vehicle and the traveler, to round out the story of the soul's journey.

Recent Americans—those of us whose forebears crossed the oceans in the last five hundred years—have lost the connection to the past and place that galvanizes many traditional communities. Yet the longer we stay here the more that world imprints itself on our psyches.

When I stood on the bridge at El Real in 1992 and first visualized my "seamless, continuous" descent, the newest Salinas-proposed dam project had yet to fail. Within months, it seemed, the industrial land-scape would claim the Usumacinta and consume the watershed, obscuring the details of its river-oriented history forever.

At the time, a half dozen or more outfits carried a few hundred customers down the Usumacinta and a few tributaries every year. For most it was the safest or the only way they would ever know the (then) wild highway in the rain forest, the haunt of monkey and croc-odile, the watery path to the Otherworld. Every one of those cus-tomers—European, American, Mexican, Guatemalan—formed a bulwark against the dams, if their voices could be made to matter. Their eyes absorbed the ancient cities in their unbridled contexts and subtly altered their sense of the world, and by extension our collec-tive sense of the world at large.

Since 1994 river business in Chiapas and Peten has been reduced by more than half. That loss has removed a growing economic factor from the region, one that employed more and more locals as time went on, and cast a shadow on the watershed's interior lowlands, especially the river corridors, where anything might now transpire, unwitnessed by outsiders. Economic pressures and political expedi-ence could resurrect massive dam proposals at any moment. The con-sequences for human rights, and for ecological and archaeological progress, could be grave.

To protect the Usumacinta, what is needed is a new model for the shape of the world, and for shaping a world. One based on the water-shed, and which echoes the ancient Mesoamerican system of enclos-ing amorphous space and declaring it special—which says that within these bounds matters will be conducted according to principles tran-scending self-interest.

A current debate in the literate journals argues over whether early humans had an impact on prehistoric megafauna populations in the western hemisphere, or manipulated nature to their own ends. Clearly they did, and conquered and displaced each other as well. It is futile to claim otherwise. Likewise, it is futile to contend—as some do—that somehow these facts (and theories) discredit natural world affinities expressed by contemporary Native Americans and their apologists, somehow negating reasoned arguments for more and larger designated wild areas. (I.e., "There never was an untrammeled landscape, so what do we mean by 'wilderness,'" etc.). Such a claim relies on a "false dichotomy," in Stephen J. Gould's phrase, denies Indians the basic human qualities of complexity, self-interest, and internal disagreement. It denies them the capacity to evolve philosophies and basic worldviews that accommodate new realities, and redress past failures.

When native people have disrupted natural balances, they have suffered, and sometimes changed. Classical and contemporary Mayas in the Usumacinta lowlands and elsewhere overpopulated their range, overreached their resources and food supply, and succumbed to conflict within and between their communities. In ancient times the survivors turned back to the land, to small, self-regulating communities based in seminomadic family agriculture, hunting, and trade. Contemporary Mayas face more complex decisions, but the awareness of limits has been brutally thrust upon them.

We may view the native affinity for nonhuman life partly as a legacy of "animist" religions, but also as an affirmation of past error (extinguishing the mastodons, overpopulating the range, wiping out the neighboring tribe). Following their apocalypses in Mesoamerica, in re-forming their world, they erected ceremonial centers that symbolized the cosmos and declared a new "here."

Differently driven (perhaps), medieval Europeans carved out raw land from amorphous old-growth oak and spruce forests according to the *Landschaft* principle (hence "landscape"), in which related land uses like crops, orchard, and pasture radiated outward from a village core, in rings. The forest formed the wild, communally held outer ring. The land-use model of contemporary conservationists reverses but essentially maintains the form, proposing rings—or sections—of various agricultural, residential, and extractive uses surrounding a wild inner core, reflecting our now-inverted relationship to wild land: we surround *it*.

The "parquistas," likewise, are changing to embrace a model of designated zones where compatible human uses may coexist in proximity to the largest possible areas of primary habitat—or just empty but exploited land, ripe for recovery.

That principle guided the conservationists I met in the Usumacinta, who worked at loose ends, though they were effective locally. Success now requires that they consolidate their efforts.

Mexico and Guatemala must cooperate to enact binding legislation to place the Usumacinta corridor, appropriate portions of its affluents and their banks, under some sort of perpetual "wild-and-scenic river" cooperative status. Current protective strategies in the lowland drainage of the Pasión, in Montes Azules, and the Sierra Lacandon of Peten, have accomplished much, despite their weaknesses. But a comprehensive, well-planned, humanitarian protection scheme based in watershed management would attract more international funding than any dam project.

A well-funded, comprehensive study of the rivers Usumacinta and their corridors—as well as Laguna Miramar and other principal lakes—must be undertaken. The study should last for years and address terrestrial and aquatic biology, archaeology, water quality, and economic development. It should expand existing protected areas into a binational but contiguous protected area extending to, or nearly to, the headwaters of the major tributaries. Existing wild cores at Montes Azules, the Sierra Lacandon, and other areas would be retained, and new ones would be designated as needed (Las Tazas Canyon on the Jatate). Village, residential, extractive, and agricultural zones would be managed by indigenous councils. The hundred miles from Corozal to Tenosique would be designated as a world heritage site—the historical, cultural core; the river running through it.

Such a structure would mean more than the currently vague constructs of industrial tourism, or the nonbinding, poorly managed, and arbitrarily designed systems of biosphere reserves and parks already established. Models could be found in the Adirondack Park, in the land-use conventions recently instituted around Siberia's Lake Baikal, and in similar areas combining public and private lands, human and wild communities. Lessons could be learned from the progressive Indian state of Kerala, and from Nunavut, the new indigenous province in Canada's Arctic. A watershed plan would create more economic activity and last longer than huge infrastructure projects, spreading its wealth for generations instead of leaving workers unemployed and stranded at its inevitable completion. But it would also require land tenure reforms and the acceptance of limits to growth.

Rivers are the binding principle of the Maya lowlands. By encouraging safe nonmotorized use; by instituting water-quality, hydrology, and aquatic biology studies; and by assuring safety from human predators, they would be restored to their former primacy, and restore a sense of continuity to the place and its people. Renewing the preexisting geocultural pattern along the Usumacinta, in a reasonable contemporary context, would provide a canopy under which regional identity and tradition could thrive, and peace could return.

FOR THREE WEEKS I tried to get back on the river, but the conditions in the hinterlands kept deteriorating. Ultimately nobody chose to join me—they thought I was crazy. Going solo required a magnitude of risk I was unwilling to assume.

My money ran out, and still the Freedom languished at Yaxchilan. It took some doing, but through a friend of Chato's, and by sending

Manuelito a second bottle of Hornitos, I was able to have it returned to Palenque with one of the daily combi drivers.

The next day, my last, I walked the mile and a half from Panchan to the ruin, past the 'shroom dealers and the new museum (lavish outside, rather empty as yet inside). There the big timber of the national park began. A paved walkway, new to me, began at an enormous mahogany encrusted with spider plants and bromelias. It climbed through the forest, crossing and recrossing the travertine pools, falls, and sculpted extrusions of the stream called the Otolum, the calcium-rich cascade that fell steeply out of the jungle and had fostered the ancient city's rise two thousand years ago.

Rich shade filtered the sunlight. It was Sunday, admission was free. The Palencanos—the children of Fray Pedro—were out in force. There were grandmothers and grandfathers, their offspring strung out around them like scattered seeds; rowdy school groups and church outings; lovers in various stages of flagrante delicto; farm laborers in rubber boots. They streamed up and down the winding brick path, rested in the shade, swam by the dozens in the national bathing costume—lingerie for women (regardless of figure) and bikini briefs for men—mingling their essences in the pearly stream with those of their undoubted ancestors, a stirring public spectacle of class homogeneity, partial nudity, and minimally contained chaos.

Soon I emerged from the woods and crossed the Otolum toward the main ruin. The Palace's eastern facade towered over the adjacent forest. I stayed in its shadow, skirting the open plaza with its crowds and sunshine, crossed the Otolum again, and followed a winding track up the overgrown pyramid base at the rear of the Temple of the Foliated Cross, one of the three main structures in the celebrated Group of the Cross. From the base of the temple I climbed to a ledge circling the roof comb and sat looking out over the Plaza of the Cross, the Temple of the Inscriptions, the Palace. Beyond, the plain fell away in a wide curve toward the gulf.

Aracaris and parrots fed in the canopy, level with my line of sight, clinging to the park's morsel of primary habitat. The steep, forested, needle-like peak of Descending-Quetzal-Big-Mountain soared directly overhead, home to the local earth lord and the souls of the ancestors.

A Chol man and his wife, both under huge tumpline loads, passed through the crowd in front of the Temple of the Inscriptions, and around it to the edge of the forest. At a trailhead they put down their loads and bought a fruit drink called a liquado from a pushcart vendor. When they finished they mounted their packs, the man looked around, and they disappeared under the canopy. Their village, Naranjo, lay eight kilometers up the narrow, slippery trail paralleling the Otolum, beneath some of the most impressive old growth in Chiapas.

Naranjo featured in one of Moises's most often-told stories, which began with the eruption in April 1982 of El Chichón, a volcano lying seventy miles southwest of Palenque. That evening Palencanos noticed an orange glow emanating from a distant charcoal-colored cloud. The next morning a fine gray ash had settled over the town. It lay six inches and more on the streets, the rooftops, the milpas. It choked the rivers. Everything ground to a halt, exactly as it does in a snowstorm.

The middle-class wives and daughters of Palenque fled to visit friends and family in the federal district or the United States, leaving the men to shovel ash, make repairs, put things back in order. There was little food to be had, Moises said, but plenty of Corona and Dos Equis. The men worked and partied. Sex workers, sensing the market gap, flooded the town. After a few days a knot of men and prostitutes had constellated around Panchan, working, playing cards, and drinking.

One day Moises looked out of the champa and saw an Indian standing on the patio below. The man, who was from Naranjo, had worked for Moises in the past. Please, the man said, help us. All the fields are ruined, the livestock are dead, the water is bad. We are dying. Moises took the man in and gave him food, and the man left for home.

It rained in the night. The next day Moises walked past the Temple of the Inscriptions and up the trail, a quagmire of ash six inches deep.

A gray viscous flood clogged the Otolum. When he reached Naranjo it stank of dead livestock. Feral dogs skulked around the house compounds and corrals. Most of the people had disappeared.

Moises walked up the short and narrow main drag until he came upon an old man, a headman of the village, kneeling in the middle of the street, his arms raised to the sky. He was covered with ash and he wept, cursing the gods like a Native American Job. Naranjo had upheld its end of the sacred contract, he cried. His people had kept the calendar, burned copal, and sacrificed. They were bad gods, who would do such a thing. He would honor them no longer.

It was a stunning scene. To Moises it felt like the harbinger of some impending cataclysm, something greater than the eruption, that echoed the selva's late classical apocalypse. It reminded him of the moment when ancient Palenque's campesinos repudiated the gods and their elite representatives for taking the corn out of their mouths, failing to protect them from foreigners, failing to uphold the contract of reciprocity, and abandoned the city.

The people scattered, as Moises had it, the campesinos up the Tulijá valley, the royals to the Usumacinta and eventually to Miramar. The forest began its thousand-year recovery.

At Miramar, the exiles built stone temples and emulated the ancestors. The scattered campesinos erected rough wood enclosures amid maize plantations (like San Vicente), simple compounds where they buried their dead, focused cosmic energies, and reframed their shattered world. Out of amorphousness they re-created space and made amends with the creators. They survived.

I looked around me at the three inward-facing pyramids of the Group of the Cross and the plaza they surrounded, agreeable in scale and proportion yet riddled with harmonious asymmetries. They emulated the three cosmic hearthstones. Their art and inscriptions replicated the events that led to the creation, and justified the reign of Palenque's greatest dynasty.

The highest pyramid, that of the Cross, celebrated the world tree, the "First-Tree-Precious" that held up the sky—a ceiba. The Temple of the Foliated Cross did the same for the first maize plant, and the emergence of the Maize God, First Father, in the center of the sky—an act accomplished through the intercession of the paddler gods. The temple's hieroglyphic text, according to Linda Schele, explicitly equated the "First-True-Mountain" of the creation myth with the widespread motif of the cleft, which first surfaced at La Venta, marked the figurines and toad imagery of Olmec times, and reached its highest expression in the pass in the Sierra Lacandon from which Yaxchilan took its name.

It struck me that this framing of the amorphous world, setting aside space meant for special consideration, was not merely a universal human impulse but a function of geography itself, which represented, perceived, and honored itself over and over, in ever-replicating mirrors: the world expressing itself outwardly through human settlement and land-use patterns.

Beside the pyramids rushed the Otolum, a surrogate for all rivers and symbol of the path to Xibalba. Just beyond the pyramids the stream entered an ancient man-made culvert in front of the Palace.

I climbed down from the temple and bought a delicious mango-and-banana liquado at the pushcart. As I stood on the small foot-bridge crossing the Otolum, my eyes followed the creek to the ancient culvert. On an impulse I discarded my paper cup in a garbage can and walked to the opening. Some tangled weeds and mala mujer (stinging nettles) grew through cracks between paving stones that lined the sloping bank. Watchful for snakes—a man had been bitten by a fer-de-lance when I was there in '92—I slid down the bank and stood on an exposed slab at the head of the culvert.

Inside, the creek fell over a small drop and kept roaring underground toward the opposite opening. It looked as if you could walk all the way through without wetting your feet, but I couldn't tell. The tunnel arched overhead, about ten feet high from bottom to top.

In a cosmogram like Palenque you could hardly have created a more perfect and concrete metaphor for the Watery Path, a place where residents and pilgrims could visualize and even practice "entering the road" into the sky, as Chan-Bahlum was shown doing on the Temple of the Foliated Cross, and Pacal on his sarcophagus lid. Many souls must have gazed down this tunnel, I thought, and perhaps followed it ritually to the end, where they emerged transformed, having conquered death, symbolically at least, like the Hero Twins.

I followed as far as the light penetrated. Bats skittered overhead. I thought of Kayaks Away, the Jatate rapid in which I had swum but survived, memorable not because I had almost drowned but because I had taken the elevator down almost as far as it would go and returned. The creek ran downstream toward the light, the fast current twisting from bank to bank around rocks and over ledges, a mostly continuous line of waves about eight or ten inches high. Out of habit I scouted the miniature rapid as if to run it. On a reduced though proportionate scale it would have rated about a class 3-plus; it had tricky moves and hazards, but without question, you could run it.

AFTERWORD

I N JUNE 1997, TWO MONTHS AFTER I LEFT PALENQUE, AN ANGRY MOB attacked a group of archaeologists and workers who were attempting to remove a seventh-century altar from El Cayo, a small ruin about halfway between Yaxchilan and Piedras Negras. The archaeologists, aware of rumors the altar would be looted, wanted to take it upstream to Frontera Corozal for safekeeping.

The mob, twenty-five or thirty Chol men armed with AK-47s, stripped and beat the members of the INAH party, led by Mayanist

Peter Mathews, and lined them up at the edge of the river. The victims expected to be executed, but the mob became distracted when six of the prisoners escaped, and by internal disagreements over what to do with the others. In the confusion Mathews and the rest of his party dove into the rain-swollen Usumacinta and swam for Guatemala through a spray of bullets. Naked, they hid in the forest of the Sierra Lacandon National Park on the Guatemalan shore, and tried to walk twenty miles to Piedras Negras. But they weakened; the river rose thirty feet. Three days later a supply boat motoring upstream from the dig at Piedras Negras answered their signal and ferried them safely back to Corozal. One of the archaeologists suffered a ruptured spleen, and Mathews himself received a broken nose.

While the party had INAH and local permission to move the altar, the kidnappers claimed their patrimonial right to the ancient monument.

The perpetrators remain unknown, their connection to the river bandits speculative. The altar's present disposition is equally unknown, though INAH representatives in Palenque are still negotiating for it.

Later that same year, in December, armed campesinos of the government supported paramilitary organization called Peace and Justice murdered forty-five Zapatista-sympathizing men, women, and children in the aldea of Acteal, in the Chiapas highlands near Ocosingo, while the victims were praying. In September 1999 twenty-four Acteal men were convicted of the massacre and sentenced to up to thirty-five years in prison. A family feud was partially blamed for the attack, and reported links from the killers to the state government were never proved.

In January of 1998 Roan McNab's pickup truck was ambushed and fired upon while he was transporting the gunshot-wounded victim of a similar feud from Uaxactún for treatment in Flores, Guatemala. Roan survived, though his truck was badly shot up. Since then he has completed his graduate work in Florida and returned to Peten and his work for WCS in the Maya Biosphere Reserve.

In 1998 wildlife biologist Ignacio March was named head of Conservation International in Chiapas, where he is implementing a comprehensive community ecotourist program for the biosphere reserves. The slow shift to wilderness tourism and organic farming continues in the villages around Lake Miramar, with the ejidos increasing their production of organic native cacao and brown rice and acquiring modern canoes. Fernando Ochoa has received international recognition for his work.

Our raft descent in 1997 was the last commercial trip on the Jatate. Since then tensions have ravaged the cañadas region, where forty thousand soldiers remain stationed and foreign Zapatista sympathizers have been deported. The conflict in Chiapas remains unresolved as of this writing.

The Usumacinta below Yaxchilan remains off limits to paddlers. Ceiba Adventures has reduced its activities in Chiapas to running day trips on the Shumulja, near Agua Azul, and lancha trips up the Pasión to Lake Petexbatun, in Peten. Tammy Ridenour's Maya Expeditions, active on other Guatemalan rivers, now carries customers to Piedras Negras by motor launch and returns them upstream to Bethel, avoiding the perilous waters downstream. The dig at Piedras Negras goes on productively under the dual auspices of Brigham Young and San Carlos universities, though hunters burned a Nature Conservancy station nearby and the CPRs near El Desempeño were ejected from the national park.

The looming privatization of the electrical power industry in Mexico jeopardizes all the rivers of Chiapas.

In 1998 southern Mexico and Guatemala suffered extensive flooding and forest fires, damaging forest around Miramar and elsewhere in the selva and wreaking havoc along the lower Jatate. Hurricane rains in 1999 raised waters to record levels in the Usumacinta and Grijalva drainages, flooding the towns and villages of the Chontalpa, displacing thousands, and sending crocodiles, reportedly, into the streets.

ACKNOWLEDGMENTS

Victor Perera invited me on my first trip to the Usumacinta and Chiapas, and introduced me to Chan K'in Viejo and Don Moises Morales. The late William Bronk provided me with the underpinnings of thought and language.

Material and moral support came from Charles Ritchie, Jon and Ellen Cody, Dick Carlson, Grace and Bob McGrath, and Ernest Berman. Alex Shoumatoff offered invaluable assistance and support early and late in the researching and writing process; Bill McKibben and Sue Halpern also supplied essential support from beginning to end. Jim Kunstler, H.B., Ellen Rocco, Martha Foley, and Lamar Bliss of North Country Public Radio added critical assistance, along with Dr. Joseph Y. and Eli Rudnick, Ed Finnerty and Nancie Battaglia, William Sweeney, Tom Paine and Shirley Reid, Pete and Kristi Grenfell, Todd Kelsey, the Alfred P. Decker Foundation, Jeanne Shaw, Sue Kavanagh, Gail Stern, Noah Shaw, Rich Liotta, "Bill" of Panchan, Maurice Kenny, Joe Cannistraci of the JMS Body Shop, in Albany, New York, John and Mike Quenell, Robert Anderle, Jacob Bernstein, Brad Watson, Nathan Farb, Manuel Oca, Hector Vasconcelos, Chato Morales. My late sister Cynthia Isdell's wise counsel kept me going over the rough spots.

Corporate support came from Rob Center and Kay Henry, of Mad River Canoe, Waitsfield, Vermont; Don and Georgia Jones, of Jones Outfitters, Lake Placid, New York; Vinnie McLellan, of The Mountaineer, Keene Valley, New York; Dave Cilley of St. Regis Canoe Outfitters, Lake Clear, New York; Backpacker's Pantry; Northwest River Supplies.

Moises Morales, Rakshita, and Susan Prins, of Palenque, Chiapas, saw the value in the idea, encouraged it, and made me feel at home. Marta Cruz Lopez, of Antigua, Guatemala, and her patient instruction, improved my rudimentary language skills.

Virginia Cazort and Herbert Brown offered numerous lodgings, insights, and fellowship.

The advice and logistical support given me by Scott Davis and Rachel Schmidt, of Ceiba Adventures, Flagstaff, Arizona, were indispensable. Helen Running, at Ceiba's home base, answered my endless questions with wit and kindness. Tammy Ridenour, of Maya Expeditions, and Mauricio Morales, of Mexico Verde, added their unqualified assistance.

Drs. Ian Graham, Gary Gossen, David Freidel, Kent Reilly, John Justeson, Nicholas Hopkins, Carolyn Tate, Ricardo Salvador, Robert Carlsen, Richard Iverson, Brent Ryals, and William Engelbrecht returned my calls and e-mails, tolerated my ignorance, and shared their work. C. Randall Daniels—Sakim—explained Muskogee canoe beliefs. Mike McBride provided helpful material on Bufo toads and hallucinogenic enemas. The listeros of the Aztlan listserv entertained and informed me every day. The librarians of Harvard University's Tozzer and Widener libraries, and the Starr Library at Middlebury College, went out of their way to assist me.

Ron Canter made sense of the geography.

Sr. Ignacio March offered me his time and important documents. Roan McNab put me up, made coffee, and shared his passion for wilderness and its human and nonhuman inhabitants. John Beavers and Mike Lara, of the Nature Conservancy, did their best to help me out, though I missed our rendezvous. Chuck Carr of the Wildlife Conservation Society offered ideas, contacts, and encouragement. I hope I have done justice to our exchanges.

The Maya people of Chiapas and Guatemala showed me the human face of the land.

Above all Alonso Mendes, Josh Lowry, David Kashinski, Todd Kelsey, Fernando Ochoa, Ronald Nigh, and Alban Pfisterer protected me, guided my thoughts, and reminded me of the pleasure of men's company in wild places.

My special thanks to Alane Salierno Mason, editor extraordinaire, without whose belief and enthusiasm this project would never have been possible.

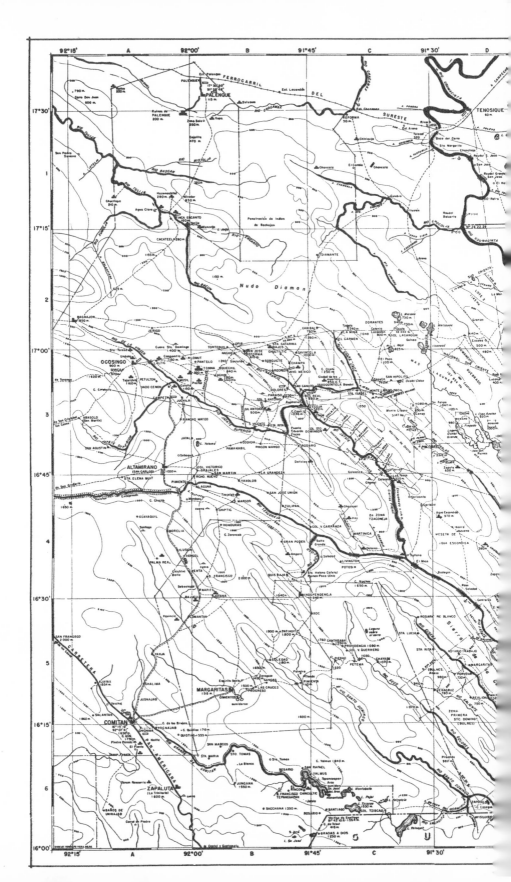